Leendert Weeda
Vergil's Political Commentary in the *Eclogues, Georgics* and *Aeneid*

Leendert Weeda

Vergil's Political Commentary in the *Eclogues, Georgics* and *Aeneid*

Managing Editor: Katarzyna Grzegorek

Associate Editor: Anna Borowska

Language Editor: Manuela Rocchi

Published by De Gruyter Open Ltd, Warsaw/Berlin
Part of Walter de Gruyter GmbH, Berlin/Munich/Boston

This work is licensed under the Creative Commons Attribution-NonCommercial-NoDerivs 3.0 license, which means that the text may be used for non-commercial purposes, provided credit is given to the author. For details go to http://creativecommons.org/licenses/by-nc-nd/3.0/.

Copyright © 2015 Leendert Weeda

ISBN 978-3-11-042641-0
e- ISBN 978-3-11-042642-7

Bibliographic information published by the Deutsche Nationalbibliothek
The Deutsche Nationalbibliothek lists this publication in the Deutsche Nationalbibliografie; detailed bibliographic data are available in the Internet at http://dnb.dnb.de.

Managing Editor: Katarzyna Grzegorek
Associate Editor: Anna Borowska
Language Editor: Manuela Rocchi

www.degruyteropen.com

Cover illustration: © Thinkstock/ The text on the front cover is from Vergil's *Georgics*, book 2, 510-523.

Contents

Preface And Acknowledgements —— VII

1	**Introduction, Political Opinions, Propaganda —— 1**	
1.1	Introduction —— 1	
1.2	Did Vergil Express Political Views? —— 5	
1.2.1	Methodological Features —— 5	
1.2.2	Political Content Of Vergil's Poems —— 6	
1.2.3	References —— 8	
1.2.3.1	The Literary Frame —— 10	
1.2.3.2	The Functional Frame —— 11	
1.3	Propaganda —— 13	

2	**The Context —— 22**	
2.1	Poetry And Visual Media In The Late Republic And Early Empire —— 23	
2.2	Literacy And Audience For Poetry —— 31	
2.3	Patronage Or Amicitia? —— 43	
2.4	Summary —— 52	

3	**The *Eclogues* And The *Georgics* —— 54**	
3.1	The *Eclogues*: Pastoral Poetry With Commentary On Octavian's Land Confiscations —— 54	
3.1.1	Introduction To The Section About The *Eclogues* —— 54	
3.1.2	The *Eclogues* —— 59	
3.1.2.1	Which River Did Lycoris See In Vergil's Tenth *Eclogue*? —— 76	
3.1.3	Summary Of The Section About The *Eclogues* —— 83	
3.2	The *Georgics*: A Didactic Poem With Political Views —— 85	
3.2.1	Summary Of The Section About The *Georgics* —— 102	

4	**The *Aeneid*: An Epic With A Commentary On Contemporary Affairs —— 104**	
4.1	References In The *Aeneid* —— 104	
4.1.1	References To Augustus —— 105	
4.1.2	References To Cleopatra —— 115	
4.2	Models In The *Aeneid* —— 120	
4.2.1	A General Introduction —— 120	
4.2.2	Dido: Was She A Historical Character? Early Myths —— 124	
4.2.3	Dido In The *Aeneid* —— 127	
4.2.4	Models For Dido —— 133	
4.2.5	Cleopatra And Dido Compared —— 135	
4.2.6	Augustus And Aeneas Compared —— 137	
4.3	Summary —— 140	

5	**Vergil's Political Views. Was He His Master's Voice?** —— 142
5.1	Vergil's Political Views —— 142
5.2	Vergil: His Master's Voice? —— 149

Bibliography —— 152

Index —— 164

Preface And Acknowledgements

I undertook the research for this book because I suspected that the Augustan poets, in particular Vergil and Horace, were much more seriously engaged in political issues than has yet been realised. The focus of this book is on Vergil, and I suppose that he, like Horace, lived and worked in the highly political ambience of the Roman social elite, consequent upon his position near the centre of power. In this book, I examine whether Vergil wrote about political issues at all and what his political views were, and whether he presented his own independent commentary on contemporary issues. I explore the importance of his poetry as an instrument of reflection on the great political changes in Rome of the period from the middle to the end of the first century B.C..

Much literary criticism of classical texts is done from the perspective of a literary frame, where the scholar investigates the literary objectives of ancient scholars: the latter are supposed to create a literary continuity with their paragon by referring to predecessors. Ancient authors may also have been inspired by objectives other than purely literary ones, namely by functional objectives, when the authors' main purpose is to deliver a *specific statement*. Consequently, I introduce the notion of a functional model, which runs next to the literary model. In this study I am looking in particular for political statements in the narrative, and/or references to political actors, when the author, in this case a poet, intends to give his commentary on political issues. In this book I explore Vergil's political views in the whole of his work. I conclude that Vergil's political engagement is visible in a great number of texts. For long periods he was consistent in his opinions about several political themes. Vergil wrote poetry which was supportive of Augustus, but at the same time he dared to be critical of him or of his policies. Vergil was a commentator with an independent mind and not a member of Augustus' putative propaganda machine.

The intended audience of this book consists of classical scholars and students who are interested in Vergil's views on socio-political issues, and those who are interested in intertextuality and classical reception. The book may also be useful for teachers in the upper forms of grammar schools. Further, students of modern languages with similar interests as those in the first category may find the book of interest, as all Latin texts have been translated. Finally, those who maintained a liking for classical literature and culture after their secondary education, may take pleasure in reading the book out of general interest.

I am especially indebted to Professor Marc van der Poel, professor of Latin at Radboud Universiteit Nijmegen, who has always been very supportive of my research challenging my ideas on the one hand, and offering useful suggestions on the other[1].

---

[1] The section on the *Ecl.*10 (3.1.2.1), and the part of chapter 4 concerning Vergil's portrayal of Dido have been written originally as separate papers to be submitted to a journal of classical studies. I

The encouragement of Professor Eric Moormann, professor of Classical Archaeology at the same university is gratefully acknowledged. I also express my gratitude to professor Joan Booth of the University of Leiden and to Dr. Stephen Heyworth of the University of Oxford for their critical questions at the time of completing my thesis. The comments of Dr. Yvan Nadeau of the University of Edinburgh have been very stimulating. I am thankful to two anonymous reviewers and the language editor of De Gruyter Open, Manuela Rocchi, for their helpful suggestions. My thanks also go to members of the staff of De Gruyter Open for their cooperation and support during the writing and publishing process: Dr. Anna Borowska, Katarzyna Grzegorek, and Dr. Agata Morka. Lisenka Fox of Radboud Universiteit assisted me greatly clearing up some secrets of the digital age. My very special gratitude is to my wife Marja who read my writings and showed me different ways of exploration.

Radboud Universiteit Nijmegen
September 2014

---

wrote these together with the supervisor of my doctorate thesis, Professor Marc van der Poel. The paper by Marc van der Poel and myself on *Ecl.*10 is inserted in the book as "Which river did Lycoris see in Vergil's tenth *Eclogue*?". Special thanks are due to my daughter Claire Weeda of Radboud Universiteit Nijmegen who suggested many improvements in both papers.

1 Introduction, Political Opinions, Propaganda

1.1 Introduction

Many fundamental changes took place in Rome in the second half of the first century B.C.. After the murder of Iulius Caesar in 44 B.C. the civil war entered a new phase and it was only after the battle of Actium in 31 B.C. that Octavian (63 B.C.-14 A.D.) could set about establishing his authority, by which order and tranquillity became possible[2]. Until that year an armed struggle had been taking place, as Octavian had directed extensive military campaigns against his major opponent Mark Antony and others. In 27 B.C. Octavian became *princeps* and from that moment onwards occupied himself with the transition that eventually transformed the Republic into a monarchy. From 26 B.C. there was relative peace in Italia and the population could begin to repair the economy. However, the Golden Age as a period of peace and restoration did not commence immediately after Octavian's victory at Actium and his assumption of power soon afterwards. The destruction of the countryside, the heavy taxes that had been levied to finance the war and the expropriations of the land of many landowners and small farmers alike, as part of the programme of resettlement of veterans, which had started during the civil war, had impoverished the population.

These events caused many leading families in the Republic to feel deep resentment towards Augustus and to resist the changes fiercely. For many others, relief that the war and the slaughtering were over took precedence over any objections they may have had that Augustus would most likely rule as *rex*. At that time kingship had a very negative connotation. The change was considerable for the senate, its members and for the elite in general. The senate was no longer the highest authority and while Augustus kept in close contact with the senate and consulted it regularly, important decisions in matters of foreign policy, military affairs or high-level appointments were taken within a small circle of confidants. The role of the senate was much reduced, and rejection of imperial decisions was impossible. There were three main areas of change which met with opposition by the senate. These were the reduction in membership of the senate, the extraordinary powers which Augustus took (or which the members of the senate assumed that he took) and the legislation which went against the privileges of the elite. However, the senate offered only firm opposition when they felt that their privileged positions were being eroded. Several members of the old patrician families had not survived the civil war or had disappeared. Those who were still alive reluctantly accepted the emperor's increasing power; the alternative – yet another destructive war between rivals – was untenable, also for them. Augustus introduced

---

[2] Although Octavian preferred to be called Gaius Iulius Caesar, I will use the name of Octavian for him until January 27 B.C., when the senate gave him the name of Augustus.

homines novi from Italia and from the Latin speaking western provinces as members of the senate and many of the non-political classes without any real influence became the new political leaders (Yavetz, 1993, 24). Thus, he appointed officers in the legions and administrators in the provinces from the class of *equites*. He succeeded in gaining and keeping the loyalty of many senators – new and old – by appointing them to the most important posts in the provinces, such as governors and chief commanders in the army[3].

This does not mean that there was no open opposition to Augustus[4]. Within several sections of Roman society there were signs of unrest, and ancient sources refer to several instances of political opposition. Tacitus dedicates a fairly long passage to this opposition in his *Ann*.1.9-1.10, and mentions the struggle with Sextus Pompeius, Lepidus and Mark Antony, and the insurrections of Licinius Varro Murena, Egnatius Rufus, and Iullus Antonius[5]. Suetonius reports in *Aug*.14-18 the uprisings of Lucius Antonius and the siege of Perusia, Sextus Pompeius and the Sicilian war, and the struggle with Marcus Lepidus and that with Mark Antony, the most dangerous of all, which ended at Actium. But this was not the end of Augustus' troubles and some attempts at revolution and other uprisings continued, as we read in *Aug*.19.1. Not all these conspiracies were equally threatening, and they were certainly not as dangerous as the power struggle between 40 and 31 B.C.. Lepidus' son (30 B.C.) had a grudge against Octavian after the experiences of his father. The case of Varro Murena and Fannius Caepio (23/22 B.C.) is a celebrated one as they had murderous intents. Nothing is known about Caepio and Varro Murena is most likely Licinius Varro Murena, the brother of Maecenas' wife Terentia. It seems that they had a following of people in influential positions in their conspiracy against the *princeps*. Marcus Egnatius Rufus (19 B.C.) is rather unknown and his conspiracy was an amateurish revolt. There were two family plots against Augustus, namely the scandal in 2 B.C. of Iulia the Elder (the daughter of Augustus and Scribonia) and Iullus Antonius, M. Antony's son, who were accused of conspiracy and of having an adulterous affair, but who presumably tried to influence future succession (Ruikes, 1966, 166-196). About ten years later (6-8 A.D.) there was a second scandal, that of the younger Iulia (Augustus' granddaughter), followed by the conspiracy of L. Aemilius Paullus and Plautius Rufus. This again had more to do with family feuds and family quarrels about

---

3 For an interesting discussion about the changes in the senatorial classes in Rome after Augustus took power and the importance of the system of *clientela* see Galsterer (1993, 16-17). For a general review of the system of *clientela* see Brunt (1988c, 382-442).

4 Raaflaub & Samons II (1993, 417-454). Ruikes (1966, 68; 78) is entirely concerned with the subject of opposition to Augustus. I differ from Ruikes' view that the estrangement of Cornelius Gallus and Mark Antony was due to the rivalry between the two for the favour of Lycoris/Cytheris. See the discussion of *Ecl*.10.

5 Licinius Varro Murena and Egnatius Rufus were executed for conspiracy in 23 and 19 B.C. Iullus Antonius became a lover of Iulia and was forced to commit suicide in 2 B.C.

succession than with opposition against the Principate or the *princeps*⁶. Obviously, any of these conspiracies could have resulted in the death of Augustus and perhaps a return to the old struggle for power between various families and factions. If one considers the whole period of Augustus' reign there was always some opposition which Augustus and his immediate circle managed to keep in check. It is a moot point, however, whether the opposition was made less serious by the success of Augustus' supposed programme of propaganda.

In general, however, the rule of Augustus was received favourably. At Rome and in the provinces there was peace and stability and as the economy became stronger, the crippling poverty of many sections of the population was relieved to some extent. For the first time after many years of armed conflicts, in which groups and individuals wrestled for power, a general feeling arose that the ruler – the *princeps* Augustus – was accessible and felt responsible for the well-being of the whole population. Common people welcomed in particular the end of the general conscription and they benefited most from the revival of the economy, which was most visible in the extensive programme of public building and infrastructure, such as roads, public offices and the many new tenement buildings, which Augustus erected. It took some time, however, for the Golden Age to arrive. War did not end with Actium and in the next decade there was still substantial unrest. It was not before June of the year 17 B.C. that Augustus felt confident to openly celebrate the new era, when he organized the *ludi saeculares* for which Horace wrote his *Carmen Saeculare*. In the meantime he succeeded in combining absolute power with the restoration of the old institutions of the Republic, which ensured that the changes could be recognised.

It is often said that there was a need to win the support of the leading classes and that convincing them and the public at large of his vision as to how to organise the state was a matter of the highest priority for Augustus. It is obvious that in this vision Augustus had assigned to himself the highest authority, and in 27 B.C. and again in 23 B.C. he received such a commission from the senate. Others would claim that he had assumed this position and therefore a propaganda programme to influence and to manipulate public opinion was a necessity, also after 27 B.C.. In the opinion of many scholars the objective of such a programme would have been to demonstrate the blessings of the new age. It is thought that for this purpose he used – apart from written propaganda – also several different means, such as the repair and aggrandizement of Rome, the building of new temples and public buildings and the commissioning of self-portraits (Galinsky, 1996, 3-41).

In this book I will analyse all the extant work of Vergil, who was born during the civil war, and experienced its horrors. I chose to study his poetry not only because he

---

6 See Ruikes (1966, 197-212). L. Aemilius Paullus was the son of Cornelia. He married Iulia, Augustus' granddaughter in 4 B.C. Plautius Rufus is unknown.

experienced the transition from the Republic to the Principate and the concomitant political change, but also because he obviously is a – if not the – leading poet of his day, and because a substantial body of his poetry is still extant. In a sequel to this book the poetry of Horace will be analysed in the same manner. The two poets cover between them the most important poetic genres. Vergil left us a didactic poem, pastoral poetry and an epic; Horace satirical poems, odes with a wide range of subjects and letters in verse. Although two established poets are the subjects of this study and its planned sequel, it would be equally interesting to examine graffiti, or the work of unknown or anonymous poets, "folk-poets" or "street-poets", who were not members of the Roman upper classes or intellectual circles. On the one hand these poets may have expressed very different views as they stood closer to the common people. On the other hand they may have been more eager to write propagandist texts as they were economically more dependent on the favours of the ruling class.

One can hypothesize that Vergil wrote political propaganda which went against his own political views or that he wrote texts without holding any political views at all. Or he may have worked by order of unscrupulous leaders. Consequently I will first examine whether Vergil expressed any political views, and whether he was consistent in some or most of his views. In addition, I will consider whether these views were critical or supportive of the leadership.

This book is divided into two main parts. The first (chapters 1 and 2) contains the theoretical cadre and the literary and socio-political context. In the second (chapters 3 till 5) I examine whether Vergil expressed political views in his poetry, and whether it is likely that he wrote propaganda[7].

Chapter 1 is a short general introduction which deals first with an exposition of the method of study of the political content of Vergil's poems (sections 1.2.1 and 1.2.2). Second, I present an explanation of the notion of references (section 1.2.3), in which a distinction is made between the concept of a literary frame (section 1.2.3.1) and a functional frame (section 1.2.3.2). At the end of chapter 1 (section 1.3) I give a short exposition of some general aspects of propaganda and of propaganda in antiquity. I present the context within which the poets wrote in the second chapter. I discuss briefly some aspects of Augustan poetry, and of the visual media such as statues, reliefs, portraits and paintings in Rome and Italia in the Late Republic and Early Empire in section 2.1. I also examine in this chapter the levels of literacy, the process of distribution and multiplication of poems, the likely audiences in the public and

---

[7] When appropriate, I will occasionally discuss texts of Horace and Propertius in the introductory chapters 1 and 2, and not restrict myself to Vergil. Chapters 1 and 2 are also meant as precursory chapters to a possible sequel to this monograph about the political views of Horace. The passages of Latin or Greek texts in this book are taken from the Oxford Classical Text (OCT) editions, where available. If the OCT text is very old or not available, the Teubner or another standard edition has been used. The renderings into English are mine. All deviations from this general rule will be clearly indicated.

private sphere (section 2.2), and the position of poets in general and their dependency on patronage (section 2.3).

The second part of the book is concerned with Vergil's poetry: chapter 3 is devoted to the *Eclogues* and the *Georgics,* and chapter 4 to the *Aeneid*. In chapter 5 I present Vergil's political views, and I also discuss in this chapter whether he contributed to a putative propaganda programme.

I give at the end of the book an extensive bibliography and an index.

1.2 Did Vergil Express Political Views?

I have subjected Vergil's texts to critical tests in order to understand their meaning with respect to the poet's political views. As an aid to these tests I developed a model of research, which is nothing more than a structured way of classifying the poems. The model offers a structure for a close reading of the poet's work enabling the reader to identify the political nature of a poem.

1.2.1 Methodological Features

When one examines the question whether Vergil wrote about political issues and whether his work was propagandistic, one moves within the triangle of three variables: poet, poem and reader. All three variables will be considered, but the emphasis will be on the poems and the audience. The poems hold the key to the poets' political views and other beliefs. The other key variable is the potential audience within the context of the political and intellectual environment of the time. Who were the groups of individuals who read the works of the poets, who did the poets want to reach, and who did in their turn possibly influence the poets?

It will become evident that I am concerned with the political and social function of the narrative within the context of contemporary events, displaying Vergil's political engagement. Eventually, my objective is to identify those texts which are concerned with the person or the policies of Octavian and later of Augustus, and to scrutinise these for the poet's political views. However, in a study like this, one cannot hope to find scientific evidence based on firm hypotheses that have been tested by experiments, as is usual in the natural sciences. The best one can hope for is to make a plausible hypothesis by a careful examination of the texts with the aid of the model described below.

Before evaluating Vergil's texts, some contextual questions will be considered in chapter 2: the conclusions drawn from these will constitute the background of the main analysis of the texts. A proper understanding of the real situation of the past will never be possible and will always remain incomplete and fragmentary[8]. The messages which the poets give us in their works can only be understood properly by placing these against the background of the time of writing, the political and social situation, the cultural climate, literacy and many other issues. Therefore, the final purpose of the chapter on about the context is to examine whether poetry in general was suitable for propagandising and whether – through exposure to the work of the poets – the audiences of the poets were likely candidates for the reception of propaganda. In addition, in chapter 2 the poets' positions in society and the likelihood that they were compelled to write propaganda through the system of patronage will be studied and the related issue of their independence will be examined.

1.2.2 Political Content Of Vergil's Poems

First, the political or social scope of a poem needs to be established. Although the poems were written by men who actively observed the developments of their time and who participated in the best of social circles, the current issues of their time are obviously not discussed in all of their work. Some of their poems are purely private and deal with their personal joys or sorrows, loves or hates, successes or failures, such as for instance *Ecl.2*.

In this section a model of analysing the poems for political content will be given. It is important to note that political content may not be readily evident. As a first step, it is necessary to ascertain whether a poem deals *explicitly and overtly* with current political matters is needed and this is where the test of *matters of current interest* will be appropriate: if the poet is clearly concerned with these matters, the poem has most likely a political content. In some poems, however, the political content is hidden and not immediately visible. This is where the test of *references* is important, and such a poem must be scrutinised for references and their likely meaning needs to be established. The subject of references will be discussed in more detail below.

If a poem deals overtly or by reference with current political or social topics, there are two possible options: the poem belongs either to the group of *"political"* or to the group of *"private political"* poems. These two definitions have been introduced in order to classify a poem about current issues more accurately. A work is a *"political"* poem when it addresses or mentions Augustus or any other prominent political figure directly and when it contains commentary on a specific political or economic decision, situation or event, or commentary on a specific issue or issues in the area of economic, moral, military or foreign policies. In addition, a work is *"political"* when the poet

---

[8] As Glenn Most expressed at a seminar (2009) at Radboud Universiteit Nijmegen: "In a larger sense, even the complete works that survive from antiquity may be considered to be fragments, inasmuch as the larger cultural context which produced and enjoyed them has been lost."

writes about specific political, economic, social or moral issues without necessarily addressing a member of the political leadership. Furthermore, a poem is *"political"* not only when the poet writes *explicitly* about major social or political questions, but also when there are *implicit* or indirect references or allusions to political issues. What do I mean by the words politics or political? The term is used in a traditional sense for the total of strategies, policies and actions which are necessary for the running of an organised society, and which are pursued by a particular group or groups who have a stake in the community; this group is not necessarily that which is in power.

A poem is *"private political"* when a poet gives his views or commentary on the current political, economic, social or moral situation without directly referring to a particular person or event. In these cases the poet may reflect in general terms on the behaviour of his fellow citizens or of a particular group, for example the *nouveaux riches*. Poems containing the poet's views on life also belong to this group. This definition of a *"private political"* poem is not all that different from what Brink calls the "indirect method." I use the words 'without directly referring' where Brink uses the expression "indirect method."[9]

"Political" poems are generally concerned with political or social issues of greater significance than those dealt with in *"private political"* poems. The classification of the poems into the groups of *"political"* and *"private political"* is meaningful and helpful in the present research. For instance, it appears that Horace wrote 27 poems (of a total of 162) which are either supportive or critical of Octavian or Augustus policies (Weeda, 2010, 238-242). Of these 27 poems, 25 belong to the category of *"political poems"*. This is to be expected since Horace would have expressed his praise or criticism in poems which were concerned with matters of substantive political weight. In the case of Propertius, 12 *"political"* poems were identified of which 10 are critical (Weeda, 2010, 326-327).

The third test concerns the *likely dates of writing* of the poem: the events presented in a poem will be confronted with the real dates that these events occurred. The idea behind this is that it is less likely that a text was written as a political commentary when this text was released years after the event.

---

9 Brink (1982, 544). The meaning of the word *"private"* in the definition of *"private political"* is similarto that in for instance *"private opinion"*. The latter is defined in the OED, 1998, as: "one's own mind or thought." In a recent essay under the title "Horace and Augustus", Lowrie (2007, 82) also writes about the general and private political: "Politics breaks into Horace's quiet and secluded lyric space from the outside, rather than occupying the centre. The dominance of the *private*, however, is a *political* stance." (my emphasis). In my definition these poems would not belong to the category of *"private political"*, as the dominance of the private sphere and the withdrawal therein are a signal of the poet's refusal to be involved in and to communicate about political matters.

1.2.3 References

As already indicated in the previous section, the interpretation of references is essential for understanding Vergil's poems, or indeed those of any poet. My starting point is the work of Thomas (1986), who presented a very valuable model of classification of references. In addition, the monograph of Hinds (1998) contains many useful observations on the subject[10]. After discussing Thomas' model I will extend this by differentiating between on the one hand the literary (section 1.2.3.1) and on the other the functional frame (section 1.2.3.2).

In Latin literature imitation is a frequently occurring feature. Quintilian devoting a whole chapter to the subject (*Inst.*10.2.4) stated that *ante omnia igitur imitatio per se ipsa non sufficit* (first, imitation alone does not suffice), and that an appropriating author should do better: one ought to find that he *propria bona adiecerit* (adds his own good things) (*Inst.*10.2.28) (Russel, 1979, 1-16; Thomas, 1986, 177, note 20). *Imitatio* is not copying. However, the frequent occurrence and importance of ancient authors' references to their literary predecessors has led presumably in the recent past to an overemphasis on the intertextuality of references, which has resulted in an abundance of secondary literature searching for possible literary sources of references. Conte (1986, 23) coined the term "comparisonitis." That is not to say that comparison is not a very worthwhile tool in literary research, such as in Harrison's (2007c) admirable study of "generic enrichment" in Vergil's and Horace's poetry. For instance, his (2007c, 48-59) analysis of the match of on the one hand the different parts of Silenus' song in Vergil's *Ecl.*6 and on the other the *Metamorphoses* of Parthenius in particular, but also of Ovid and the works of Hellenistic poets, illustrates the contrast between a study in the literary frame and the functional frame, as I will explain in the next sections. Harrison's interpretation of Silenus in the poem is wholly within the literary frame, when he (2007c, 48) states: "The character of Silenus, I would argue, could be presented in this poem as performing Parthenius' actual role in literary history, forming a crucial conduit between the Roman poets of the mid-first century BC and the great Hellenistic poetry of Alexandria." Needless to say those different perspectives will often lead to different interpretations, which are supplementary and not contradictory. I work in this study chiefly within the functional frame and I will interpret Silenus' song very differently from Harrison, as I will explain in section 3.1[11]. Hinds (1998, 18-19) concurs with Thomas' view (1986, 173) "deploring the promiscuous citing of literary 'parallels' in old-fashioned commentaries, 'whose importance goes uninterpreted and whose

---

10 I will not enter into a discussion about the merits of using the word "allusion" or "reference". Hinds (1998, 17-25), has many interesting things to say about the subject. I will use the word "reference" for two specific reasons. First, it is the term used by Thomas. Second, the word "reference" is more appropriate for my argument, when I develop my model of the functional frame.
11 See also note 82 in section 3.1.2.

provenance seems to matter little."' Paraphrasing Thomas' summary (1982, 163) Hinds (1998, 18) states: "in his [Catullus'] self-presentation the alluding author was seen (variously) to reject, correct, or pay homage to his antecedents [Euripides, Apollonius, Callimachus, Ennius and Accius], acknowledging their importance but ultimately claiming his own version as superior." The dynamics of appropriating appear in the variety of referring actions (rejection, correction, paying homage) and the variety of intertextuality, from Euripides to Accius[12].

Thomas' model of "the art of reference," which he expounds in his 1986 paper, is particularly useful for this study. In his exposé, Thomas (1986, 173) says: "What I propose to do is to take Virgil, specifically the *Georgics*, and to use the poem as a basis for establishing a typology of reference." He (1986, 175) suggests:

> a typology with several categories, and although certain of these overlap and others have their own subcategories, the issue is most conveniently approached with recourse to the following types: **casual reference, single reference, self-reference, correction, apparent reference**, and **multiple reference** or **conflation** (this last being the most sophisticated form of the art and often including within it a number of other categories).

With the exception of the single reference (and to some extent the casual reference and the self-reference), Thomas allocates literary qualities to the remainder of the categories, such as enriching the narrative, instilling veracity, or making the story more lively, thus assigning these references to what I call the literary frame. For reasons of economy the remainder of Thomas' categories are mentioned only briefly in the footnote[13]. Here, I intend to discuss only his notion of the single reference (Thomas, 1986, 177-182) in some detail in the section about the functional frame (1.2.3.2), as his conception of single reference fits well into my notion of appropriations within the functional frame; however, my contribution has some important extensions to Thomas' concept.

---

[12] Hinds (1998, 17-34). See also Conte, 1986; Thomas, 1982 and 1986. The term "dynamics of ap¬propriating" is used by Hinds. Martindale (2000, 2), when discussing literary canon making through the ages, suggested that "authors elect their own precursors, by allusion, quotation, imitation, translation, homage, at once creating a canon and making a claim for their own inclusion in it."

[13] The casual reference (Thomas, 1986, 175) "recalls a specific antecedent, but only in a general sense", with minimal importance to the new context and is often meant to "instill generic veracity." For self-reference see note 17. Correction (Thomas, 1986, 185) is a form of reference when "the poet provides unmistakable indications of his source, then proceeds to offer detail which contradicts or alters that source." The term apparent reference (Thomas, 1986, 190) is used by Thomas "of a context which seems clearly to recall a specific model but which on closer investigation frustrates that expectation."

1.2.3.1 The Literary Frame

In these cases the author, inspired by a literary objective, wants to create a literary continuity with his paragon by referring to a predecessor or an admired fellow-author. The referring author's aim can be to establish his literary credibility, demonstrate his erudition, or achieve his inclusion in the literary canon. Conte (1986, 23-95), reviewing Pasquali's approach, brought new insight. Conte (1986, 27), discussing the "decidedly unfruitful" predominance of the position of the author over the text, remarks that "if one concentrates on the text rather than on the author, on the relation between texts (intertextuality) rather than on imitation, then one will be less likely to fall into the common philological trap of seeing all textual resemblances as produced by the intentionality of a literary subject whose only desire is to emulate." The referring author engages into conversation with the system of his literary colleague(s) or predecessor(s). In the words of Conte (1986, 28): "One text may resemble another not because it derives directly from it nor because the poet deliberately seeks to emulate but because both poets [the original and the 'referring' author] have recourse to a common literary codification." In the next section (1.2.3.2), I will argue that an author can also step outside the literary frame by referring to models which are taken from real life persons or events, or from expressions of the visual arts.

In general, the literary objective is achieved in practice by referring to texts from the literary tradition, and, as stated in the previous section, Thomas' typologies are a valuable instrument studying the characteristics of the literary frame. The appropriating author describing for instance a person or event has a person or situation in mind whose "parallel" from previous texts he uses, and in many cases adapts. From the abundance of studies, I have selected two examples. Nelis (2001), searching for a model for Dido in the *Aeneid* has demonstrated that there is much literary continuity between Vergil and Apollonius, arguing that Medea as portrayed by Apollonius in the *Argonautica* was the (literary) model for Dido[14]. When an author describes an event, he may use events as a literary model, as Vergil likely did in the case of "all the martial encounters in the second half of Virgil's *Aeneid* [which] involve some allusive doubling of Iliadic battle action" (Hinds 1998, 116).

References can also be discriminated on the basis of how transparent and recognisable they are. I will use "refer to" or "reference to" when a word or words apply directly to a person or a thing. There is no doubt in the reader's mind who or what is meant. An "indirect reference" means that the word or words apply obliquely or covertly, i.e. by suggestion or by a hidden or obscure meaning. An example of an indirect reference to Cleopatra is G.3.26-29, telling part of the story of the triumphs of the Romans under Octavian, that of Actium over Antony and Cleopatra (see further section 3.2). A third type is an allusive reference, which "is a covert, implied or indirect

---

[14] Nelis (2001, 184): "The sheer weight of the evidence set out in the two preceding chapters suggests that the Medea of Apollonius is the central model for the creation of Vergil's Dido."

reference" and is often symbolical or is achieved by using a metaphor, parable or allegory. The main difference between an indirect and an allusive reference lies in the use of symbols or myths by the latter. An allusive reference requires a greater power of association by the reader than a (indirect) reference[15]. Examples of allusive references – both concerning brutal killings – are the one to Augustus in *A*.12.945-952 through the story about Aeneas killing Turnus (see section 4.1.1), and the one to Cleopatra in a passage in *A*.10.495-498 through the story about the sword-belt of Pallas (see section 4.1.2). Allusive references were quite common in Augustan Rome and were used in all kinds of visual media, particularly in sculpture, architecture and painting. These were understood by the Romans and were seen as a form of commentary on the events of the day. "Augustan culture, and especially the arts, architecture and poetry, were a sophisticated and cosmopolitan blend of many traditions." (Galinsky, 1996, 148; Lowrie, 2009, 21-22; Zanker, 2010, 3). This is very visible for example in the *Ara Pacis Augustae*, in Augustus' *Prima Porta* statue, in wall paintings and in the Forum of Augustus. Similarly, allusive references were very common in Latin poetry and a reading of these poems with alertness for these references can reveal hidden themes.

1.2.3.2 The Functional Frame

The references within the literary frame discussed above are appropriations of a written text: poetic, historiographic, rhetoric, or any other literary text. Appropriating authors can refer for several reasons, ranging from the wish of exhibiting their work to the wish of making a statement. However, in Latin literature – as in any literature – references to persons, pictures, events or places that are not written down are also much in evidence.

Above, I indicated that Thomas' conception of the single reference should be considered in some detail as it may have a bearing on my notion of the functional reference. But first, what is a single reference?[16]. In Thomas' words (1986, 177): "Virgil's chief purpose in referring to a single *locus* is simply stated: he intends that the reader recall the context of the model and apply that context to the new situation; *such reference thereby becomes a means of imparting great significance, of making*

---

[15] Contrary to Claes (1988, 103-112) I see the significance of allusion as a mental stimulus of associative interpretation and less as a rendering of intertextuality.
[16] Thomas (1986, 177-182) considers considers 12 instances of single references. Without wishing to discuss the merits of these references I only note these: *G*.1.50-53 re. to CATUL.64.12; *G*.1.32 re. to CATUL.66.64 and to Callim.*Aet*.4, fr. 110 Pf; *G*.104-110 re. to Hom.*Il*.21.257-262; *G*.3.485 re. to LUCR.6.1191; *G*.3.556 re. to LUCR.6.1144; *G*.3.480-481 re. to LUCR.6.1140; *G*.1.247-248 re. to ENN.*Ann*.33, 160 Skutsch; *G*.4.447 re to Hom.*Od*.4.463; Euphrates in *G*.1.509, in *G*.4.561, and in *A*.8.726 re. to Callim. *Ap*.108; *G*.1.252-256 re. to ENN.*Ann*.384-385, to Eur.*Med*.1-5, and to ENN.*scen*.246-251 V².

connections or conveying ideas on a level of intense subtlety."[17] And as Thomas (1986, 178) further remarks "reference to a single author or passage is often such that the full force of the reference and significance for the new setting can only be recov- ered through consultation of a larger context of the model than has in fact been recalled." Thomas presents his notion of single reference only within the context of referring to fellow authors (see note 16). While his concept is very close to my notion of a functional reference, there is however one crucial difference. A functional reference is not restricted to only referring to a written text by another author, but can also refer to stories about or pictures of mythical or contemporary persons, places or events that have not been recorded in a written form.

In my notion of a functional reference the appropriating author does not primarily have a literary objective, but a functional one. The author works within a different frame of mind than the literary one. His main purpose is to deliver a *specific statement* creating a functional description of persons or events. The appropriating author intends to portray with a functional description the characteristics of a person, such as the political motivation or views of a person. In addition, the author may search for the nature of a (political) issue, and/or the manner in which his *persona* acts. In this study I am looking for political statements in the narrative, and/or references to political actors. In the case of both persons and events the author may select a model generally renowned for the characteristics he wants to illustrate. I call such a model a functional model. The choice of model for persons is often either a contemporary (often not recorded in a written form) or a well-known historical or mythical person who generates associations in the readers' minds. As a consequence, when the model in the author's mind is an illustrious contemporary person, the author by implication refers to this contemporary person. It is likely that in such a case a reader will associate the narrative with contemporary events and/or persons. Similarly, the referring author's choice of model for describing an event may be a contemporary event. The dynamics of appropriation in using a functional model is similar to my interpretation of Thomas' (1986, 177) idea of the single reference: "recall the context of the model and apply that context to the new situation", and "making connections or conveying ideas on a level of intense subtlety." The key words are "context", "making connections", and "conveying ideas", meaning that a single reference invites the reader to contemplate a wider vista, that of the conceptual and ideational themes which motivate the author.

---

[17] My emphasis. Acc. to Thomas (1986, 176) some casual references can have similar characteristics as single references. He gives an example of *G*.3.453-454 which "in reality [...] belongs in the paragraph to follow [about single references], and is anything but 'casual'." Self-reference (Thomas, 1986, 182-183) "belongs to the same realm as single reference, but the fact that the recalled *locus* is the poet's own work creates the potential for highly allusive statement." See also Conte (1986, 25-26), and Campbell (1970, 56-81), writing in 1924 about Horace's view on poetry's function in the community.

Conte (1986, 38), discussing allusion within the conception of the 'poetic langue', states:

> When a past text is summoned up allusively [by a referring poet] and its latent vitality spreads through a new poem, allusion works as an extension of the other weapons in the poet's armory. Allusion, in fact, exploits a device well known to classical rhetoric, 'figurae elocutionis' (tropes). If a poem uses 'golden scythe' to denote 'moon', rhetoric teaches me that this is a figure – more precisely, a metaphor. The verbum proprium 'moon' and the figurative expression 'golden scythe' denote exactly the same object, but the difference in function is crucial.

Conte (1986, 38) argues that the "poet sets up a tension. A gap is created between the letter (the literal meaning of the sign) and the sense (the meaning)." I argue that in the case of Conte's example the different frames (the literary or the functional) are crucial for the "sense" that the author wants to convey. The use of "golden scythe" as described by Conte can be seen as an instance of both the referring and original poet "having recourse to a common literary codification" (Conte, 1986, 28) and belongs – according to my definition – to the literary frame. The poet may want to describe the beauty of the bright moon on the increase. However, if the referring poet were in a functional frame of mind he would refer to the real celestial body on the increase and not to a past text, thus suggesting a very different "sense." For instance, the new context would show that the poet wishes to refer to the promise of the future greatness of a bright young man.

In addition to the above case of a functional model of the "scythe," two more examples may illustrate my point. In the first case the appropriating author (Horace) refers to a text by a preceding author (Pindar). In his panegyric *Carm.*1.12, Horace quotes almost to the letter the opening lines of Pindar's second *Olympian Ode*. In a forthcoming paper I will argue that Horace uses the second *Olympian* not as a literary model but as a functional one. He lauds Augustus by referring to Theron of Acragas and thus implying that the former is of the same stature as the Sicilian king. In the second example the author (Vergil) does not refer to a written text by a predecessor. In the *Aeneid* Vergil created mythical persons and placed these back in time to more than a thousand years before his own. He probably used models from his own day for these mythical beings. In this way, Vergil combined myth and reality in order to interpret his own time and thus the use of the particular functional model becomes the origin of references to contemporaneous persons or events (Griffin, 2004, 183-197). In the case of the *Aeneid*, Vergil probably used Cleopatra as a functional model for Dido in order to refer to current events in the 30s B.C.. I will discuss this in more detail in section 4.2.

1.3 Propaganda

Before presenting some general observations about propaganda in antiquity the notion of propaganda needs defining. For the discussion in this book I have adopted the following definition of propaganda, which is a modification of the definition in the Oxford English Dictionary (OED): "propaganda is the systematic and managed propagation of information, images or ideas by an interested party in order to encourage or instil a particular attitude or response[18]." I have added the word "managed to" the definition given in the OED, as propaganda generally emanates from a central source which maintains control of the process. Control of the process is especially relevant in the case of putative Augustan propaganda, as the question whether some of the literary output was "court inspired" literature under Maecenas as minister of propaganda is still a matter of debate. White (2005, 335) observes rightly that

> One reason that Augustan poetry is rarely discussed as court poetry nowadays is that royal courts have become alien to our experience. But even if that were not so, the model would be inadequate because Augustus went out of his way to dissociate his regime from contemporary monarchies and because Roman poets who might have wished to represent him as a monarch lacked an established idiom in which to do so.

I have also added to the definition of propaganda the word "images," as information or ideas may also be transmitted through images in visual media. In contrast to the definition in the dictionary I have deleted the words "especially in a tendentious way" since this gives propaganda too much of a negative connotation. I refrain from using modern theoretical concepts about propaganda, as these rely heavily on our present-day assumptions about the ease of communication through different means, about the understanding of messages on different levels and above all about the desirability to reach as many people as possible. In addition, modern theories about propaganda suppose the application of techniques of psychological manipulation, combined with techniques of organisation, which were not developed before the 19th century (Ellul, 1965, 3-6; White, 2005, 335-337).

Many scholars – particularly in the 1930s – assert that Octavian started a propaganda programme[19]. In the second half of the twentieth century this view was expressed by, among others, Gordon Williams. According to him (1968, 41-51), propaganda should be considered within the context of patronage, especially that

---

18 Ellul (1965, ix-xvii), quotes the following definition: "propaganda is the expression of opinions or actions carried out deliberately by individuals or groups with a view to influencing opinions or actions of other individuals or groups for predetermined ends and *through psychological manipulations*" (my emphasis). I omit the psychological manipulations as these techniques, common in today's propaganda, were probably unknown in the Augustan age.

19 In chronological order: Syme, 1939/2002. Scholars, who discuss Syme's views without necessarily agreeing with him, are: Millar (1981, 146-147); Linderski (1993, 42-43); Yavetz (1993, 27); Galinsky (1996, 3); Stahl (1998, xx-xxi); Williams (1968, 41-51); Williams (1982, 13-14); Williams (1993, 258-275); Wyke (2004, 98-140, esp. 113;reprint of the original of 1992); Janan (2001, 19). For a position in between see for example Binder (1971, 5).

of Maecenas, involving "a dependence, both financial and social, of the poet on the patron." (1968, 44). In the 1980's Williams stated (1982, 13-14):

> That policy [Octavian's policy of land confiscations after 44 B.C.], among a whole series of other effects, produced a number of poets who needed patronage to help them regain their fortune and status; among them were the greatest of Roman poets, Virgil, Horace, and Propertius. Octavian (Augustus from 27 B.C.) was lucky in finding Maecenas to manage that patronage [,' and...] 'What Maecenas had to work on was the fact that the situation of these poets [...] could readily be seen by them to be the direct result of the social and political evils that had to be the prime concern of anyone who aspired to, or held, power. Their own personal interests coincided with those of the state in the solution of those problems. What needed to be done for these poets [...] was to convince them that Augustus – and Augustus alone – had both the insight and the capacity to solve the problems. That was the function of Maecenas.

Although much is written about propaganda in our day, only very few references to the subject exist in the sources from Augustus' time. Wyke (2004, 116) states: "In the absence of substantial extracts of both Augustus' [so called] autobiography and contemporary prose histories, few later statements regarding his direct propagandist strategies can now be corroborated except, perhaps, by their widespread repetition." Although Wyke's statement concerns Octavian's propagandist strategies with respect to Cleopatra, her remark has general validity. There are some passages in Augustus' *Res Gestae* which may be considered as dealing with the subject. For instance, in *Res Gestae*.19.1 and 20.1 Augustus summarises his building and restoration program in Rome, starting with the temple of Apollo Palatinus. He also refers to the rebuilding of the Capitolium and the theatre of Pompey, *sine ulla insriptione nominis mei* (without any inscription of my own name), which suggests that such an inscription was common. The *Res Gestae* is a piece of self-glorification and not a propagandist work. Later examples referring to propagandist writing can be found with Cassius Dio and Suetonius. Cassius Dio.52.30.9, however, should not be interpreted as concerning propaganda, although for reasons different from those which Galinsky puts forward[20]. A passage in Suetonius' *Vita Horati* concerns propagandist writing, when Augustus clearly requests poems on a specific subject by Horace: *Scripta quidem eius usque adeo probauit [...]ut non modo Seculare carmen componendum iniunxerit sed et Vindelicam uictoriam Tiberii Drusique* (He [Augustus] approved his [Horace's] writings so much, [...] that he not only ordered him to write the *Carmen Seculare*, but also [the odes] about Tiberius' and Drusus' victory over the Vindelici). A further example is a passage in Suetonius' *Divus Augustus*.70-71 where he discusses *sive criminibus sive maledictis*

---

20 Galinsky (1996, 40-41). In this passage Maecenas counsels Augustus not to let cities in the provinces have their own coinage, weights and measures. This does not refer to the potential of imperial coinage to transmit propaganda messages throughout the whole empire, but it should be regarded as an advice for prudent financial management by the cities and for standardisation with other regions in the interest of trade.

(either criminations or slanders) quoting a slanderous epigram about Octavian's failures in the Sicilian war: *[...] epigramma vulgatum est: Postquam bis classe victus naves perdidit, Aliquando ut vincat, ludit assidue aleam* ([...] an epigram was common: 'After two times been defeated at sea and having lost his fleet, he [Octavian] plays a game of dice, hoping to win at some time.'). These two passages are cited here to show that Suetonius recognised propagandist products. Whether Horace was forced into propagandist writing or not is a question that will be left for the planned sequel to this monograph

But did Octavian actually organise any propaganda at all? Was he really interested in managing the propagation of information in order to instil the elite or the general population with a particular attitude? Had propaganda any role to play in Roman politics in the second half of the first century B.C? It remains to be seen whether propaganda really produced changes in the outlook of ordinary Romans of Octavian's and later Augustus' time. Today it is taken for granted that written propaganda can shift public opinion. Are our opinions too preconceived by our experiences of the twentieth and twenty-first centuries in assuming that convincing people was necessary and that this was achieved by propaganda? Did the average educated Roman read poetry, or did the average common Roman listen to poetry readings or study coinage and reliefs? According to Manders (2008, 12), the emperor's use of various media was meant to represent power, and the representation of power was aimed at "information, glorification and legitimation." Information and legitimation can certainly be seen as driving forces of propaganda, as the essence of propaganda is the aim of instilling a particular attitude or response in the recipient. Glorification was often the result of the "offerings of respect by subjects to the emperor" and self-glorification by the ruler can perhaps enhance the attraction and thus the perceptions of the regime. However, it is doubtful whether these were motivated by a desire to propagandise in order to commit others to the ruler's views or to receive approval for his achievements[21]. Whether some forms of propaganda (not necessarily literary) were exercised in fact, and the related notions of the representation of power in Augustan time are in need of reappraisal, even if Galinsky (1996, 40) has indicated in his book that "more recent explanations of propaganda have become more careful and nuanced." Some nuance was already visible when Williams (1968, 75) stated: "the conception of the poet as interpreter and critic of his own society is represented by many Augustan poems." This latter view demonstrates the shift to the school which sees the Augustan poets as

---

21 Manders (2008, 12). In her dissertation (Radboud Universiteit Nijmegen) Manders looked at the use of coinage by the emperors in the period of 193-284 A.D. Although she describes a situation of two or three centuries after Augustus, she makes some general points which were probably also valid at the time of Augustus. See also Hekster (2009, 13-21); Levick (1982, 104-116, esp. at 107); Veyne (1990, 293-482, esp. at 295-302).

commentators[22]. For example DuQuesnay – admittedly writing about Horace's *Satires* I – moves towards this view. His interpretation of the poems is inconsistent with the prevailing view of most scholars at the time, namely that Maecenas had assembled a group of talented young poets to praise Octavian. DuQuesnay sees the poets of the time differently, as cultured and intelligent watchers of events. Even though, Horace is "not writing as a detached observer, but as the friend of Maecenas," his writing never turned into a form of propaganda (DuQuesnay, 1984, 57; see also Yavetz, 1993, 40). Powell (2004/1992, 143) argued that the *Aeneid* "was meant among other things as a complex set of arguments to the effect that Augustus and his settlement would last." Putnam (1995,14), writing about the *Aeneid*, also subscribes to the view of the poet as commentator when he writes:

> In partially rejecting the nineteenth-century attitude about the *Aeneid* as the glorification of Augustan Rome, with Virgil merely pulling the strings at the emperor's puppet show, we are also disposing of a basic critical fallacy, namely that distinguished poetry emanates directly from the fabric of society. [...] The poet, on the other hand, comments, teaches, argues from an intellectual and emotional distance which prods society by applying the goad of quality.

After the nineties of the last century the school which sees the Augustan poets as commentators gained strength. Stahl (1998, xxv) described this in the following words:

> Today there is also a tendency to discount the possibility of officious directives given to the poets. Some interpreters will argue in favor of mutual respect and of the Augustan poets' intellectual independence rather than resume the *unpalatable line of court-inspired literary production*, which prevailed largely unquestioned before World War II (and even World War I) when and wherever the first European emperor was held in high esteem.

However, one should not conclude that the matter has been settled and that the general opinion has progressed to the view that the poets acted as commentators and not as propagandists. If that were the case, it is surprising to observe that many scholars of today still see the need to address the old question whether the works of the Augustan poets were written as propaganda or not. A few examples of books which were published or reprinted since the year 2000 tell a different story[23]. In two relatively recent (2009 and 2010) collections of essays the authors also address questions related to patronage and propaganda[24]. For example, in the first collection

---

22 See Brink (1982, 523-577, esp. at 531, 551-552); although writing about Horace: DuQuesnay (1984, 19-58, esp. at 56-58). See also: Brown (2007, 13-14) and Muecke (2007, 115-116), where they discuss DuQuesnay's views; Galinsky (1996, 10-41, 80-140, 225-287); Powell 2004/1992; Putnam (1995, 9-25, esp. at 14, 22); Zanker, 2010/1987.
23 In chronological order: Powell (2004, 141-174: a reprint in 2004 of the original in 1992); White (2005, 321-339); Davis (2006, 9-14; 16-18); Brown (2007, 13-14; originally from 1993); Watson (2007, 93-104).
24 Dominik, Garthwaite & Roche (Eds.), 2009; Davis, G. (Ed.), 2010; Le Doze, 2014.

Bond (2009, 141) asserts in his essay entitled "Horace's Political Journey" that Horace produced the *Satires* "to order, after his adoption into the circle of Maecenas, and at the critical time of the conflict with Sextus Pompeius, *when the organization of opinion in favour of Octavian was of the utmost importance.*"[25] The second collection is entitled *A Companion to Horace*, edited by Davis (2010). Leading themes in three of the four chapters in Part 1 of the book are patronage and Horace's putative consequential lack of independence from the donor of gifts (Maecenas), which is thought to have stifled the poet's own convictions and forced him to write according to the wishes of the leadership. The chapters' titles are telling: chapter 2, "Horace's Friendship: Adaptation of a Circular Argument," chapter 3, "Horace and Imperial Patronage," and chapter 4, "The Roman Site Identified as Horace's Villa at Licenza, Italy." (Anderson, 2010, 34-52; Bowditch, 2010, 53-74; Frischer, 2010, 75-90).

When poets are regarded as commentators their position should be judged within a wider perspective. The relations between them and their milieu, the views they may have held and their backgrounds should also be considered. In addition the literary outputs should be studied within the context of other forms of art, such as statues, portraits, architecture and painting and should be compared with those. This implies that the question of propaganda is approached differently and that the putative propagandist effects of the works of Vergil and others be judged in conjunction with the effects of other art. This more integrated approach requires that not only literary critics, scholars of classical history and classicists occupy themselves with the question of propaganda, but also the art historians and scholars of political sciences also join the debate. Particularly since the work of Zanker (1987) who looks at the many nuances and facets of Augustan art in general, the clichés of simple propaganda were replaced by the view that in the time of the change from the Republic to the Principate a much more complicated process had taken place. At this time ideology and propaganda were not pre-eminent, compared to ideas of restoration and a new beginning[26].

Examining the question whether Vergil's poems contained propaganda may also contribute towards finding an answer to the general problem of the existence of propaganda in the Augustan age. Indeed, if it can be shown that the poems were not propagandist, Vergil's writings at least can no longer be used to support the "propagandist" point of view.

Although it is a moot point whether or to what extent the written word had a place in propaganda, one finds poetry which is supportive of the ruler. A large body of panegyric poetry does indeed exist, but this is not to be equated with written

---

[25] Bond (2009, 141-142); my emphasis. Dominik's (2009, 111-132) essay in the same collection about the political content of the *Eclogues*, particularly from a detailed examination of *Ecl.*1, will be discussed in chapter 3.

[26] Galinsky (1996, 30) regards the poets as "active discussants".

propaganda. Panegyric is defined here as the (generally) voluntary writing in praise of someone to express admiration for or gratitude towards the addressee. Panegyrics were generally of a private nature, and generally on the writer's own initiative, or upon suggestion by someone else and they were about the person or about the views of the praisee. In works of propaganda the interested party had to be portrayed *"as he wished to be seen"*, while in panegyric poems the poet portrayed the addressee *as he sees him*[27]. It is often said that the text itself does not show whether it has been written by order of the "interested party" or whether it is a creation by the poet, on his own initiative. In general, however, the poets of the period clearly show their true colours. For instance, some poems have both a panegyric and opposite tone, such as Horace's *Carm*.1.37, which lauds Octavian's victory over Cleopatra whilst at the same time expressing admiration for the queen. It is unlikely that the praise for the queen was written by order of Octavian. Furthermore, there are times when the poets criticise current affairs, whilst at the same time writing an eulogy of the *princeps*. For example, in the same year (27 B.C.), Horace criticises Augustus in the form of a *recusatio* in *Carm*.2.12, but in *Carm*.3.4 writes an eulogy of the *princeps* who brought peace to Italia[28]. If a poet writes a critical poem and a supportive one in the same year, the latter is not necessarily propaganda. It is equally possible that on both occasions he simply expressed his own views.

A method of establishing whether Vergil's poems have political content has been presented in sections 1.2.1 and 1.2.2, and I intend to show that his poems have indeed significant political content. The next step is an assessment of the likelihood that he wrote propaganda for Octavian/Augustus. It is rather unlikely that a poet is a propagandist writer when only a minor part of his output concerns contemporary social or political issues. But the reverse – a high percentage of poems

---

[27] Nauta (2006, 302-305). Nauta discusses, among other things, the views of ancient commentators as Aelius Donatus and Servius. He quotes for example Donatus, who says that Vergil wrote his *Eclogues* with the following intention: *etiam in laude Caesaris et principum ceterorum per quos in sedes suas atque agros rediit* ('also in the praise of Caesar [Octavian, the later Augustus] and the other leaders through whom he [Vergil] returned to his home and his lands'). For the putative loss of Vergil's 'home and his lands', see notes 66 and 68. An interesting discussion of panegyric epic in the Augustan age is by White (1993, 78-82) and White (1993, 99); on panegyrics: "It is the writers themselves who crowd forward with panegyrics" on the grounds of a passage in SUET.*Aug*.89.3.

[28] Wilson (299, 200). I concur with Wilson's exposition of the *recusatio*. The gist of his argument is "that the function of the *recusatio* is, as the term itself informs us, to say 'no,' yet to defuse annoyance by attributing the refusal to the author's own lack of aptitude for the task." The function of the *recusatio* is not to say 'yes' reluctantly (Nisbet and Hubbard, 2001, 81-83). Wilson (2009, 200), writing about Propertius and Tibullus, makes also the point that the *recusatio* "is a vehicle for preserving the sense of distance between the addressee's mindset and the poet's. The *recusatio* is to the relation between the elegist and his 'patron' as the *paraclausithyron* is to the relation between the elegist and his mistress." I would add that by its very nature one often finds a *recusatio* in a poem with a critical attitude towards the addressee.

about contemporary social and political issues – is not automatically a sign of the writing of propaganda. In all cases the poems need to be scrutinised on their subject matter and on the question whether the poem is supportive of Augustus' views or his regime, or whether the poem is critical. Many "private political" poems in particular are supportive of Augustus simply because the views of the poet and of the *princeps* happen to coincide.

I will identify whether a poem is supportive, neutral or critical of Octavian and later Augustus, his regime, his relatives or the circle of men and women in his direct vicinity, or about his policies. It is not necessarily the case that all that a poet writes has been part of his personal experience or is his firm personal opinion. The poet may decide to express a view different from his own: for instance because he intends to use poetic licence or because he wishes to stimulate the reader by showing another side. In the case of propagandist output, he is asked or forced to express a view that is not his own. Poems which are neutral or critical of Octavian are unlikely to be propaganda, even if the views expressed in the poems are not those of the poet. However, poems which are supportive of the *princeps* or his regime should not be automatically seen as panegyrics or as propagandist. In order to resolve this dilemma the supportive poems will be scrutinised on the durability of the poets' opinions: if the conclusion is that the poet has expressed a particular view consistently over a long time, it is more likely that this was either his personal opinion or his poetic posture. Thus, the poet can present views on certain issues which happen to coincide with those of the *princeps* without having been ordered to write about these as a propagandist.

In summary, the total scheme of analysis is as follows. By applying the test of matters of current interest and the test of references, the poems can be placed in either the group of "political" or the group of "private political" poems. Together these two groups constitute the body of poems in which, in principle, propagandist content may be found. In addition, the supportive or critical nature of a poem, and the years in which the poems were written (if known) are taken into account. All texts have been subjected to this schematic approach. However, the presentation of the results of the *Eclogues* differs from that of the *Georgics* and the *Aeneid*, as the last two do not consist of distinct single poems which can be classified along these lines. The schematic approach makes it possible to characterise individual poems and compare these. Another advantage of this classification is the opportunity it provides to compare poets. In a planned monograph about the political views of Horace the "political" and "private political" poems will be arranged in five categories according to their content. The categories are: (1) The poet writes about his own experience. (2) The poet writes about his (own) poetry. (3) The poet writes about the civil war. (4) The poet hopes for better times. (5) The poet gives his view on moral issues.

Applying the tests above have led to a number of new insights into the meaning of several poems. These new interpretations can be read in the relevant parts of the book. A few examples are: in *Ecl*.4 Vergil reveals his preference for a hereditary kingship; in *Ecl*.6 he refers to the destruction of nature by human aberrations, and in *Ecl*.8 to the destruction of the countryside and of the social order in Italia. The *Aristaeus' epyllion* in book 4 of the *Georgics* has a much more radical political message than has been recognised in most, if not all, scholarly commentaries. Cleopatra being the functional model for Dido shows Vergil's high regard for the Egyptian queen and his positive attitude towards a more meaningful role for women in society.

2 The Context

In this book Vergil's political views and the topics of Vergil writing propaganda for Octavian (later for Augustus) are discussed. Before analysing the poems in detail, the background against which Vergil worked will be examined: which political message did he want to convey, if any, and whom did he want to reach? It cannot be taken for granted that he wrote propaganda, but if this was the case did he write for Augustus who wanted different strata of the population to accept his policies and if so, which groups did he have in mind? Was it the population at large that he wanted to convince, not only at Rome but also in the provinces? Or was he only interested in the elite, that is, the opinion leaders?

In this chapter I will examine two main topics: (1) whether poetry in general was suitable for a propaganda tool for the person and policies of Octavian/Augustus, and (2) whether Vergil's (and other poets') audiences were the right candidates for the reception of such putative propaganda. This leads to several questions about the context in which Vergil worked, not just in az general sense, such as the course of the struggle for power after 44 B.C. and the political developments at Rome, but also, more specifically, in relation to the audiences for which he wrote. Of course these can not be investigated in detail in a study like this. However, an overview will be presented in this chapter and some appropriate aspects will be discussed in the following sections[29].

The chapter is structured as follows. In section 2.1, I will briefly discuss some general aspects of Augustan poetry, such as the influence of archaic Greek and Hellenistic literature, the use of references, and poetic representation. This will be followed, in the same section, by a brief overview of the use of visual media in Rome and Italia in the Late Republic and the Early Empire. I will explore whether visual images served more widely as instruments of representation of power and of propaganda and I will examine the relationship between poetry and visual media. In section 2.2, issues like levels of literacy, education and the likely audiences in the public and private area will be briefly discussed. Next, in section 2.3 patronage will be considered. Most of the established poets belonged to the circles of different leading figures, for instance Maecenas and Messalla, whom are often said to have been instrumental in putting pressure on the poets to write propaganda. This chapter will close with a summary and with some conclusions on the suitability of poetry in a supposed programme of propaganda (section 2.4).

---

[29] I have not included a section about the historical context. I refer to a number of recent general textbooks and specialised books which deal with the Late Republic and the Augustan Age, such as: Boatwright, Gargola & Talbert (2004, 267-316); Bowman, Champlin & Lintott, 1996; Brunt, 1988; Crook, Lintot & Rawson, 1994; Earl, 1968; Galinsky (1996, 80-140); Galinsky, 2005; Hekster (2009, 25-68); Raaflaub & Toher, 1993; Stahl, 1998; Wallace-Hadrill, 2005; Yavetz (1993, 21-41); Zanker, 2010.

2.1 Poetry And Visual Media In The Late Republic And Early Empire

Augustan poetry was not created in a vacuum, but had its roots in the Latin literary tradition with its many Classical Greek and Hellenistic influences, and existed in conjunction with the arts in general, which in turn consisted of an intricate construction of tradition, taste and fashion, foreign influence (again mainly from Greece and the Hellenistic world), politics, social and economic developments and other elements. I will consider parallels between Augustan poetry and the visual media of that period both in the public space and in the private domain. In the public space there were the portraits, statues, and reliefs forming part of the new urban design and restoration programme by Augustus, and coins. The first three of these were generally erected in Rome and in the major cities of the empire, while coins were used and minted through all the lands under Roman rule. The public readings of poetry, which occasionally took place, also belong to the public domain. In the private domain one finds, among other things, mural paintings and ornamental pieces, vases and goblets. To this domain also belong readings of poetry in private or small gatherings, for instance at a meal or at a symposion.

Some general aspects of Latin poetry in the Augustan age will be discussed first, followed by some characteristics of visual media, in particular the way in which it was used to refer to contemporary issues.

In the Republican age Greek literary creations served as sources of inspiration for Roman authors. In the beginning there was much experimentation. What were originally Greek metres were applied to a modified Latin language, Greek mythical subjects were reworked and Greek poetic genres were adopted by Latin authors. The end of the Republic saw the rise of the *poetae novi* or *Neoterici*, of whom Catullus (about 84-54 B.C.) was the most important. They formed as it were an artistic bridge between Greek Hellenistic and Latin poetry and they no longer wrote grand poetry such as epic, but concentrated on poetry whose subject matter was to be found in their own microcosm and in which they could express their own feelings. Genres such as elegiac and lyric poetry became the vogue. Hellenistic poetry was obviously a new discovery found as a result of Roman military expansion, and as such formed the second source of inspiration. Towards the end of the first century B.C. these two main sources often resulted in poems in which many Greek archaic – for instance Alcaeus or Pindar – and Hellenistic poets – for instance Callimachus – can be traced.

Although poetry in the Augustan age remained under the influence of Republican tradition, it developed into a very sophisticated form and showed a high degree of involvement with contemporaneous issues. "The poets, then, were creative participants in the ongoing discussion about ideals and values, and they had their own minds about them" (Galinsky, 1996, 225). Bowra (1945, 34) notes that the *Aeneid* had helped many to see the main problems of life. A major characteristic of Augustan poetry was what Galinsky (1996, 229-234) describes as "complexity and multiplicity of meanings" (see also Conte, 1986, 23-31). The Augustan poets made reference to Greek mythical figures who were then given a place in contemporary events. The choice of references would also indicate the poet's approval or disapproval of a certain issue, and the audience was able to understand this. Thus, one could read or listen to a poem on different levels. The "aesthetic" level consisted of appreciating the characters in the poem on their own poetic merits and experiencing the beauty of their personalities or actions. On the "associative" level, the reader's thoughts were directed towards the events and issues of the day, whereby the reader or listener would often be invited to contemplate moral or ethical questions. Later in this book I will argue that the poets of the Augustan age made extensive use of several forms of references and associations. The use of references was not exclusive to the poets: it was common in Roman art in general, and references were widely used also in the visual arts (see below). The significance of references, therefore, canot be over-estimated.

Before moving on, it is worth considering whether the poets expressed their own opinions about political or social issues or whether their views were a result of the performative stance which they took. This has been examined in great detail in a recent book by Lowrie (2009, vii), who opens her book as follows:

> This book argues that the power poets attribute to words in Augustan Rome is intimately related to the language they use to describe the representing media. Although interest in the relation of the means of representation to power can be traced to the earliest Roman poetry, the historical crisis of the transition from Republic to Empire opened new avenues for literary production and offered fertile ground for an examination of the modes of cultural production, their respective powers and inadequacies.

Not all the avenues which Lowrie explores can be discussed in this book. I want to focus very briefly on the phenomenon of *personae*, about which Lowrie (2009, 102) remarks: "In Oliensis' words (1998:1-2), 'Horace's poetry is itself a performance venue… Horace is present in his personae, that is, not because these personae are authentic and accurate impressions of his true self, but because they effectively construct that self.'" Lowrie adds that a similar point can be made regarding the poem's address. She acknowledges the difficulty of the question whether the poets perform or teach, when she states: "Can it [poetry] teach (*Epist*. 2.1.124-8)? Horace repeatedly makes the gesture of poetic efficacy, and repeatedly pulls it back. Performativity is a topic, but does poetry actually perform?"[30] (Lowrie 2009, 103). However, the choice of the performative medium determines the effectiveness. Lowrie (2009, 215) makes this point for literature: "Closeness to the word of god, an active intervention in society, pragmatic effectiveness – the advantages of literature figured as song, as living presence [contrary to the writing of letters], as performative in all the word's senses overwhelm and seduce."

---

30 Lowrie (2009, 101-111). A different view can be found in Davis (1991, 1-10, esp. at 6-7).

Does this mean that the opinions which Horace, and equally Vergil and Propertius, express through *personae* are therefore not authentic? Is a *persona* a performative medium which is used by the poet to heighten the poem's strength? The poet's choice of the performative medium is indeed important for the power and impact of representation. How should the poet write about or sing of the *princeps*, who after all controls the centre of power? How can it be done in a manner worthy of a responsible citizen? Is therefore the use of a *persona* a way of hiding? I suggest that the poets did not hide or submit themselves to authority or fear, or that their choices of poetic expression or genre were for the "performative effect" only, and that consequently the views expressed are a construct and not authentic. In the course of this study I will demonstrate that the poets persisted in many of their political opinions during many decades, and expressed these continuously over time and consistently over several genres. Often their views were critical of Octavian and later of Augustus and his policies, and they gave these views without prompting by a third party. It is unlikely that they would have done so if these opinions were not their genuine personal views.

Next, some characteristics of the visual media will be examined, beginning with the Republican era, followed by the years of the transition from the Republic to the Principate and finally during Augustus' reign. Examples in the public area such as statues, coins, reliefs and architecture, and, in the private space, such as mural paintings and ornamental pieces will be presented. The focus will be on characteristics such as the context of the creation and the nature of the images. This will be done in rather general terms and for detailed studies the reader is referred to the well-known standard works, such as Zanker's "The Power of Images in the Age of Augustus"[31].

In the Late Republic one can find several examples of what Zanker (2010, 1-25) calls "political imagery" on monuments, which in addition to visual images often carried texts as well. These generally revealed who had erected or repaired the monument and occasionally why. Many coins also carried political images, for instance the ten coins issued in 66 B.C. by Q. Pomponius Musa with Apollo on the obverse side and Hercules with the nine Muses on the reverse side. The latter is an obvious allusion to his name. Another form of allusion in the Republican age was the building of many temples for their patron deities by victorious generals; these contained many statues of the gods taken home as a loot from Greece or from the East. At the centre of these temples would stand a statue of the general himself bigger than those of the divinities.

Octavian was quick to learn from his predecessors. On 2 January 43, within a year of Caesar's murder and at the age of only nineteen, he was voted by the Senate a statue on the speaker's platform. Although the statue has been lost, we know of it because its picture was shown on a coin soon after. The equestrian statue was to stand next

---

31 See also: Galinsky, 1996, and Kleiner, 1992. For the relationship of Augustan poetry and visual representation see Barchiesi (2005, 281-305).

to those of Sulla, Pompeius and Iulius Caesar, and so the object of the statue itself became an instrument of allusion: Octavian was as great a general as his illustrious predecessors. A second statue exemplifies this even stronger. Again, the statue is only known from coins, which were minted after Naulochus in 36 B.C.. Octavian was shown "in a pose familiar from late Classical Greek art. The model may have been a famous statue of Poseidon by Lysippus. The victor in a sea battle, he [Octavian] holds in his right hand the stern (*aphlaston*) of an enemy ship as a trophy, while the lance in his left hand marks him as a general. He rests his right foot on a *sphaira*, symbol of all-embracing rule over land and sea" (Zanker, 2010, 39). This statue of Octavian was full of allusions to Sextus Pompeius, who was defeated in the final sea battle at Naulochus, after he had been victorious over Octavian at a number of earlier occasions[32]. Sextus claimed that he had been adopted by Neptune as a son, and thus Sextus used many maritime symbols, one of which was a statue – again known to us from a coin from 42-40 B.C. – where Sextus places his foot on the beak of a ship and which shows an allusion to *pietas*. This was clearly a sneer in the direction of Octavian which the latter paid back on the statue erected after his victory over Sextus at Naulochus; one could say that there was a "battle of allusions" between the two. In addition, Octavian may have referred to a second statue and this reference may be more important still. According to Cassius Dio (43.14.6), around the year 46 B.C. Iulius Caesar had erected a bronze statue with his foot placed on the globe, expressing power over the whole world. The "father" and the *"divi filius"* stood there for all to see.

Whether manifestations of "political images" in the public domain can be found on coins is a vexed question. Giving propaganda messages on coins differs from the use of coins for self-presentation and image building by the ruler (see also Hekster, 2009). Coinage was often used for the latter purpose. At least people should know that a ruler existed, who he was and what he looked like. At worst there was the desire for self-glorification by the ruler. For the purpose of this study, propaganda through coinage will be considered only briefly. Firstly, there are no indications that Octavian and later Augustus managed personally or through an intermediary the production of coins and their minting. His focus was on economic priorities, such as the money supply and not on the form (Levick, 1982, 104-116). Secondly, more than two hundred cities in the Roman Empire had a mint. In most cases there was no tradition to put portraits on the coins, let alone Roman portraits. However, Augustus appears regularly on coins, most likely on the initiative of the local authorities: this was probably to honour the emperor, or to use the *auctoritas* of Augustus as a means to facilitate acceptance and enhance the economic value of the coins. The portraits and symbols on the coins were

---

[32] Powell (2004, 156). Octavian was defeated by Sextus in 42 B.C. in or near the strait of Messina, later near Sardinia, in 38 B.C. near Cumae and again in the strait of Messina and in 36 B.C. near Tauromenium. "The number of defeats inflicted on Octavian and his subordinates by the sea power of Sextus had enduring consequences for the reputation of Caesar's heir."

not the result of a message from Augustus, but rather an ingratiation or at best a sign of respect by the local elite[33]. This resulted in an informal interaction between Augustus and the designers of the coins, who gave their commentary on general moral themes (frugality, responsibility, trust, peace and stability) transmitted by Augustus: all this with a relatively great freedom.

The following issues of coins may serve as examples of this interpretation. Before 31 B.C. Octavian had issued a set of six *denarii* consisting of three pairs. Three coins carry the portraits of Octavian and on the reverse sides a picture of either Pax, Venus Genetrix or Victoria. The three other coins have the heads of the same divinities and on the reverse side a full-length portrait of Octavian either addressing his troops with an *adlocutio*, giving the signal to attack, or celebrating his triumph. The message is clear: Pax is the goal of the battle, Victoria is the result, and Venus is the protector of the admirable general. Apart from these six coins, there is also a series of three coins from the same period. Two of these commemorate the victory over Sextus and one shows the *Curia*. The latter symbolizes Octavian's promise to restore the Republic. Another example may be the so called *Numa* coins, issued in 3 B.C. These carry the head of Numa and are an allusion to the *Pax Numana* (that is the *Pax Augusta*). According to Galinsky (1996, 37):

> Augustus' direct control over this highly unusual series of Numa bronzes can be safely ruled out [as the bronzes were produced by a young Piso ('who did not know to obey', TAC.*Ann*.2.46)]. His [Augustus'] actions suggested the broad themes; in this case the revival of old religion, the ree-stablishment of peace and Republican traditions, and the importance of a new *saeculum*. These were expressed, elaborated and extended by individuals in their own way.

Galinsky (1996, 39) summarises the function of coins in Augustus' time as follows: "At most coin types can serve as a reflection on, and as a record and affirmation of, something that is already known through other sources. Conversely, some of Augustus' major programs, such as the legislation on morals and marriage, found no expression in his coinage."

The third type of public images, that of reliefs, and in particular those of the temple of Apollo on the Palatine and those found on the *Ara Pacis Augustae*, is important. Octavian had promised Apollo a temple after the defeat of Sextus in 36 B.C. and it is estimated that the temple was dedicated in 28 B.C.. Some terracotta plaques of the temple have been recovered and one shows the battle of Apollo and Hercules for the Delphic tripod. Some authors see in this an allusion to the struggle for hegemony between Octavian and Antony. Another interesting political image, the death of Niobe's children, was shown in a prominent place on the temple doors. According to Kleiner (1992, 84): "In sum, it is apparent from scholarly interpretation of the

---

[33] Burnett, Amandry, & Ripollès, et al. (1994, 593-594); Levick (1982, 107).

sculptural program of the Temple of Apollo Palatinus that it was carefully orchestrated by Octavian, in concert with a master designer, to underscore his personal rapport with the god Apollo, and to make reference to his momentous victory over Antony and Cleopatra at Actium" (see also Kleiner, 2005a, 220-221). Octavian's temple for Apollo competed with the rebuilding of the temple for Apollo *in Circo* by C. Sosius, who had fought on Antony's side, but had been pardoned. But Sosius understood the new political realities: a frieze of the rebuilt temple showed Octavian's triple triumph and not Sosius' own triumph *ex Judaea* in 34 B.C.. His newly-found loyalty went even further when he placed an Amazonomachy in the pediment of the temple. This was generally seen as referring to Octavian's victory at Actium, which was often compared with the defeat of the Amazons by the Athenians (Zanker, 2010, 84-85).

The *Ara Pacis Augustae*, which was built by order of the Senate between 13 and 9 B.C. is the apex of political references. The "Altar of Augustan Peace" had been voted to the *princeps* as a monument to peace after his safe return in 13 B.C. from Gallic and Spanish campaigns. Of interest here are the reliefs that tell the history of Rome and the emerging new dynasty. History was represented by a panel on the front of the building, on the west side; to the right of the entrance Aeneas together with Ascanius is seen sacrificing after their safe arrival in Latium. Aeneas is shown as a ruler with a spear and in Roman dress, whereas Ascanius is represented as a youth still in Trojan dress and holding a shepherd's staff. Immediately around the corner of Aeneas' panel, we find Augustus together with the young Gaius and Lucius, Augustus' adopted sons, also in Trojan dress. In this way Augustus was linked to Aeneas and the boys Gaius and Lucius to Ascanius. The scene referred to Augustus' "descent" from Aeneas and to the continuation of this historic line in Gaius and Lucius. More mythological figures were placed on the east side of the monument, the goddess Roma sitting on a pile of discarded armour and what is most probably Pax with all kinds of fertility symbols. The message is clear and Zanker (2010, 175) summarises this as showing "that the blessings of peace had been won and made secure by the newly fortified *virtus* of Roman arms."[34]

The north side of the altar depicts a procession of senators and families. This is repeated on the south side with the addition of the extended imperial family, including children, led by Augustus in his office of *pontifex*, who, together with a group of priests, performs the rites and sacrifices to the household gods. The two processions were presumably intended to be seen as one. These two friezes represented a powerful political message. Firstly, the pride of place was given to Augustus and the family, symbolising the elevated position of the emerging dynasty, while the Senate is to be found at the tail end of the procession. Secondly, the coming together of Aeneas

---

[34] There are various identifications of the goddess: Tellus, Venus, Italia, Ceres or Pax. Zanker considers Pax the most likely as the monument is the *Ara Pacis* and the neighbour panel is that of Roma with the discarded armour.

and Augustus symbolised not only Augustus' divine descent, but also his task of establishing a new order and restoring peace, as Aeneas had done before him [35].

The political images just mentioned were very much in the public space and I will now turn briefly to some of those in the private domain. Antony's identification with Dionysus was an easy target for political attacks. Supporters of Octavian used it to denounce Antony as a man whom Cleopatra held in her evil clutches. Their Alexandrian parties were portrayed as foreign and decadent orgies typical of the East, and all over Rome effeminate statues of Dionysus – for instance in private gardens – were given Antony's features. As a protégé of Apollo, on the other hand, Octavian was perceived as a paradigm of order and good morals and many owners of great houses set up portraits of Augustus and his family.

Several examples of scorn for Antony can be found. The same mockery which had been used against Pericles centuries earlier was now used against Antony, as several clay bowls produced in a pottery in Arezzo show. In one of them, Heracles, dressed as a woman, sits in a chariot drawn by centaurs and Omphale follows in his lion skin in a second chariot. Heracles looks longingly back at Omphale. At the same time, he is well looked after by servant girls while she is offered a large drinking cup. The allusion is clear: the spear-carrying guards behind the second chariot and the large drinking cup were seen as referring to Cleopatra, and the effeminate Heracles is obviously Antony[36]. Hekster (2004, 164) offered the interesting view that "without any direct evidence that the figures on display refer to Mark Antony and Cleopatra, and without any evidence that the design originated from Augustus or the circle surrounding him, it becomes hazardous to use the motif on the pottery as evidence for a grand Augustan [propaganda] programme." I share his opinion that this and other images of Heracles and Omphale were not part of Augustan propaganda – if that existed at all – but I differ from him when he testifies in the summary of his article that "it seems that a political reading of the images is stretching the evidence too far." These kinds of images in the visual media or words in literature may never have been meant to refer to a topical political issue, but may have become symbols of what discerning and educated Romans were very apt at interpreting as allusions to contemporaneous political events. It is not only in the Arezzo pottery that the Omphale-Cleopatra connection appears, but also in the poetry of Vergil, Horace and Propertius. A particular case in point is PROP.3.11, probably written in 24 B.C.. In the elegy, Omphale joins other (mythical) women, who represent the (evil) female powers of oriental women with ambitions to dominate the world, a well-known theme in Rome. The poem concerns the threat of Cleopatra, the decadence of the queen and of Egypt in general, the battle of Actium and the events which followed, and above all

---

[35] For the *Ara Pacis* see Galinsky (1996, 106-109 and 141-150); Kleiner (1992, 90-99; 2005a, 212-217 and 221-225); Zanker, 2010.
[36] Zanker (2010, 59-60). Plutarch referred to this in *Demetrius and Antony* 3.3.

the contrast between Antony's enslavement and Octavian's sense of duty. It is unlikely that the poem was propagandist as it was written so many years after the events, when the threat from Alexandria had long been removed. PROP.3.11 is an example of allusions to similar feelings as are expressed in the Arezzo Hercules-Omphale bowl: feelings which were presumably widely felt and which could be recognised in the visual media and in literature by the Roman cultural and social elite. Of course the elegy has also a second (non-political) theme: one should not wonder that a woman (Cynthia) governs Propertius' life when one sees that so many great heroes and men were dominated by women.

At home, in a private villa, a patrician – or a parvenu – could explain the scene to his guests and show them where he stood. To quote Zanker (2010, 62):

> Mythological symbols and parallels also offered contemporary Romans the chance to express their affinity with one side and its lifestyle or the other. It is becoming increasingly clear that the political affiliations that can be detected in poetry are intimately related to those expressed in the visual arts, even in the private sphere, as in the decorative scheme of a room or in such diverse objects as tableware and seal rings.

Finally, this section will be closed with a fine example of political imagery in the private sphere, namely in the decorations of a room, the use of wall paintings. In Boscotrecase, near Pompeii, Agrippa's family owned a large estate with a beautifully decorated villa. In one of the rooms, a wall painting in the Third Style has been discovered, probably dating from 10 B.C.. The scene is a pastoral idyll, a bucolic fantasy in the words of Zanker (2010, 285), which was not uncommon at the time (Zanker, 2010, 283-287). The painting displays a sacrifice before an enthroned goddess in an idealised pastoral landscape where no toiling farmer is visible. The landscape is a park with some trees dominated by a temple and a villa. The pastoral element is a herdsman with his goats. The picture exudes the happiness of life in the countryside when one has escaped from the moral decay of the city. The image is much in vogue as mythical elements are absent in this picture. Yet, the painting gives a powerful political message in support of Augustus, which was to be expected in a villa of this family. It alludes to a peaceful and tranquil life in the countryside which can be found now that order and peace have been restored by Augustus. It is possible to escape the bustle of the city where the *princeps* is at work establishing his empire and managing the affairs of state.

To summarise, different forms of visual images proliferated both in the public and in the private areas. Through these the patrons of the arts wanted to express their views or to broadcast their political messages in public spaces and their wealth and allegiances in private spaces. This was achieved by a subtle artistic representation of well-known figures or events from the mythical or historical past, which either alluded to the patron's successful behaviour in contemporaneous events or showed the patron or his policies in the most flattering light. In principle, this was not different from the situation in the last decades of the Republic; it was only the scale which differed. The *princeps* was a major patron and many manifestations of his political image are known. "Reading" references and allusions in the visual media was not all that different from reading those in poetry.

2.2 Literacy And Audience For Poetry

At the time of Vergil both in poetry and in the visual arts references to contemporary issues were not uncommon. In subsequent chapters I will show several examples of those in Vergil's poetry, making up part of the political messages he sent out in both the public and in the private spheres. But before conclusions about the impact of political poetry can be drawn, two different issues must be considered first. These are the questions of the ability to read Latin poetry in different social strata of Rome and Italia in the first century B.C., and the related one of the audiences of poetry. The point is of course that impact of poetry was dependent on the size and type of its audience. A situation where hardly anyone was able to read poetry, or where poems were only read by or recited to certain groups, would have been very different from one where poetry enjoyed a wide and socially diverse audience.

The question of literacy is fraught with difficulties. There has been much scholarly research on this matter, which has been summarized by W.V. Harris[37]. Before discussing literacy a few points need attention. Firstly, confusion can arise about the use of the word *literate*, which can mean two things: either "cultured" or "capable of reading and writing." I am concerned with the latter meaning. Most likely there was a great difference between reading and writing levels in Rome. In this book, the focus will be on reading for the reception of Latin poetry by contemporaries. Secondly, in antiquity, literacy differed greatly between men and women; there were only a few women of the upper classes who could read and write. Thirdly, and most importantly, the definition of literacy is very unclear. This makes the results of the many studies of the historical development of literacy and the recent official surveys by UNESCO or others unreliable[38]. The figures which will be given in this part are therefore estimates with a wide range of uncertainty. Fourthly, in view of these uncertainties, Harris (1991, 3-8) suggests to divide people into three groups according to their reading and writing ability: a first group of *illiterates*, a second of *literates* and a third middle group

---

[37] Harris, 1991; the following chapters are of particular interest: I. Introduction: Levels of Greek and Roman Literacy; II. Introduction: The Functions of Literacy in the Graeco-Roman World, and VII. Literacy and Illiteracy in the Roman World: The Late Republic and the High Empire, 100 B.C.-250 A.D.
[38] Harris (1991, 3-8). In Harris' opinion the definition of UNESCO is the most acceptable. This definition is: "an illiterate should be defined as someone 'who cannot with understanding both read and write a short simple statement on his everyday life.'" The problem however is that this definition is not respected by many officials in several countries. Harris is sceptical about the measurement of literacy by the use of people's ability to sign for instance a marriage certificate or by counting the number of years of some form of elementary schooling.

of what he (1991, 5) calls *semi-literates*, who are the "persons who can write slowly or not at all, and who can read without being able to read complex or very lengthy texts." This third group of semi-literates belongs, for the purpose of this study, to the group of illiterates, as poems are generally complex or very lengthy texts.

In our Western, industrialised world the ability to read and write is generally seen as something natural. However, "in rural Greece in 1951 the illiteracy rate among males was 14.9 %, that among females 49.9 %. Greece at the time, however, was a country in rapid transition; more typical of an early-modern setting would be Sicily in 1871, with 79 % male and 91 % female illiteracy."[39] Societies can only achieve mass literacy when some preconditions have been fulfilled, such as the cheap mass production of reading material, schooling on a large scale, and economic necessity. The cheap mass production of reading material only started after the introduction of the printing press in the fifteenth century and an extensive school system was not in place before the nineteenth century. For instance, during the period of the industrial revolution, in eighteenth-century England, the literacy rate of the male population shot up when the factory owners started to want a literate workforce. Another impulse for the growth of literacy can be religious or ideological in nature, such was the case of the increase in Protestant Germany and Holland in the sixteenth and seventeenth centuries when people wanted to read the Bible at home.

It is clear that none of these preconditions existed in Rome in the first century B.C.. Although there were competent copyists and there existed a level of trade in books, there was nothing like mass production, and the costs of the raw materials were such that only the rich could afford to buy books. A school system as such existed only on a limited scale and presumably only in the cities. The education in the privately run "primary" schools was only for boys whose parents could afford the fees. Here they were taught reading, writing and some arithmetic. "Secondary" education was given by a *grammaticus* who taught Latin and Greek grammar through the reading of the great classical writers. Yet, it is unlikely that the writers who are the subject of my study were read in schools in the last decades of the first century B.C.. Horace was outspoken about the subject. In his literary *Satire* (*S*.1.10), probably written in the year 35 B.C., he writes about his own expectations as a poet. In the lines 74-76 he says: *an tua demens/vilibus in ludis dictari carmina malis?/non ego* (What, would you be a fool, wanting your poems dictated in common schools? Not for me). And in 21 B.C. he reflected on the fate of his poems by writing in *Ep*.1.20, 17-18 (the final lines of his first book of *Epistulae*): *hoc quoque te manet, ut pueros elementa docentem/occupet extremis in vicis balba senectus.* (This awaits you too, that stuttering old age takes possession of you as you teach boys their basics in the city's outskirts). Horace was scornful about a future for his poetry as teaching material, and he rather saw himself

---

[39] Professionals in orthopedagogy in The Hague estimated in 2008 that the illiteracy rate of children in their later years of primary education living in certain deprived areas is in the order of 20 %.

as *me primis Vrbis belli placuisse domique* (that I was welcome, in war and at home, with the most excellent in the State) (*Ep*.1.20.23). Eventually, he was unable to prevent the use of his poetry in schools, but it appears that he did not encourage it and perhaps it took until after his death in 8 B.C. before it was part of the curriculum.

Remnants of school buildings have hardly been found. Generally teaching took place in makeshift classrooms, outdoors, at the corner of the forum or on the street. Boys and girls of the upper classes and of the new rich were often educated within the family walls by itinerant teachers, often learned slaves. Boys learned to read and write and were prepared for the typical elite forms of "higher" education in rhetoric and law, again at home (Harris, 1991, 233-248).

Two driving forces in Roman society had a positive effect on the literacy rates, the army and international trade. Both the army and international trade required the services of a considerable number of literates, but the effects on general literacy were limited. Harris (1991, 18-19) states rightly:

> We must distinguish between, on the one hand, an economy [like the Roman one] which provides a certain number of clerical jobs and gives some incentives, though not an overwhelming one, to an artisan or shopkeeper to read and write, and, on the other hand, an economy [like ours] in which the mass literacy of its workers and its consumers is an integral feature. It is obvious that the Romans never went beyond the former of these situations.

Establishing literacy rates in the Augustan age has given rise to much conjecture, and in general high estimates of literacy rates in Roman society prevailed before 1970[40]. Harris (1991, 9) quotes Guillemin (1937, 77), "that there were few illiterates in Roman antiquity, 'even among slaves,'" and Harris (1991, 14) quotes Marichal (1963, 208) who testified that "many Romans read newspapers." It is Harris' (1991, 22) view that "the likely overall illiteracy level of the Roman Empire under the principate is almost certain to have been above 90 %." This refers to the overall level. In much of the empire, including Italia, the written word was never encountered. However, the written word had spread considerably within the administration, the army and international trade. There were many specialist literates in these areas due to the increased need for written documents such as wills and marriage contracts, as well as due to the requirements of the management of the state and of the army in documents such as tax and property records and rosters of army personnel. Anyone who wanted to draw up a contract or record a transaction could use the professional services of these specialist scribes, often slaves, who would write up the document. Transactions of a

---

40 Harris estimates much lower literacy rates than other scholars. I give two quotes out of many. Harris (1991, 270) discusses rates in Roman Britain: "Unawareness of ancient educational conditions, tinged perhaps by patriotic optimism, has allowed some *exaggerations*," and Harris (1991, 280) mentions that the costs of education prohibited many to learn to read and write " – which would hardly need saying but for persistent *lack of realism on this subject among scholars*." (my emphasis).

modest size, however, were seldom put in writing. Apart from the corps of specialist scribes, one encountered a high degree of literacy with the legionaries, while the auxiliaries were in the main illiterate. Officers in both armies could read and write[41].

Much official communication with the public at large was not written but oral, for instance through town criers, the *praecones*. They announced public meetings and voting results, and gave general information. As a rule, official decrees and edicts were posted at public places such as the forum for anyone to read and if one could not read there was generally someone who could read it aloud.

The writing of letters was very common, not only in the private domain. The communication between Rome and the governors in the provinces or between the provincial administrative centres and the commanders of the army was generally by letter, which had the advantage that it could overcome distance. The same held for communication with and between traders in the provinces.

The overall literacy level of 10% then, will almost certainly have included a very high literacy level among the educated elite who wrote and read Greek and Latin literature, studied philosophy, wrote letters, prepared and made legal pleas, addressed political meetings and so forth. The aristocracy and the new rich constituted the elite, and the senators and higher officials were recruited from this class. Examples from the Augustan age are C. Asinius Pollio and C. Cornelius Gallus, both literary men prominent in public life. Contrary to the standards of today's prosperous Western world and of parts of the Eastern world with its increasing prosperity, the Roman Empire as a whole had a relatively small middle-class of, among others, successful freedmen, professionals and officials, craftsmen and middle-ranking army personnel. This was also true for Rome and Italia. Within this class there was a fair degree of at least the ability to read. The group of people who were poor or very poor was much larger than it is commonly believed. Needless to say that the widespread poverty meant that many children – boys – remained illiterate; not dissimilar to some of the poorest countries we know today.

Thus far the level of literacy in the Roman Empire at the end of the first century B.C. has been considered. What matters for our subject is not just literacy as such, but more specifically the ability to read Latin, as the poetry of Vergil, Horace and other poets was not translated into other languages at the time. This raises the questions

---

41 Harris (1991, 253, note 413). Harris gives an amusing anecdote which shows that the army in general had a rather high degree of literacy. There were attempts in the late 40s and 30s B.C. to propagandise the soldiery. I quote Harris: "In 46 Caesar tried to subvert both the local and Roman troops of Scipio Nasica in Africa by means of brief *biblia*, with some success; Nasica replied in kind (Dio xliii.5; cf. *Bell. Afr.* 32). Octavian tried the same technique on Antony's army in 44 (App. *BC* iii.44: many *biblia*), as the Caesarians did against Brutus before the second battle of Philippi (Dio xlvii.48.1). When Antony had such leaflets shot into Octavian's camp outside Alexandria in 30 B.C. (which, incidentally, shows what a lightweight object a *biblion* could be), Octavian read them out to the soldiers himself (Dio li.10.2-3)." So much for written propaganda.

of Latinisation and bilingualism: for the purpose of this study I define the latter as the ability to speak and read Latin, next to the ability to speak, read and possibly write another, generally indigenous, language. In a large geographical area as the Roman Empire many local and generally very old and long-established languages of old civilisations existed. The situation differed greatly between Rome and some other large cities in Italia and the countryside, for instance in southern Italia. As an aside, this was also the case in Rome itself with her many immigrants and a large imported population and the resulting great social differences. The Latinisation in many Gallic and Spanish cities was much more advanced than in Alexandria and other cities of Hellenistic origin, where Greek was the language of the upper classes and the administration, and education was seen as natural. During the reign of Augustus' successor Tiberius (14-37 A.D.) – admittedly a few decades later than the period which I discuss – a boarding school for sons of the aristocracy in Gallia was established in Augustodunum (modern Autun). In the backwoods of, say, Cappadocia or Cantabria literacy was virtually zero, Latinisation was minimal and bilingualism hardly existed. In general, the presence of the army was an important factor[42].

In summary, it is not possible to come to precise figures of the ability to read Latin in either Rome and the other towns of Italia, or the Italian countryside, or the different cities and regions of the empire in the Augustan age or to specify these for the different social strata of Roman society. However, two general conclusions may be drawn. Firstly, with respect to the overall levels of literacy, Harris gives the following estimates for the various regions. In Rome and Italia the overall level of literacy was below 15%, and he gives a similar figure, for instance, for Gallia Narbonensis and Baetica (modern Andalusia and Granada) and for the cities in the African provinces of Numidia (modern Northern Algeria) and Africa (region of Carthage; modern Tunisia). Harris estimates the average literacy level for the Western provinces as a whole as between 5 and 10%. In Rome and Italia literacy is defined as the ability to read and write Latin and in the Western and African provinces as being bilingual according to the definition given above. However, the situation in the Eastern provinces is very different as the main language for literates was Greek. Thus, an estimate that the overall level of literacy in the latter provinces was similar to Rome and Italia does not mean that the ability to read and write Latin was similar as well. Secondly, considering the literacy in different social strata, Harris states that the social and intellectual elite of Rome and the larger towns of Italia could generally read and write, often both in Latin and in Greek, although there were still many members of the upper classes who were illiterate. An appreciable part of the successful freedmen, craftsmen and traders of these cities could read Latin. Since the Roman elite spent much time on their estates in different parts of Italia, small pockets of Roman culture came into being there. In the provinces however, the great majority of people was not latinised and did not

---

42 Harris (1991, 175-193). In these pages, Harris discusses all geographical areas of the Empire.

participate in the Latin cultural manifestations. There were pockets of acculturisation in the towns where groups of originally Roman administrators, traders and others mixed with the indigenous populations, who together formed the elite and who could read and write Latin. This was a small minority and constituted a much smaller percentage of the total population than in Rome[43].

Who were the audiences of poetry and how much were they in touch with poetry? Did they read poetry or did they listen to public or private recitations? Did people purchase books? Was Latin poetry read in places outside Rome, in Italia or perhaps far away in the provinces? Horace referred to this latter question in his *Ep*.1.20 and his *Carm*.2.20. In the former he reflected on the fate of his poems and in *Ep*.1.20.10-13 he says to his book:

> *carus eris Romae, donec te deserat aetas;*
> *contrectatus ubi manibus sordescere vulgi*
> *coeperis, aut tineas pasces taciturnus inertis,*
> *aut fugies Vticam aut vinctus mitteris Ilerdam.*
> (you will be precious in Rome, till your youth deserts you; when you've been touched by vulgar hands and begin to grow filthy, you will either in silence feed artless bookworms, or will run away to Utica, or be sent in chains to Ilerda)

Horace was proud of his success in Rome, but feared that this might change and that his book of poems might be disregarded and would turn up in Utica, North Africa or Ilerda (modern Lerida) in Spain: just like a master who sells off his ageing slave. A few years earlier, in 25 B.C., he had finished his second book of *Odes* and in *Carm.* 2.20 he referred to his hope that after his death his work might survive and that he would visit the outermost borders of the known lands as a *canorus ales* ('a tuneful swan'). In the two passages Horace did not necessarily refer to an international readership; his words express, in the *Epistula* (*donec te deserat aetas*) the fear of future obscurity, and in the *Ode*, the hope of future fame. In line 13 of the latter he compared himself to another famous flyer *Daedaleo Icaro* (Daedalus' Icarus) and wished to become *notior* (more renowned) than him (Icarus). Nisbet and Hubbard's (2004, 337) commentary on this line is: "in choosing bizarre symbols to express his thought, he [Horace] shows an agreeable detachment from a deeply felt aspiration."

Before discussing the audiences of poetry, the process of the making and distribution of books will be first considered. How did a book of poetry come about? Was it published and then sold through the book trade? Was there a market for books?

According to Starr (1987, 213-223) not much is known about the book trade in Vergil's age. Perhaps this lack of knowledge is not all that serious as we have a fair idea about what Starr calls "book circulation." He (1987, 213) states that "Romans

---

[43] Harris (1991, 259-282); MacMullen (2004, 215-231); Woolf (2004, 231-242).

circulated texts in a series of widening concentric circles determined primarily by friendship, which might, of course, be influenced by literary interests, and by the forces of social status that regulated friendship." Starr offers a credible model suggesting that an author sent gift copies of the finished work to his circle of friends and that this was effectively the point of release of the book, and after that it was openly accessible. The author had these copies made at his own costs and under his own management, and there was no commercial copying at this stage. When the text had been released, other people were free to make their own copies. There were no commercial transactions, and if someone wanted a copy made they had to pay for the creation of a copy, with no copyrights payment to the author. Most readers depended largely if not entirely on privately made copies, not only for new, but also for older work.

Libraries formed another source from which work could be obtained for copying. A number of private libraries existed in the Roman townhouses and country villas of the upper classes. It is generally held that L. Aemilius Paullus Macedonicus was the first to bring books to Rome, those of king Perseus after the take of Pydna in 168 B.C.. Faustus, the son of Sulla, continued his father's library after his return from Athens in 86 B.C.. This library contained a considerable part of Aristotle's private collection. Lucullus created a private library in Rome and Tusculum which was stocked with books he had brought back from *Asia Minor*. These libraries lost parts, or perhaps the whole of their collections through confiscations in the late 40s or early 30s B.C.. A well-known library outside Rome is that of Piso, which was found in Herculaneum. Others like Cicero and his friend Atticus held large collections of books. Cicero mentions in his letters that he consulted the libraries of his friends and that he borrowed books to have them copied[44].

Apart from private libraries, some public libraries were also established in Rome. The first one was the library which Iulius Caesar had planned, but which was built by Asinius Pollio in the *Atrium Libertatis* in the late 30s or early 20s B.C., quickly followed by two libraries by Augustus, one next to the temple of Apollo on the Palatine in 28 B.C and one in the Porticus Octaviae which was built after 23 B.C. [45]. Public libraries

---

[44] Casson (2001, 61-108). Cicero wrote about the library of Lucullus in *Fin.* 3.2.7: *Nam in Tusculano cum essem vellemque e bibliotheca pueri Luculli quibusdam libris uti* (for when I was down at Tusculum, and wanted to consult some books from the library of the young Lucullus); about the library of Sulla in *Att.*4.10.1: *Ego hic pascor bibliotheca Fausti* (I am nourished here by Faustus' [Faustus Sulla's] library) About borrowing books from Atticus he wrote in *Att.* 8.11.7; 8.12.6; 13.31.2 and 13.32.2. Some examples are: *Att.*13.31.2: *Quoniam etiamnum abes, Dicaearchi quos scribis libros sane velim mi mittas, addas etiam 'καταβάσεως.'* (Because you are still absent, I would like you very much to send me Dicaearchus' books of which you write, and add also his 'Descent'.) and in *Att.*13.32 he repeats his request: *Dicaearchi 'περι ψυχης' utrosque velim mittas et 'καταβάσεως'* ('Please send me both books of Dicaearchus 'On the Soul,' and the 'Descent.'). See also Quinn (1982, 125-128).

[45] Horace referred to this library in his *Epistula ad Augustum* (*Ep.* 2.1.216-217). Although there were libraries in Rome, Gallia for instance did not have a single library at the end of the first century B.C.

held contemporaneous authors, as a passage from Ovid's *Tristia* shows. When Ovid was banished in 8 A.D., his books were forbidden and their author was no longer able to visit the library on the Palatine. About this library Ovid says in *Tr.*3.1.63-64: *quaeque viri docto veteres cepere novique/pectore, lecturis inspicienda patent* (all those things which men of old and of today have come to in their learned minds are open for inspection by readers).

Distribution of copies from a master copy held in a public library cannot have started earlier than about 30 B.C., when Vergil had finished his *Eclogues* and Horace his *Satires* and *Epodes*. In 30 B.C. only the public library of Pollio had been opened and therefore the supposed dissemination of propagandist literature at the time before Actium and the fall of Alexandria was not possible through these channels.

Book dealers were a third option. It is assumed that they stocked older works and a limited selection of recent work. Normally, the book dealer made only the copies he sold, a kind of copying on demand. In Cicero's time there were some booksellers at Rome whose copies were often of a dubious quality. Cicero complained about this poor quality in one of his letters to his brother Quintus (*Q.fr.*3.6.1), where he writes: *de Latinis vero quo me vertam nescio; ita mendose et scribuntur et veneunt.* (Regarding Latin books, I don't know where to turn; the copies are written and sold full of faults). Horace referred in *Ep.*1.20.1-2 to the possible sale of his book in a bookshop. He says:

> VERTVMNVM Ianumque, liber, spectare videris,
> *scilicet ut prostes Sosiorum pumice mundus.*
> (Toward Vertumnus and Ianus, my book, you seem to look, in order, of course, that you may be offered for sale, polished smartly with Sosii's pumice)

The *Vortumnus* was a well-known shopping street in Rome with some book trade and the Sosii were booksellers. When Horace wrote these lines in 21 B.C., he reckoned with the possibility that a number of copies of his book would be distributed through the book trade. However, he had his reservations about that option. He used indeed words related to young male prostitution, such as *prostes* and *pumex* (pumice); the latter was used by boys for scraping off their bodily hair in order to look younger, but also for smoothing the ends of the book rolls. Horace referred to the Sosii again in his *Ars Poetica* (*Ars.*344-346), when he wrote about "international best sellers". I interpret these lines not only as a description of the bookseller's work but also as a reference to his own desire to keep away from the cheap writing for the masses. He implies that there is nothing wrong with a poem that both delights and instructs, but it should not be judged on those criteria alone. There ought to be a place for other poetry as well. Horace seems to suggest in these lines that only poems which were expected to do well commercially were selected by booksellers. The lines say:

> *lectorem delectando pariterque monendo;*
> *hic meret aera liber Sosiis; hic et mare transit*
> *et longum noto scriptori prorogat aevum.*
> (Delighting and equally instructing a reader; such a book earns the Sosii money; this crosses the sea and preserves for a long time its author's name)

It is obvious that this system of dissemination of literary work could not create a great number of copies. It was expensive and out of most people's reach, and one had to find a "master copy" to be able to make a duplicate. Thus, obtaining a literary work was a matter of a specific search. Any form of advertising and hard selling was completely absent, and thus one needed to have active knowledge of, or at least interest in, the work of the author. One could gain this knowledge from friends, hearsay or private and public recitations. In many cases the acquaintance of and affinity with the work was the result of contacts within a limited circle with shared interests and ideas. Therefore, it seems probable that most copies of, for instance, the poetry of Vergil or Horace were read or recited within a limited group of people, generally men, who shared the poet's culture and education, and who could discuss the ideas expressed by the poets. Moreover, as I will discuss below in the section about patronage, most poets belonged to the upper class. Starr (1987, 223) makes the point that

> for older Roman writers [for instance Vergil and Horace], literature was always seen as merely one facet of the life of an aristocrat, albeit a very important one. Although writing and reading undoubtedly affected their social relationships, those relationships were also based on other ties such as politics, marriage alliances, and family traditions.

Above I have touched only lightly on the question of which people or groups formed a poet's audience, the final stage in the process of transmitting his (political) views or feelings[46]. If poetry was being used for propagandist purposes, the question whose minds were targeted – the public at large, the soldiers, the middle class, the upper class, the senate or all these groups at once – should be addressed. According to Quinn (1979, 35; see also 1982, 140-165) literature in Roman society reveals a fundamental dichotomy:

> On the one hand, there is the possibility of a large audience, the possibility of a viable social function; if the writer is appreciated, he can feel he is worth his salt. On the other hand, there is the likelihood of no more than a small hypercritical élite more interested in technique than in what the writer has to say and the frustrating feeling of fulfilling no social function.[...]. The conflict is occasioned in large measure by the shift from an oral literature to a written literature: Plautus had a wide audience, for whom he had an immediate appeal; Horace wrote for a small audience of those seriously interested in difficult poetry.

---

46 Goold (1992, 110-123); Quinn, 1979; Quinn (1982, 75-180); Woodman & Powell (1992, 204-215).

Plautus' audience, made up of craftsmen and soldiers or ex-soldiers, could not read well enough to appreciate a long and difficult text, and they relied only on oral transmission. However, it is not Plautus' time we are interested in, but the last decades of the first century B.C.. At that time only a few tragedies and comedies of consequence seem to have been written, and drama did not hold a similar position in Roman life as it had done in previous centuries. According to Quinn (1979, 92) mime, comparable to our "music-hall shows ranging from striptease to political satire", became fashionable and was the entertainment for the general public[47]. The writers of drama were members of the upper class who did not write for the stage and did not want to be associated with organized performances (Quinn, 1979, 113; White, 1993, 47-63). Pliny the Younger (*Ep.*6.21) wrote about the reading of a comedy to a select few (*paucis*) by Vergilius Romanus in a letter to his friend Caninius Rufus[48]. Although Pliny wrote in the first century A.D., he described a custom which had started a hundred years earlier. Ovid's *Medea* was presumably never performed on stage, "since later in life Ovid boasted he had never written for the stage." (Quinn, 1979, 113). The same holds presumably for the tragedies of Asinius Pollio. Large audiences could also be reached through performances in which the poems were sung. Lowrie (2009, 83-97) examines this thoroughly for the case of Horace's *Odes*. She notes, however, that it is not clear whether sung performances actually took place, even taking into account Horace's own references to music. She (Lowrie 2009, 83) states: "we cannot determine whether Horace's self-referential musical vocabulary is figurative or literal," although in her opinion this does not exclude "their historical performances." Yet, it remains uncertain if, in the case of poems being sung, large popular audiences were reached.

Unlike the writers of comedy, Vergil and Horace – writers of serious poetry –had to find a new position for themselves and their poetry. They had no contacts at all with

---

[47] Horsfall (2003, 15; 56); Quinn (1982, 152-158). Lowrie (2009, 83) states: "Vergil's *Eclogues* were performed as mime." Three ancient texts refer to theatre performances of the *Eclogues*. The first is found in *Vita Donati*.26 (Hardie, 1966, 8): *Bucolica eo successu edidit, ut in scena quoque per cantores crebro pronuntiarentur* (He produced the *Bucolica* with such a success, that these were also frequently performed on stage by singing actors). The second is in Servius' commentary on *Ecl.*6.11 (Thilo, 1887, 66): *[...] hanc eclogam constat in honorem Vari esse praescriptam. dicitur autem ingenti favore a Vergilio esse recitata, adeo ut, cum eam postea Cytheris meretrix cantasset in theatro, quam in fine Lycoridem vocat, stupefactus Cicero, cuius esset, requireret.* (it is certain that this eclogue was written in honour of Varus. It is said however, that the poem was recited by Vergil under very great applause, so much so that, when later the prostitute Cytheris, who eventually was called Lycoris, declaimed it in the theatre, a stupefied Cicero demanded to know whose it was). "Cytheris was the most famous *mima*." (Quinn, 1982, 156). We will meet Cytheris/Lycoris again later in relation to Cornelius Gallus. The third text is from St. Augustine who writes of Vergil; '"few of you have known him from the text, many, from theatres"; that could mean, either from public readings or from dramatic performances' (Horsfall, 2003, 15). It is known that public readings of the *Aeneid* continued until the seventh century A.D., but this does not prove that it was widespread in the first century B.C..

[48] Not much is known about Vergilius Romanus; this mention in Pliny's letter is the only source.

popular audiences: the contacts within their circles of *amici* helped them to find new audiences.

Private readings of plays and poems to invited audiences and solitary reading became fashionable with the elite, who looked down on popular theatre. Readings to small groups were social as much as literary events (Quinn, 1982, 140-145). Servius testifies to this in his commentary on *A*.4.323: *cui me moribundam deseris, hospes?* (To whose mercy do you abandon me, who will soon die, guest?), the lines which Dido spoke when Aeneas deserted her. Servius writes that, when the passage was read to Augustus *cum privatim paucis praesentibus* (at his home with a few people present), the *princeps* was greatly affected. Such recitations were generally held among groups of social and intellectual equals, and this could certainly lead to social interaction, for instance by commenting on the texts.

Lowrie (2009, 14) testifies: "It is generally agreed that elite, literary reading was a kind of performance rather than the solitary activity now standard, although there has been something of a backlash against a purely oral understanding of reading: silent and solitary reading did exist and was presumably common among the well-educated." She (Lowrie 2009, 52) states also: "scholarship in antiquity did not occur in a social vacuum. [...], much research entailed social interaction, whether the company of a slave, a friend, or a group of peers, in person or by correspondence. Cicero and his friends circulated and discussed texts. Even solitary reading is a social practice."

It is well known that Vergil read his work in private sessions (Goold, 1992, 110-112; White, 2005, 322-323). Some testify that he was shy and soft-spoken. In *Vita Donati*.16 we read that Melissus, Maecenas' freedman, said: *in sermone tardissimum ac paene indocto similem* (speaking very slowly and almost like an uneducated man)[49]. More evidence can be found in an episode reported in the *Vita Donati* referring to an occurrence after the battle of Actium. In the *Vita Donati*.27 we read:

> *Georgica reverso post Actiacam victoriam Augusto atque Atellae reficiendarum faucium causa commoranti per continuum quadriduum legit, suscipiente Maecenate legendi vicem, quotiens interpellaretur ipse vocis offensione.*
> (He [Vergil] read the *Georgics* to Augustus during four successive days when he returned after his victory at Actium and stopped at Atella for curing his throat, and Maecenas took his turn at reading as often as he [Vergil] had to stop speaking by the loss of his voice).

Another mention of private readings by Vergil to Augustus is in Servius' commentary on *A*.6.861, where he notes that Vergil read book 6 to Augustus and Octavia, and probably others as well. One of the listeners, perhaps Octavia, broke out *fletu nimio* (in excessive weeping).

Horace has testified which kind of audiences he preferred. In *S*.1.10.73-74, which he probably wrote in the year 35 B.C., he says that he does not attempt to reach large

---

[49] The texts from the *Vita Donati* is in: Hardie (1966, 5; 8).

audiences: *neque te ut miretur turba labores,/contentus paucis lectoribus* (and that you should not strive to be admired by the crowd, but that you be content with the select few as your readers). Horace made the same point in *S*.1.10.39; *nec redeant iterum atque iterum spectanda theatris* (these [his satires] should not come back again and again to be seen on stage). About twenty-five years later he still held the same opinion[50]. In 12 or 11 B.C. he wrote a lengthy passage about three forms of poetry in his *Epistula ad Augustum* (*Ep*.2.1.156-218) in which he asks Augustus to look favourably on his art, which is poetry for private reading (*lectori credere*) (to entrust themselves to a reader) (2.1.214). In his earlier *Ep*.1.19, written between 23 and 19 B.C., he expressed similar feelings. In the lines 41-44 he says: *spissis indigna theatris/scripta pudet recitare [...]'/si dixi, 'rides,' ait, 'et Iovis auribus ista/servas* (If I said, 'I feel ashamed to recite my unworthy work in your crowded theatres,' says he 'You are merry, and preserve your work for the ears of Iove [Augustus]'). At the end of his life, when he wrote his *Ars Poetica*, he again poured scorn on the writing for large audiences and showed to be dismissive of the taste of large crowds, be it in the theatre or in someone's townhouse. In *Ars*.212-213 he writes: *indoctus quid enim saperet liberque laborum/rusticus urbano confusus, turpis honesto?* (What taste indeed would the man, ignorant and just finished with his hard work, have, a peasant mixed up with a man from town, the man without breeding with the respectable?). Lowrie (2009, 11) takes a similar line when she argues on the ground of the opening line of the first Roman Ode: "When Horace sets a premium on poetry's aesthetic quality, he makes a similar gesture against entertainment in favour of a higher standard that separates him from popular culture (*odi profanum vulgus* (I despise the vulgar throng), Odes 3.1.1)."

The passages from Horace discussed above tell us, firstly, that large-scale recitations (*spissis theatris*) of poetry took place and that Horace detested them. Secondly, that he did not have much regard for the typical theatre crowds and did not want to cater for their tastes (*Ep*.1.19 and 2.1). Thirdly, that he was lucky as he could read his poetry to *auribus Iovis*, Augustus' ears. Propertius writes also obliquely about his preferred audience in the sixteenth Elegy of the third book (PROP.3.16.29-30), where, discussing his burial place, he expresses his wish to be remembered as a poet who was read by a select group of friends and admirers.

Probably as a result of the new political situation, after 30 B.C. the composition of the Senate changed considerably, and the traditional political rhetoric, practiced by for instance Cicero, gradually disappeared. Rhetoricians had developed the practice of declamation, and when the opportunity for political oratory in the Senate dried up, declamation became a successful form of entertainment. Poets followed the example

---

50 Quinn (1982, 146, note 232), argues that Horace may have used the words *contentus paucis lectoribus* in *S*.1.10.74 as a way of answering public criticism of his fourth *Satire* and that the words do not represent his preferred kind of audience. This is unlikely, as Horace repeats his preference several times during a period of 25 years or more.

of rhetoricians and sought large live audiences (White, 1993, 59-63; 2005, 322-323). White (1993, 60) quotes Seneca (Maior) who testifies in his *Controversiae* (*Con*.4.2) that in the 30s or 20s Pollio "became 'the first of the Romans to recite his works to an invited general audience.'"

In the last chapter of this book the question whether Vergil's work was part of a programme of propaganda will be briefly discussed. At this stage, I wish to make two points about his – and likewise other Augustan poets' – audiences. My first point is that the manner in which works of poetry were selected and received by these audiences did not create ideal conditions for Octavian's and later Augustus' putative propaganda. These people had other ways of forming their opinions and they chose their allegiance on the grounds of their political and social interests. It is doubtful that these men were easily convinced by the poets to either adopt or change a long-held view. I suspect that the convictions of these people were not a result of information, but had been formed by their class, their family and their position. In addition, the works of the poets were merely a small part of the total of information which they received, and probably not the most important part. This brings me to my second point: the growing *auctoritas* of the *princeps*. As time went on, Augustus' rule grew firmer, which meant that he became more and more a force to be reckoned with. His greater authority was not just a function of his position, but also of his personality, and many people within the elite were starting to appreciate the peace and stability that he had brought (Galinsky, 1996, 10-41). It is not inconceivable that many began thinking along the same lines as Augustus and actually approved of his actions. These men did not need any propaganda. In the chapters to come, which deal with Vergil's poetry, I will argue that there are clear indications that over time Vergil adopted a similar acceptance of the *princeps*.

In summary, the conclusion about the nature of the audience or readership of poetry is that, in general, only the members of the elite could read, and that for most other people the usual way of receiving information was through oral channels. The distribution of books was an expensive business, and therefore only members of the upper classes could afford to buy them. This meant that poetry circulated only within a small circle of people. Poems were used for private reading or for recitation in small gatherings of members of the political and intellectual elite for whom poetry was not the most likely means of forming their opinions. According to White (1993, 60) the poets acted in large-scale recitations of poetry as literary performers with the "ostensible motive to test critical reaction to work in progress." There is no evidence that these were used as a platform to deliver political messages.

2.3 Patronage Or Amicitia?

When examining propaganda by the poets of the first century B.C., their position in society and their "patronage" have to be considered, as these have a bearing on the issue of their independence. The social background of the poet, his way of raising an income, and the nature of the system in which the "patrons" and the poet operated are all relevant[51]. The word "patronage" has become the common expression in secondary literature to describe the relationship between a wealthy man and a poet in Augustan Rome and later. For the purpose of this study the nature of these relationships need to be determined more comprehensively. White (1978, 78-79; 1993, 32-34) pointed out that the word *patronus* is never used in Latin to describe the literary relationship. White (1978, 79) states: "A *patronus* is somebody who has manumitted a slave, the formally designated sponsor of a town or corporation, or a lawyer who has undertaken a defence. The word does not denote the man who maintains a circle of friends and dependants." The use of the word "patron" or "patronage" originated in the Middle Ages to denote the men and women who founded and endowed churches and who had rights of appointment over them. White, (2007, 196) remarks that Horace "applies the word [*amicus*] to these relationships [socializing with others] more than twice as often as all other terms combined, and without apparent regard for status differences. 'Friend' is how he describes himself in relation to, among others, his junior protégé Septimius [*Carm*.2.6.24], the influential knight Maecenas [*Carm*.3.8.13], the senators Pollio and Messalla [*S*.1.10.85-87], and the prince Tiberius [*Ep*.1.9.5]." In this section, I will explore whether the terms suggested by White, *amicitia* and *amicus*, are not a more appropriate way of defining the relationships between men in influential positions and poets than the terms patronage and patron. Most of the poets of Augustus' days were members of the elite. Several belonged to the equestrian class, namely Tibullus, Propertius and Ovid, and Vergil was probably an *eques*; in any case it is very likely that his father was a landowner. Horace was probably the son of a member of the upper middle class of a town in Apulia and it is not unlikely that he also had been admitted to the equestrian ranks. Horace himself provides us with evidence that his father and he were not poor. Firstly, in *S*.2.7.53-54, he lets his slave Davus refer to his status as an *eques*: *tu cum proiectis insignibus, anulo equestri/Romanoque habitu* (You, when you have thrown away your regalia, the knight's ring, and your Roman dress). Secondly, in *S*.1.6.76-78, he refers to his own expensive education: *sed puerum est ausus Romam portare, docendum/artis, quas doceat quivis eques atque senator/semet prognatos* (but he dared to take his boy off to Rome, to be taught those studies which any knight or senator would have his own children taught). Although Horace was an exception, he was probably not an isolated case[52].

---

51 Gold, 1982, 1987, 2012a; Tarrant (2000, 183); White, 1978, 1982, 1993, 2005 and 2007; Williams (1968, 41-46).
52 White (1993, 5-14, esp. at 8-12); White (1993, 211-222) (Appendix 1) gives an overview of the social status of the Latin poets from the third century B.C. to approximately 140 A.D., and White (1993, 223-265) (Appendix 2) presents the connections of the Augustan poets. See also Ross Taylor (1925, 161-170).

Unlike in today's society, where paid work is standard for the elite, this was not common in late Republican and Augustan Rome and Italia. *Equites* and candidate senators had to satisfy a property qualification in order to belong to the senatorial ranks, and the required property was of such a level that one could live on it reasonably well. Therefore, for the elite not working was the norm, and it was this elite that supplied the leading politicians, army officers and intellectuals[53]. It goes without saying that for the rest of the population a life of hard toil, if not slavery, was the norm. The leading classes and their extended families lived a comfortable life in townhouses in Rome and other cities, supported by a great number of servants and surrounded by a large retinue who were dependent on them in one form or another. In addition, most had one or more estates in Italia and lived the life of the landed gentry. The large estates could accommodate many hundreds, including members of the family, tenants, servants and slaves. The economic and social relationships at the level of the extended family encouraged mutual dependencies of the family members, where the services of many were bartered for food and protection by the few. The result was that in the economic unit of the family barter was the norm, just as this form of economic exchange was common in many parts of society at large. Such was the economic environment which the poet knew and of which he was a privileged member. The nature of this membership, in particular being the *amicus* of the head or of a leading member of the family will be discussed below after some other economic aspects of being a poet have been considered.

Did the poet have any earning potential? The answer is clearly that this was not the case. Firstly, in a time when the mass production of books did not exist and where the markets for selling books were minimal, the turnover of the few booksellers and therefore the opportunity for the poets to generate an income were limited. A source of income was writing for the stage, particularly for pantomime, which had become popular. However, this was not regarded a serious occupation for a serious poet and was frowned upon. In some cases, poets seem to have received payment for theatre productions, the best known case being Horace's *Carmen Saeculare* in 17 B.C.; but these cases were few and far between. Secondly, the poets came from and worked in an environment where payment for any service was uncommon. In particular, payment for intellectual services, such as writing poetry or oratory, was seen as demeaning, as it brought the artist or professional down to the level of a trader. Thirdly, as argued above, most of the poets did not need any payment for their work anyway, as they had sufficient income from other sources, especially Vergil and Horace, who were relatively rich. White (2007, 198) makes some interesting points with respect to Horace's financial position: "about four years before they [Maecenas and Horace] met, Horace had already wangled a pardon for fighting at Philippi, and

---

[53] Veyne (1990, 5-69, esp. at 46-54, and 293-482). In his book, which concerns euergetism and the gift economy, he gives a detailed description of the social and economic environment.

a salaried clerkship that installed him in 'the status group which lies just below the rank of *eques.*' Subsequent largesse from Maecenas and others is best seen as an enhancement of his income rather than the foundation of it."[54]

The ancient sources tell us little about the precise nature of patronage at the end of the first century B.C., but it is unlikely that the relationships between the poets and the members of the Roman elite fit the *patronus-cliens* model. Although the economic and social background of a rich and often influential man differed greatly from that of a poet, the special bond between the two was generally founded on *amicitia*. In this section, the concept of *amicitia* will be discussed in more detail and will be set against the model of patronage. As argued above, the poets belonged broadly to the social upper class and moved as easily within this group as orators, lawyers and philosophers did. Charging for services rendered was not done, and a different but much more subtle mechanism transferred forms of recompense from the wealthy and influential to the professionals. White (1982, 56) says the following about this[55]:

> At least in Rome, these professions involved not simply the independent pursuit of an art or discipline but engagement in the life and interests of well-to-do society. Their practitioners provided services which beguiled the leisure or abetted the business of the leading citizens. By these services they established ties of *amicitia* which yielded far greater rewards than any system of fees or commissions would have done. Testamentary bequests, gifts of cash or property, and large loans on easy terms might fall into the lap of a rich man's friend. [...] The exchange of gifts and benefits had an important and well-defined place in the Roman code of friendship; and the wealth which accumulated in the hands of the rich during the early empire gave them rare means of putting in practice the virtue of liberality.

Amicitia therefore was more than just mere affection; Brunt (1988b, 355) notes that it bound people together "in bonds of obligation and honour." Amici did not take for granted that they were members of the same social set or held the same political conviction. Brunt (1988b, 356) also states that "*Amicitia* often purports to describe sincere affection based on a community of tastes, feelings and principles, and taking the form, where opportunity permits, of continuous and intimate association." There is often a shared intellectual interest and familiarity between the members of a circle of *amici*. *Amicitia* is not the same as *clientela*; the latter is generally based on a difference in social status and a *cliens* pays respect to his *patronus* and there is no feeling of being equals. A *cliens* is expected to fulfil his duties for his *patronus* in return for his protection.

---

54 Armstrong (2010, 13-14) presents some estimations of the wealth of Vergil and Horace. He asserts that both men easily met the property requirements to be *eques* or *senator*; "Vergil, another rich knight, died worth twenty million sesterces, richer even than Atticus [who was very rich]." See also White (2007, 197-198); Williams (1995, 295-296).
55 See also Brunt (1988b, 351-381); DuQuesnay (1984, 24-27); White (1993, 3-34); Gold (2012a, 303-310).

Descriptions of this form of *amicitia* can be found in several works of the Augustan poets, such as Horace's *Odes* and *Satires* and Propertius' poetry[56]. A good example is the following selection from the *Odes*. The opening lines of the *Odes* testify to Horace's feelings of friendship for Maecenas; *Carm*.1.1.1-2, a dedication to Maecenas, reads: *MAECENAS [...],/ o et praesidium et dulce decus meum*, (Maecenas, my protection, my pleasure and my glory). In *Carm*.1.20.1-5, Horace invites Maecenas to drink wine with him[57]:

> VILE potabis modicis Sabinum
> cantharis, Graeca quod ego ipse testa
> conditum levi, datus in theatro
> cum tibi plausus,
> care Maecenas eques,
> (A cheap Sabine you will drink from ordinary cups, a seasoned wine that I myself sealed with pitch in a Greek jar on the day when you were given an applause in the theatre, dear knight Maecenas)

In this short poem of twelve lines, Horace expresses his feelings of *amicitia* towards Maecenas. He offers him good wine, that has been stored away since the day of Maecenas' return to public life after a dangerous illness. This shows how much Maecenas had been in the poet's thoughts.

In *Carm*.2.17.3-4, which describes that the destinies of Maecenas and Horace are linked, one reads: *Maecenas, mearum/grande decus columenque rerum* (Maecenas, you are the great glory and pillar of my existence). Further in book 3, in *Carm*.3.16.29-30, Horace voices his joy with the Sabine estate, a "gift" by Maecenas (see below): *purae rivus aquae silvaque iugerum/paucorum et segetis certa fides meae* (A stream of clear water, and a few acres of woodland, a promise of my cornfield that never fails). In the Ode to Maecenas (*Carm*.3.29.25-26, 32-34) Horace expresses his concern for Maecenas' well-being:

> tu civitatem quis deceat status
> curas et Vrbi sollicitus times
> [...]. quod adest memento
> componere aequus; cetera fluminis
> ritu feruntur,
> (You trouble yourself about what form of government is suitable for the state, and being anxious for the capital you are fearful of [...]. Do not fail to put right what arises with even mind. Everything else is taken away like a river does)

---

56 See also Heyworth (2007b, 102-103), who gives a different view concerning Propertius.
57 The Loeb edition has *clare* in line 5, and the translation given is: 'Maecenas, illustrious knight.'

Horace tells his friend not to fret about matters of state and counsels him to take life more calmly. In *Carm*.4.11.18-20 he expresses joy for the celebration of Maecenas' birthday: *ex hac/ luce Maecenas meus adfluentis/ordinat annos* (from this day my dear Maecenas records the increase of his years).

Yet another source of the *amicitia* of Horace and Maecenas is a passage of Suetonius in his *Vita Horati* 2.2 (Rostagni, 1944, 112-113):

> Maecenas quantopere eum dilexerit satis testatur illo epigrammate:
> Ni te visceribus meis, Horati,
> plus iam diligo, tu tuum sodalem
> nimio videas strigosiorem;
> sed multo magis extremis indiciis tali ad Augustum elogio: "Horati Flacci ut mei esto memor".
> (How much Maecenas loved him is demonstrated sufficiently by this epigram: If I do not love you, my Horace, more than my own flesh, you may consider your comrade very much poorer than a scrag; But he said this much more strongly to Augustus in this short sentence in his last will: "Remember Horatius Flaccus as much as you will me.").

Finally, in *S*.1.5.40-42 Horace describes the value he attaches to being in the company of friends. The party is on the way to Brundisium to attend a meeting between Octavian and Mark Antony. Maecenas has joined them early and a few days later the other *amici* arrive. About the reunion with the latter, among them Vergil, he writes:

> *Plotius et Varius Sinuessae Vergiliusque*
> *occurrunt, animae qualis neque candidiores*
> *terra tulit neque quis me sit devinctior alter.*
> (Plotius and Varius meet us at Sinuessa, and Vergil, men such as neither the earth bore brighter, nor to whom another is more devoted than I)

As for Propertius, it is not certain whether his patron was a Volcacius Tullus, nephew of L. Volcacius Tullus, who was consul in 33 B.C., or Maecenas. I concur with Heyworth (2007b, 95-97, 103) that Propertius did not write seriously about any patron at all. Heyworth (2007b, 96) says: "In fact there is nothing to suggest closeness between Tullus and Propertius." and "my conclusion is that Tullus is intended to be read not as a real patron in either book [*Elegiae* book 1 and 3] but as a poetic imitation of one." In *Elegia* 1.22.2, Propertius refers to his *amicitia* with Tullus. Heyworth (2007b, 98), however, pours scorn on this *amicitia* and sees Tullus as "scarcily more than an acquaintance, not a life-long friend" of him[58]. Propertius refers in only two poems

---

[58] Heyworth (2007a, 94, note 57) discusses the relationship between Propertius and Tullus. Although he does not address explicitly the question of patronage versus *amicitia*, I interpret his view on the relationship of the two men as a neutral one, that is, neither a patronage nor an *amicitia*. He states: "there is no adequate evidence to suppose the patronage of Tullus was important to Propertius: he explicitly rejects the opportunity to accompany him as part of his uncle's *cohors* in I vi, and in other poems in which he features (I i, xiv, xxii; III xxii) the relationship is one of distance and contrast, not

(*Elegiae* 2.1 and 3.9) to a relationship with Maecenas. Heyworth (2007b, 103) states that "it seems to me bizarre to base an unquestioning belief in Propertius's acceptance of Maecenas's patronage on such a foundation."

Thus, generally the poets were part of circles of friends, and belonged to the retinue of members of the Roman elite, together with other intellectuals who had not wished to pursue or had not been accepted in a political or judicial career[59]. Although gifts from the magnates were forthcoming, as Maecenas' gift of the Sabine farm to Horace shows, it was not financial support that the poets expected. In a barter economy such as the Roman one, the transfer of goods was common, and people were used to this form of exchange, but this is not to say that I see the gift as a form of payment for services rendered. Bowditch (2010, 56) discusses this system of benefaction and states the following:

> In many ways, the Roman system of benefaction, and its subset of literary patronage, displays features of what anthropologists analyze as a "gift economy" (Veyne 1990; Dixon 1993; Bowditch 2001: 31-63). These characteristics include expenditure for the purpose of establishing prestige and status, the social cohesion that arises from gift-giving, an obligation to make a return gift, a perpetual disequilibrium of indebtedness – who is more indebted to whom? – and, perhaps most tellingly, a delay between an initial gift and its reciprocation, a temporal lag that, as Bourdieu points out (1977: 171), serves to mystify the economic aspect underlying an ideology of voluntarism in this form of exchange.

Murray (1990, vii-xxii), in his introduction to the translation of Veyne's *Le pain et le cirque*, notes that Veyne rejected rightly the use of modern economic theories for understanding ancient economic structures. Murray (1990, xv) states that Veyne understood that interpretations based upon modern theories

> do not correspond to the perceptions of those [in ancient societies] engaged in these [economic] activities, and because they do not explain either the specific forms of social response or the ways such forms change in history. These were the arguments that led Veyne to reject modern theories, and to assert the difference, the essential otherness, of ancient economic organization [from ours]. In order to understand ancient economic history, we must forget economics.

---

intimacy and respect." Gold (2012a, 310-314, esp. at 313) shades the traditional view of Maecenas' patronage of Propertius. She states: "*Thus the patron here* [PROP.2.1 and 3.9] *functions doubly*, in both a poetic setting, as a theme for Propertius' poetry and his Muse, and as the historical figure to whom this poetic gift might be presented." (my emphasis).

59 White (1993, 35-63) gives a list of recorded friendships of poets. To the circle of Maecenas belonged: Domitius Marsus (latter half of first century B.C.), Fundanius (comic poet), Horace, Melissus (comic poet), Plotius Tucca, Propertius, L. Varius Rufus (latter half of the first century B.C.), Vergil and the brothers Visci. To the circle of Messalla Corvinus belonged: Horace, Ovid, Sextilius Ena (latter half of the first century B.C.), Sulpicia (late first century B.C.; in the Tibullan corpus there are some poems about a romance; see White, 1993, 91), Tibullus, Valgius Rufus (consul in 12 B.C.; see Horace's *Carmen* 2.9) and Vergil.

This view has much to commend it, and the Roman gift economy can be seen as a development of the original Greek concept of public euergetism. In the Greek *polis*, giving to the community was a regularly occurring act of social responsibility[60]. This was also the case in Roman society, but in addition another group of receivers appeared: *clientes* and *amici*. Murray (1990, xiv) explains that

> A gift economy is not one based on gift *exchange*: that would be a society half-way to becoming [economically speaking] "rational" in our sense [...]. The first essential in a gift economy is that return, reciprocity, should be unequal and incommensurable: I give to you because you cannot give to me, being poor; or I give to you so that you may give to me something quite different, incapable of being measured against my gift.

According to Bowditch (2001, 22-23, 31-63; 2010, 53-74) the rich elite, the "patrons" (rather *amici*) of the poets, expected the companionship of the latter and a place in the poet's verse. One might rightly ask whether the gift of an estate in the Sabine hills is not rather excessive compared to the return gift of being the addressee in a few poems or of being in the presence of poets[61]. However, the nature of this "gift" is often misunderstood. Maecenas, who was at the centre of power, "gave" the villa at a time when much property was being expropriated, for various reasons, and perhaps Horace's Sabine estate was one of such properties. The ownership of the villa was presumably not transferred to Horace, but the poet enjoyed the free use of the property.

Through their association with the powerful, the poets hoped to receive recognition and publicity for their work. In these "salons", they recited their work, but presumably also discussed all kinds of subjects and their opinions might be sought once they had acquired the confidence of their *amicus*. Consequently, it is not surprising that the poets expressed their views in their poems.

Obviously, this raises the question about the independence of the poets. Maecenas, for instance, may have encouraged poetry in praise of Augustus, and White (2005, 331) states: "Maecenas' implication in the panegyrical slant of Augustan poetry is likely."[62]

---

60 Veyne (1990, 5-69; 293-482); see also Mauss, 1954.
61 Gold (2012a, 309-310); White (2007, 198, note 13), quotes Bradshaw (1989, 160-186) with respect to Maecenas' gift of the Sabine estate: "Bradshaw (1989) rightly insists that Horace does not unambiguously describe the Sabine farm as a gift from Maecenas and that the scholiasts, who do, cannot be proved to have possessed information independent of Horace's words. Cairns (1992) 107-9 is equally right to say that the conventional view may nevertheless be correct."
62 Anderson (2010, 34-52): this essay concerns the *amicitia* between Horace and Maecenas. The author (2010, 51) states that "book 1 of the Epistles [of Horace] is a decisive refutation of the theory of Horace's incorporation in the so-called Circle of Maecenas," and "he [Horace] is polite and friendly to Maecenas in three letters, but Maecenas does not control them, and indeed Horace presents himself from the start as choosing the genre [*Epistles*] in spite of Maecenas' wishes." Hekster (2009, 48-50), and White (2005, 331) do not regard the Augustan poets as propagandists, but emphasise the panegyric aspects of their poetry.

This does not make the poets dependent lackeys, and I differ from Bowditch, who argues that Horace traded his independence away for the gift of the Sabine estate. She (Bowditch 2001, 15) argues that "philosophers and poets alike avoid the language of patronage, and the corresponding diction of *clientela* or clientship, when describing relations between those of elite social status. Literary patronage, as I discuss in more detail below, was referred to almost exclusively in terms of *amicitia* or friendship." In her (Bowditch 2001, 16) opinion, Horace was only autonomous on "the level of poetic representation," and he felt all the "obligation – the sense of debt, gratitude, and compulsion to return" – that the gift economy would impose. In a recent (Bowditch 2010, 73) essay she also states that "whether in response to such power [the power which compels, not only if it invites but even if it beseeches] or to the more subtle persuasion of gifts, Horace wrote poems that cannot be dissociated from the socioeconomics of patronage." She overlooks, however, Horace's' independent attitude, which is evident through the contents of the many critical poems which he wrote until the end of his career. Bowditch (2001) analyses a total of 49 of Horace's poems: I consider 8 of these as critical, but she does not discuss the critical content of any of these[63].

Contrary to what has often been stated, the involvement as an *amicus* in a circle of *amici* worked as a guarantee of their independence. As accepted members of the circle of friends, the poets, who were financially independent, were seen as having a contribution to make, and the writing of poems about political or social questions emanated naturally from their position of intelligent observers and participants in the arguments, and not from an order to write propagandist material. This is a very different picture than that of what Nadeau (2004) in the title of his book calls the "safe and subsidized" poet by a patron: the scenario of *amicitia* is far more subtle. It is part and parcel of the social relationships in the late Republic and the early Empire. As White (1978, 92) says: "Once established in the *amicitia* of a rich man, poets received material benefits which were the perquisites of friends rather than the due of poetry."

Of course, there are other points of view. For instance, several scholars argue that Maecenas and Augustus put pressure on Horace. Watson (2003, 2-3) states that Horace's introduction to Maecenas' circle in 38 B.C. gave "obligations to trade mutual benefactions – on Maecenas' side the treasured gift of the Sabine farm," causing an "ideological sea-change which Horace now undergoes." In the planned sequel

---

63 Bowditch (2001, 278-280). She has analysed 4 *Sermones* (1.1, 1.6, 2.2 and 2.6, of which 2.2 is critical), 3 *Iambi* (1, 7 and 16, of which 7 and 16 are critical), 28 *Carmina* (1.1, 1.2, 1.3, 1.9, 1.12, 1.16, 1.17, 1.20, 1.22, 1.30, 1.35, 1.37, 2.1, 2.7, 2.13, 2.16, 2.18, 3.1-3.6, 3.22. 3.29, 3.30, 4.11 and *Carm. Saec.*, of which 1.35, 2.1, 3.6 and 3.29 are critical) and 14 *Epistulae* (1.1, 1.2, 1.7, 1.12, 1.13, 1.14, 1.16, 1.17, 1.18, 1.19, 1.20, 2.1, 2.2 and *Ars Poetica*, of which 2.1 is critical). I will discuss these in a planned sequel to this book on Horace's poetry.

to this book I will argue that Horace remained critical of Octavian/Augustus after 38 B.C.. Brink (1982, 558-560) sees a new period in Roman literature after 19 B.C.. He considers the withdrawal from public life of Maecenas as one of the significant factors of Horace's writing "official and panegyrical verse" (1982, 559). In the planned sequel I will also argue that Horace probably wrote his panegyrics for Augustus because he genuinely believed that the *princeps* brought peace and stability.

The issue of freedom of speech and libel laws in Augustan Rome is also relevant in this context. Raaflaub (2004, 57-58), discussing Cicero, touches on the exclusive character of the Roman aristocracy and their ways of dealing with power. Although the essay is about freedom of speech, the conclusions may also be relevant for the restrictions which the Roman elite put on dissenting opinions, thus making the poets feel less free to express their points of view. Raaflaub (2004, 57) states:

> It [freedom of speech] was not, however, a primary political value in aristocratic communities, even if at least the political elites claimed it as their natural right, based on their social distinction. [...] What mattered to them was that they were part of an exclusive group who shared power and government and in that sense were equal – even if within this framework they competed fiercely for primacy.

Rutledge (2009, 41-42) makes a relevant commentary from a sociological viewpoint:

> Hence under Augustus it seems that libel laws – which had existed previously, though perhaps with less rigorous application – were at last enforced. In general there was a pecking order: plebs must not attack their superiors; senators must not attack one another; nor must they attack the *princeps* – though again some of this was contingent on the context in which a particular remark was made. The relationship between the addressor and addressee, the social milieu, or the political situation could variously determine or qualify what could and could not be said.

Pagán (2004, 382) remarks: "Rather, in a way familiar even to us who prize freedom of speech, there was a growing acknowledgement of a gentlemen's agreement as to what can and cannot be said," In the next chapters I will argue that Vergil, who moved in the intellectual and social elite, claimed similar rights on freedom of speech as the members of the aristocracy.

2.4 Summary

Before drawing the different sections of this chapter to a close, I will quote the final passage of a book by Woodman and West (1984, 195) as I believe that this summarises and supports my conclusions of the relevant contextual factors:

> We set about this collection [*Poetry and politics in the age of Augustus*] in the hope that it would shed some light on an interesting subject which is important both to literary scholars and to historians. Our contributors show that easy distinctions such as 'Is this poetry or propaganda?'

and 'Are the poets sincere or are they puppets?' take us nowhere. The matter is complicated by the genuine friendships within the circle of writers and *principes uiri*, by the delicacy with which Maecenas treats his poets, by the recognition that Augustus had restored peace, order and idealism to a society which had lost them, by the significance of the form a poem takes and of the time when it was written. There can have been few ages in which poets were so intimately and affectionately connected with the holders of political power, few regimes with a richer iconography, few poets so profoundly moved by a political ideal and so equipped to sing its praises with subtlety, humour, learning and rapture. The reader of these poems needs a touch of all these.

The subject matters upon which Woodman and West touch have been broadly discussed in the present chapter. The conclusions of my chapter are that Vergil, Horace and Propertius had lived through a time of great political and social upheaval and change, and in Octavian saw the first signs of some stability. When peace arrived, new intellectual and artistic values in poetry emerged, such as a high degree of involvement in contemporary issues. References to mythical and historical subjects were used widely in the Augustan visual media and in poetry to present messages, often with a political content, about contemporary events. The poets were involved in circles of *amici* and belonged to the retinue of members of the Roman elite, together with other intellectuals. The reading or the recitation of their poetry took place in these privileged circles, where the poets' views and commentary on political matters were neither exceptional nor, perhaps, the most authoritative. One might therefore seriously doubt whether poetry with a propagandist character was an effective means of communicating political messages within the Roman elite.

3 The *Eclogues* And The *Georgics*

In the present and next chapter the focus will be on the political content of Vergil's poems, which will be read and analysed according to the scheme of analysis presented in section 1.2. Chapter 3 is divided in two parts: section 3.1 deals with the analysis of the *Eclogues* and 3.2 with the *Georgics*. Chapter 4 contains my observations and conclusions of the political content of the *Aeneid*.

3.1 The *Eclogues*: Pastoral Poetry With Commentary On Octavian's Land Confiscations[64]

3.1.1 Introduction To The Section About The *Eclogues*

The question whether Vergil expressed real personal experiences in the book of *Eclogues* has been explored extensively[65]. I will argue that the majority of the *Eclogues* contains the poet's commentary on two major political events: Octavian's resettlement of army veterans and the land expropriations after Philippi in 42 B.C., and their effects on the Italian countryside. These were very much part of his personal knowledge. Presumably, Vergil tapped into his own observations – and those of people he knew – of the land expropriations and its effects, using these for portraying the political and social state of affairs in Italia. This does not mean that parts of the *Eclogues* are Vergil's autobiography, in the sense that the poet is portraying directly his own experiences. For instance, Tityrus' visit to Rome in *Ecl*.1. to plead his case is not a description of the poet's own visit to the city to prevent the expropriation of his or his family's property. This visit probably never took place[66]. In narrating Tityrus' story in *Ecl*.1, Vergil does, however, use his personal experience of the expropriations. In the words of Perutelli (1995, 45): "Virgil adds a new level of reference, beyond Theocritus,

---

64 This section intended as a paper to be submitted to a journal was written in close cooperation with Marc van der Poel as co-author. I am grateful to Claire Weeda and Els van Thiel for their helpful comments.

65 Boucher (1966, 16-26); Clausen, 2003; Coleman (1981, 21-36); Dominik (2009, 111-132); Hermes (1980, 212-234); Nauta, 2006; Otis (1966, 109-128); Page (1960, xv-xvii); Perutelli (1995, 36-42); Tarrant (2000, 173-175); Wilkinson (1997, 24-39); Williams (1968, 303-329); Zetzel (2006, 38-52).

66 Boucher (1966, 17) also interprets Tityrus as a poetic *persona*, and not as representing Vergil himself. He states that "dans la première [*Eclogue*], Virgile, par l'intermédiaire de Tityre [...] témoigne de ses sentiments envers Octavien." (Vergil, through the intermediary of Tityrus, [...] speaks in the first [*Eclogue*] of his views of Octavian). All renderings of French text into English are mine. Cf. Jenkyns (1998, 169-172),, I hold that Vergil was indeed "concerned for the distresses of his fellow countrymen, the Mantuans – so much is explicit – and to that extent personal experience enters into his allusions to the confiscations; and of course it remains possible that he himself lost some land, possible even that Caesar restored it, or compensated him in some other way. But that is pure speculation, nothing more; *Virgil does not suggest this to us, either directly or by implication.*" (Jenkyns, 1998, 171; my emphasis). See also the discussion of *Ecl*.1 in section 3.1.2.

that to historical [but not autobiographical] events, which he transforms into a source of pathos. The confiscations of land introduce and explain suffering, sorrow and the sense of an end which in Theocritus' pastoral world was only aroused by the natural cycle of life and death." Vergil's literary debt, in his book of *Eclogues*, to his Hellenistic predecessors, chiefly to Theocritus, has long been recognised, and many scholars from the nineteenth century onwards have identified Vergil's Hellenistic model or models for the *Eclogues*. Generally, scholars have explored the subject from the perspective of literary models[67]. In addition to expressing his love of the Italian country, Vergil had a second objective when he wrote pastoral poems. Clausen (2003, xix-xx) hints at this when he compares Vergil with Theocritus:

> In one important aspect, however, Theocritus is more strictly pastoral, more realistic – more considerate, that is, of his fiction – than Virgil: very rarely does he [Theocritus] allow an extraneous reference to obtrude, [...]. Yet these few references in Theocritus, together with his [Vergil's] own sense of the sufficiency of the country, enabled Virgil, apparently, to include a wider range of experience – politics and politicians, the ravages of civil war, religion, poetry, literary criticism – in a pastoral definition.

Scholars who explored whether Vergil expressed real personal experiences concluded that this is only the case in a limited number of *Eclogues*. In addition, they are divided as to which poems these experiences can be found in[68]. In an introduction

---

67 It is probable that Vergil had access to a collection of pastoral poetry by Artemidorus of Tarsus. This edition contained ten poems attributed to Theocritus (*Idylls* 1 and 3-11). See Clausen (2003, xx); Gow (1986, lix-lxii, esp. lx). In the case of the Eclogues Harrison (2007c, 34-74), writing about generic enrichment and/or generic departure in Vergil (and Horace), examines particularly Vergil's inspiration by Theocritus, although Harrison (2007c, 39) also points out that "often we can see a connection between generic enrichment and [reference to] political circumstances." An anonymous reviewer of the manuscript made the comment that "the most important scholarly debates and literature" on the literary tradition are not sufficiently acknowledged in this book. I do not enter the discussion on the literary tradition on purpose, as the focus of the book is very different from most, if not all existing scholarly work. I do not examine Vergil's poetry from a literary perspective. My focus is on the functional frame – in this case his political views – which explains why the reviewer did not find a comprehensive discussion of the scholarly literature, which generally is concerned with the literary.

68 Page (1960, xv-xvii) identified *Ecl*.1, 6, 9 and 10 as a "group distinctly connected with the poet's personal experiences." Boucher (1966, 17), who explores in detail the question whether the *Eclogues* were "pour les Romains de l'époque augustéenne le symbole de la poésie personelle, du refus de la vie politique" (for Romans of the Augustan age the symbol of personal poetry, of the refusal of the political life), argues that both are present. Williams (1968, 303-329) is ambiguous however, whether the dispossessions in the Mantua region are necessary to the interpretation of *Ecl*.1 (see Williams, 1968, 308) or *Ecl*.9. (see Williams, 1968, 321). Coleman (1981, 21-36) describes Vergil's notion of pastoral as a "synthesis of myth and reality" (see Coleman, 1981, 33). He (1981, 28) also refers to the "intrusions of real persons", and acknowledges Vergil's personal experiences. Because Hermes, 1980 is concerned with book 4 of the *Georgics*, we do not know his view on all the *Eclogues*, as he discusses only *Ecl*.1 and 9 in his dissertation. However, he (Hermes, 1980, 234) states: "Deshalb geht auch die Auffassung

to his essay about the interpretation of the tenth *Eclogue*, Conte (1986, 102, note 8) asserts: "I do not wish to deny completely the legitimacy of studies based on biographical or historical data, but in general one must be extremely wary, as the damage done often exceeds the benefits obtained." I trust that I will not damage Vergilian scholarship too much, when I suggest that the historical context – in which Vergil places most of his *Eclogues* – functions as the frame for his political opinions and cannot be ignored. In the following section (3.1.2) I argue that in the majority (8 of 10) of the poems – many more instances than generally recognised – Vergil uses his personal knowledge and experience in order to expose the social and political situation caused by the decline of the rural order. Vergil did not describe historical events precisely, but adapted these using them as functional references. For instance, in a number of places Vergil mentions historical persons who are supposed to be actively involved in the dispossessions in his own area and specific events in his own region. Examples are: Alfenus Varus in *Ecl*.6.7, 6.10 and 6.12 (Vergil ingratiates himself with the land commission or with Varus, who represents the man in charge of the expropriations) and *Ecl*.9.26-27 (Varus is active in the Mantua region), and C. Cornelius Gallus in *Ecl*.6.64 (typifying Vergil's hope that someone may intervene on behalf of the suffering Mantuans) and *Ecl*.10 (Gallus' loss of his mistress). Specific events are referred to in *Ecl*.9.27-28 (Varus, spare Mantua), and in *Ecl*.10.47 where Vergil mentions the river Rhenus in Northern Italia. Bowersock (1971, 76) argued persuasively that "the scholia [Servius, Donatus and others] are worthless evidence for details of the land commission, and so is Virgil. That can only redound to the poet's credit. He has caught a mood, an atmosphere in his poems." There is no independent confirmation of their involvement and the scholiast had presumably no other source than the poems[69]. However, Vergil certainly

---

zunehmend dahin, daß auch Vergil irgendwie von den Ereignissen [the land appropriations] betroffen worden sein muß, und daß dies auch in den Eclogen zum Ausdruck kommt." (Therefore, the opinion, that Vergil must also have been affected somehow by the events [the land appropriations], and that this also finds expression in the *Eclogues*, recedes progressively). All renderings of German text into English are mine. Clausen (2003, xxx, 29-30, 121-126, 236-237, 266, 289) identifies only *Eclogues* 1, 8, 9 and 10 as having a theme which is the result of Vergil's knowledge of the land confiscations and the ensuing social problems. In addition he discusses a bearing on contemporary political issues in *Ecl*.4. Wilkinson (1997, 24-39) concludes that *Eclogues* 1, 4, 5, 6 and 9 show Vergil's engagement with contemporary political issues. See also the discussion of the views of Servius and Donatus in Patterson (1987, 24-40), which raises similar questions, for instance: "Donatus professed uncertainty as to whether the *causa* of the *Eclogues*, which he merges with *intention*, was a desire to imitate Theocritus or to make a statement about the progress of civilization or, rather, to gain the indulgence of Caesar and the recovery of Virgil's lands" (Patterson, 1987, 31). For the supposed loss of Virgil's lands see note 66.

69 Boucher (1966, 16-26); Clausen (2003, 181); Jenkyns (1998, 170-171); Nauta (2006, 303 note 8) does not commit himself, and argues rightly: "It has been endlessly debated what may and what may not be deduced from these sources (see Horsfall (1995) 12-13, with references), and I will not presume on any

introduced historical persons. I suggest that Varus, Pollio and Gallus represent a special kind of historical allegories symbolizing the involvement of high-ranking officials without exactly specifying who was involved where. Thus, Vergil showed the gravity of the situation. A number of passages can be interpreted as referring to events affecting people who the poet knew well (see note 66), such as *Ecl.*1 (Tityrus' attempt to extract a promise that his farm would not be confiscated in line 42), or *Ecl.*9.10 (Menalcas having won a reprieve for the family farm or other farms). There is evidence, which has so far been neglected, that Vergil referred to the new reality of the social and economic relations in the countryside through his choice of names of *personae*. Examples are the impertinent Thyrsis, in *Ecl.*7.33-34, used to refer to new arrogant landowners, or Mopsus in *Eclogues* 5 and 8 to refer to the new-comer soldiers, who replaced or exploited the traditional farming population. Further, the river *Rhenus* in *Ecl.*10 refers to the Reno (near Mantua), which Lycoris saw when she left Gallus, symbolising Gallus' loneliness as a result of the misfortunes of war. Finally, in *Ecl.*4, one can read in Vergil's preferred new constitutional order once the war was over.

Vergil was much concerned about the disappearance of farming and small holdings in Italia. In his poetry he voiced not only his concern and compassion with the suffering farmers, but also pointed out political responsibilities, often through allusions. Vergil did not hold back in naming the men whom he held responsible. In the book of *Eclogues* I read less praise of Octavian and his associates than for example Nauta argues[70]. Zetzel (2006, 50), in an essay about Horace's *Sermones*, writes that Vergil "does indeed deal with substantial problems and with the realities of Roman and Italian life in the Triumviral age." However, his (2006, 50) conclusion that "it might be argued (as I [Zetzel] think Horace does argue), that to veil the moral and social issues under the mask of pastoral, to emphasize poetics rather than politics, to construct a smooth, elegant, and artificial world and diction [as Vergil does] is *not the best way to write or to live in Rome of the mid-30s*" (my emphasis) is not supported by the results of this study. Vergil is an elegant poet indeed, who, through his allusions in virtually every *Eclogue*, presents his political messages in a pastoral wrapping, thus subtly shrouding his viewpoint.

In a relatively recent essay (2009), entitled "Vergil's Geopolitics," Dominik also discusses the political content of the *Eclogues*, particularly on the ground of a detailed examination of *Ecl.*1[71]. Dominik (2009, 111) states: "My application of geopolitics

---

specific reconstruction of 'what really happened.'" I concur with Nauta. See also notes 81 and 91.

70 Nauta (2006, 301-332) states that Octavian is praised in *Ecl.*1 (2006, 305-310) and in *Ecl.*8 (2006, 310-316), and 'other nobles' (Pollio, Varus and Gallus) in *Ecl.*3, 6, 10 and 9 (2006, 316-324). I will discuss these at the appropriate places in the next section. See also note 112.

71 Dominik (2009, 115-117; 121-124; 125-126 and 127-129). *Ecl.* 2, 3, 6, 7, 9 and 10 are touched very briefly (2009, 129).

involves this nexus of political and geographical factors but emphasizes specifically the political aspects that relate to, influence, weigh upon or literally cast their shadow upon a particular geographical space, in the case of Vergil, the countryside." He (2009, 112) describes his "investigation of Vergilian geopolitics" as follows:

> Vergil uses nature to explore political issues throughout his *oeuvre*. Although Vergil's pastoral world has been viewed generally as a place of co-operation between man and the natural environment, the essential features of Vergil's commentary in exposing the vulnerability of the environment and its denizens to the ever-encroaching politico-military and urban worlds are not just generally sustained – despite moments of optimism and hope – but rather increase in magnitude and gravity as his narrative progresses.

According to Dominik (2009, 117-122), this is a matter not only of Vergil writing green politics, such as "rural exploitation" (2009, 117), and "destruction [of the landscape], often as the result of politico-military force and the shameless consumption of the civilized world" (2009, 119), but also of Vergil pointing out that "disintegration of the *locus amoenus* in the *Eclogues* is afforded political import not just by its manifest association to the intrusion of the urban superstructure, but especially by the personal tragedies of its inhabitants" (2009, 122)[72]. This study not only adds to Dominik's argument, as I am examining all *Eclogues*, but also has a different emphasis. I will argue that Vergil intended to deliver a political statement about the destruction of rural communities, tapping into his own knowledge and experience of the land expropriations. Martindale (2000, 107-124) also considers the issue of "green politics" in the *Eclogues*. He (2000, 118) contends that "at the very least one must recognise that Vergil's green spaces are somewhat 'lordly possessions.' Vergil shapes his rustic world into a form that allows him and his friends and patrons to make their own appearance there without embarrassment alongside the shepherds." In Martindale's view an important aspect of Vergil's "greenness" is his protest against the evils of the city. I intend to demonstrate that Vergil's concern went much deeper, originating in what he saw as the fundamental destruction of the way of life of the crofters and the substantial change, even loss of, traditional rural values.

Most scholars (note 68) hold the view that *Ecl*.1 and *Ecl*.9 contain elements of Vergil's personal experience and portray contemporary social and political issues, and that *Ecl*.2 and *Ecl*.3 are bucolic poems without any reference to political topics. Concerning *Ecl*.1 and *Ecl*.9 I concur with the above views. However, I read *Ecl*.2 and *Ecl*.3 as bucolic poems indeed, but specifically referring to the noble values of country life, which were in danger of extinction. *Eclogues* 1, 2, 3 and 9 will be discussed only briefly, and I will focus on six poems (*Eclogues* 4, 5, 6, 7, 8 and 10), offering some new arguments and interpretations.

---

72 Cf. Jenkyns (1998, 171); see also note 66.

3.1.2 The *Eclogues*

In this section each *Eclogue* will be examined with a view to establish whether a particular poem has a political content, and its nature. This will be done not only by close reading of the poems, but also by referring to the appropriate political and social context.

The first *Eclogue* is written as a conversation between, on the one hand, Meliboeus, who has to leave for foreign lands as his farm has been expropriated and who wonders if he will ever return, and on the other hand Tityrus, who has the good fortune that he can remain, albeit on a small plot of infertile land. In the poem, land has been confiscated after the battle of Philippi (42 B.C.) and Vergil depicts the contrast between the two men, the unhappy Meliboeus for whom there is no future (as for many others) and the lucky Tityrus. Meliboeus asks why Tityrus has been absent and Tityrus answers that he was in Rome. Now that he is living with frugal Amaryllis, he can save enough from his property (*peculium*) to purchase his freedom, also he gained the ownership of the small piece of land. This is the first of several examples, where Vergil expresses his positive opinion of the role of women: frugal Amaryllis enables Tityrus to be free. Yet the threat of expropriation remains. Thus, Tityrus goes to Rome to plead his case and in Rome *hic illum uidi iuuenem, Meliboee, quotannis/bis senos cui nostra dies altaria fumant* (Here I saw him, Meliboeus, the youth for whom our altars smoke twelve days each year) (*Ecl.*1.42-43). The youth is Octavian and the altars refer to Tityrus celebrating the ruler's birthday every month[73]. Octavian gives Tityrus his "freedom", a promise that he can stay on his land, and tells him to continue with farming as of old: Tityrus enjoys his "double freedom" in the shade of a beech tree. That is why in lines 6-7 Tityrus cries out: *O Meliboee, deus nobis haec otia fecit./ namque erit ille mihi semper deus* (O Meliboeus, a god has given us this ease. For truly, to me this man shall always be a god). The interpretation that Tityrus' visit to Rome may be an allusion to Vergil's own efforts to prevent the expropriation of the family property is very likely erroneous (see note 66). In this poem, Vergil acknowledges the relative peace which Octavian has brought after Perusia (40 B.C.). However, the poem is also somewhat ambiguous. On the one hand, there is praise for Octavian as the new benign ruler, on the other there is Tityrus' visit to Rome, where his future is decided by the same benign ruler (or elite) who carried out the dispossessions after Philippi: a serious criticism of Octavian. It is most likely that the poem was written in 41 or 40 B.C., when Vergil presumably was still harbouring the memory of his negative experiences regarding Octavian's role in the land confiscations[74].

---

[73] Clausen (2003, 48); Nauta (2006, 305-310); Williams (1968, 307-312, esp. 310-311); Wissowa (1902, 157-159).
[74] Nauta (2006, 309-310). Nauta's literary frame: "Tityrus had to go to Rome to meet his 'god.'. Whether Tityrus may sing or not is decided in the city, and this demonstrates that Virgil's *bucolic*

The second half of the poem is about the contrast in the fortunes of the two characters. In lines 46-47, Meliboeus says to Tityrus in lines 46-47: *M. Fortunate senex, ergo tua rura manebunt/et tibi magna satis, quamuis lapis omnia nudus* (Meliboeus: Happy old man, so these fields will remain yours, and large enough for you, although everywhere there are exposed stones). In lines 67-72, Meliboeus bewails the misfortune of never seeing his homestead again and having to leave his native place. The poet's sympathy is for the loser, Meliboeus, who in *Ecl*.1.67-72 says:

> M. en umquam patrios longo post tempore finis
> pauperis et tuguri congestum caespite culmen,
> post aliquot, mea regna, uidens mirabor aristas?
> impius haec tam culta noualia miles habebit,
> barbarus has segetes: en quo discordia ciuis
> produxit miseros: his nos conseuimus agros!
> (Meliboeus: Tell me, shall I ever, in future, see again with amazement the land of my family and my humble cottage's roof covered with turf; shall I, after I don't know how many years, see with amazement my ears of corn, my kingdom? For a godless soldier will own this well-tended fallow land, a bloody soldier these crops! See where civil war has brought us, wretched citizens! For these people we have planted our fields!)

In the first *Eclogue*, Vergil praises Octavian for bringing hope of peace and stability, but the six lines near the end of the poem suggest that it is also a sad poem marked by embitterment and despair caused by the expulsion of the small farmers. The word *barbarus* in line 71 does not refer to a foreigner, but to a brutal Italian soldier who has received Meliboeus' land in the resettlement programme. These last lines make it a poem with political content, and show criticism of Octavian, who was personally involved in the resettlement programme[75].

Scholars generally accept that *Ecl*.2 (together with 3) belongs to Vergil's earliest work[76]. The second *Eclogue* is a love poem in Hellenistic fashion against a Vergilian background showing the contrast between the simple and good life in the country and the imminent corruption of the city. The poem tells us that the shepherd Corydon, modelled on Polyphemus of Theocritus' eleventh Idyll, is hopelessly in love with the boy Alexis, who is kept by their master in town. Apart from the Vergilian theme of

---

poetry as well is dependent on forces beyond it." Nauta however also makes the functional point: "And indeed the praise for Octavian is inextricably linked with the criticism: *if there were no dispossessions, there would be no need for the saving grace of an intervention by a beneficient ruler.*" I interpret the criticism as the dominant mood of the poet. (emphasis is mine).

75 Cf. Dominik (2009, 122): "Octavian, who presided over the land evictions of 41 BCE in the aftermath of the triumviral settlement imposed on Italy after the battle of Philippi."

76 The book of *Eclogues* was presumably written between 42 B.C. and 35 B.C. The year 42 is derived from the assumption that *Ecl*.2 and 3 were probably the earliest and were written before *Ecl*.9, which was written in 41 or 40 B.C. The year 35 B.C. results from the reference to Octavian in *Ecl*.8.6-13. See also: Clausen (2003, xxii-xxiii); Perutelli (1995, 28-31).

the pure country and the evil town, the poem also expresses the power of the absentee landlord over the life of the farmer.

The third *Eclogue* is influenced by Theocritus' fifth *Idyll*. *Ecl*.3 has two parts: the first contains the conversation between two herdsmen preparing for their singing contest and the second concerns the contest proper. In the third *Eclogue* the theme of the threat to pastoral life which we saw in the second *Eclogue* is maintained and expanded. The opening portrays the lack of care of the herdsmen, Menalcas and Damoetas, for their sheep and the suffering of the flocks. It presents the dark side of their work when they destroy the vines (line 11) *atque mala uitis incidere falce nouellas* (and wrongfully cutting through newly planted vines with an evil pruning-hook), or try to steal goats (lines 17-18) *non ego te uidi Damonis, pessime, caprum/excipere insidiis* (Didn't I see you, mischief, ambushing Damon's goat).

In the second part of the poem, the two herdsmen decide to turn to poetry and commence a singing match. They settle on the prizes. Menalcas' prize is a pair of beautiful beech cups and Damoetas also brings a pair of goblets along; according to Putnam "these are strange objects for a humble shepherd to be carrying around – esoteric and highly cultivated" (Putnam, 1970, 125). Thus, these simple country folk possess unexpected qualities of appreciation of the beauty of the arts, and this is one of the ways in which Vergil glorifies the simple country life. Towards the end of the poem Asinius Pollio, lover of pastoral poetry and poet of tragedy himself, appears. At the time of writing this *Eclogue* Vergil and Pollio were friends. By introducing him, Vergil makes the point that in fine poetry simple rural people can engage with the sophistication of the elite. In fact, unsophisticated people can attain Pollio's poetic grandeur and reap the fruits of honey-sweet success; lines 88-89 say: *D.Qui te, Pollio, amat, ueniat quo te quoque gaudet;/mella fluant illi, ferat et rubus asper amomum* (Damoetas: he who loves you, Pollio, may he come where he is glad that you are also there; honey may flow for him and the bramble may bear fragrant fruit). The poem ends in a positive vein. Poetry has a stimulating effect on the two men: Vergil shows in lines 92-103 how, after they had lost themselves in poetry, they appear to change into caring herdsmen. Their singing match ends in a draw. When Vergil wrote this poem, probably in late 42 or early 41 B.C., he had just witnessed or was still close to the traumatic experiences caused by the expropriation of the land and farm of many people in his immediate environment. He expresses the wish to be a poet of pastoral song and to reach the same heights as his friend Pollio. But in *Ecl*.3 Vergil also shows his resolve to depict the farmers' life, reflecting on the noble values of life in the countryside which were under siege.

The fourth *Eclogue* was probably written in 40 B.C., or at least no later than 37 B.C., when Mark Antony broke with Octavia. *Ecl*.4 is the famous poem in which Vergil writes about the birth of a saviour, and about his vision that the Golden Age was to be restored to man. In lines 4-5 he refers to the prophecy of the Sybil of Cumae: *Vltima Cumaei uenit iam carminis aetas;/magnus ab integro saeclorum nascitur ordo* (The last age of Cumaean song has now come; the great line of centuries is born afresh).

Harrison (2007c, 38) refers to the possibility that some Sibylline oracles "may possibly treat Roman political issues of the period of *Eclogue* 4 (41-40 BC), even an Egyptian queen who may be Cleopatra." However, he (note 12) also mentions "recent scepticism on the identification." Indeed, the pact of Brundisium between Antony and Octavian had brought hope of a lasting peace (Cf. Clausen, 2003, 120-121). The restoration would begin at the time of Asinius Pollio's consulship in 40 B.C. and coincide with the birth of a child (lines 8-10), the hoped-for son of Octavia and Antony: the latter can be deduced from lines 15-17, which refer to Hercules, whom Antony claimed to be his ancestor. Although *Ecl*.4.17 *pacatumque reget patriis uirtutibus orbem* (and he shall rule the world pacified by his father's bravery) could be interpreted as referring to just Antony, it is more likely that Vergil refers to Antony and his hoped-for son. Similarly, it should be noted that the reference to Hercules in the last two lines of *Ecl*.4 is a functional model, confirming the identity of the expected child, who, as Antony's son, descended from Hercules[77]. These final lines (*Ecl*.4.62-63) are: *incipe, parue puer: qui non risere parenti,/nec deus hunc mensa, dea nec dignata cubili est* (Begin, little boy: at whom his parents did not smile, and whom no god deemed worthy of his table, and no goddess of her bed). Vergil thus expected that Antony – and not Octavian – would bring peace to Italia. This is not surprising as Antony was in reality the prominent leader in the years immediately after Iulius Caesar's death. Vergil belonged to Antony's party and was a friend of Pollio, at that time one of Antony's most trusted lieutenants. Vergil also testified that he expected that the son would assume power (*reget orbem*) after his father, thus accepting some form of hereditary succession in a quasi-royal line, that of Antony. However, Antony's and Octavia's wedlock produced a daughter and was dissolved soon after, when Antony returned to Cleopatra.

Ecl.4 is a poem of hope for peace and the return of order to the farming lands of Italia and, as the child grows up, the expansion of Roman power, particularly in the East: *iterum ad Troiam magnus mittetur Achilles* (great Achilles will be sent again to

---

[77] Cf. Clausen (2003, 121-125, and 144-145). *Ecl*.4.15-17 and *Ecl*.4.62-63 refer to Hercules; the last line specifically to *Odysseia*.11.602-604. Antony should be considered the father of the child. Nisbet (1978, 70) states: "the mother is presumably Octavia." See also Nauta (2006, 329). Three other views are relevant. Gordon Williams (1974, 45), states that the child could have been born either from the marriage of Antony and Octavia or from that of Octavian and Scribonia, who had married a few weeks before Brundisium. He prefers the second option. Veyne (1997, 25) asserts that the annunciation had nothing to do with reality and that "the Child does not exist, or rather it is every child at once." I do not concur with either Williams' or Veyne's view on the child's descent. Both scholars overlook the significance of the clear reference to Hercules in the last two lines of the poem. The third view is that of Harrison (2007c, 40-42), who leaves the question whether Antony or Octavian was "the more likely sire of a great dynasty" open "for it would be a brave poet who would have made a firm choice in 40 B.C.." I argue that Vergil made this choice as it reflected the political situation in 40 B.C. Thus, Clausen and Goold's (1992, 110) suggestion that the poem is about a child of Antony and Octavia is very credible. See also also Wilkinson (1997, 35-39). In the words of Clausen (2003, 125): "*Failure of historical perspective vitiates much that has been written about the Fourth Eclogue."* (my emphasis).

Troy) (line 36). The blessings of the "Golden Age" were to spread over the whole earth and the land would bring forth the produce without hard labour. However, things worked out differently. The Pact of Brundisium did not hold, Octavian had to continue fighting the civil war and eventually had to confront Mark Antony; in the end the power struggle was decided in the sea battle near Actium[78]. The lines 53-54 suggest that Vergil intended to eulogise the newly born prince. In *Ecl*.4 Vergil gave a powerful political statement about his preference for a hereditary form of non-elected political authority and one-man rule. Nauta (2006, 327) interprets *Ecl*.4 as "praise of an unborn boy." Indeed, Vergil expresses his expectations for Antony's unborn child, who turns out to be a girl. If the poem is classified as panegyric, I would label it as praise of a political view, the kingship. At the time of writing, Vergil did not know that he was later to transfer his allegiance to Octavian.

In the fifth *Eclogue*, Vergil demonstrates again his leaning towards pastoral poetry. However, this poem also contains references to contemporary themes, which lie deeply hidden in the text, for example Vergil's love for the countryside, the simple and honest life of the shepherd and the suffering of the land and the farmer.

Ecl.5 is about two men, the young newcomer Mopsus, and the older shepherd Menalcas, who decide to make music and to sing. The name of Mopsus returns in *Ecl*.8 and in both poems the name is Vergil's functional model to indicate a stranger[79]. "Mopsus" alludes to the men who, following the recent expropriations, had moved to areas where previously only small farmers and herdsmen worked and lived. In this *Eclogue* one finds several indications of this. The first is in the opening lines of the poem: *Me. CVR non, Mopse, boni quoniam conuenimus ambo,/[...] consedimus [...]?* (Menalcas: Mopsus, why do the two of us not sit down, [...] since we have come together, both good at ...?). The formality of the opening may be the result of Menalcas' apprehension about the intentions of the recently arrived Mopsus and their short acquaintance. There is a second indication in the manner in which Menalcas

---

[78] Nauta (2006, 330-332) points out an interesting intertextuality between on the one hand *Ecl*.4 and on the other the beginnings of the sixth and seventh books of the *Aeneid* (*A*.6.86-94 and *A*.7.41-45). He (2006, 332) sees a clash between the two. *Ecl*.4 concerns the "wars that would lead to the restoration of the Golden Age." The two passages in the Aeneid concern "the wars that Aeneas will wage in Italy."
[79] Clausen (2003, 155). Vergil's inspiration from Theocritus can be seen in his choice of the shepherd's names in the *Eclogues*. Many of these (12 of 19), such as Amyntas, Corydon, Daphnis, Menalcas, Tityrus, and others, come from Theocritus' *Idylls*. But not Mopsus. Mopsus (Μόψος) was a mythological hunter and warrior mentioned by Apollonius Rhodos. He was a member of the crew of the Argo and also a seer who counselled Iason. Ovid (*Met*.8.350) mentions Mopsus who joined Meleager as a hunter. See also: Perutelli (1995, 42-44). Clausen (2003, 155) says of Mopsus' name: "Mopse, not a pastoral name before Vergilius; perhaps borrowed from Ap. Rhod. 3.916-18." See also the discussion on *Ecl*.8 below. It is of course possible that Theocritus used the name of Mopsus in work that has been lost to us, but was still extant in Vergil's time and not part of Artemidorus' anthology. However, when Mopsus features in other work than Vergil's he is not a shepherd but a fighter or at least a member of a group of fighters.

grovels before young Mopsus, and pays him compliments, by comparing him to the best singer in the region, Amyntas. During the wrangling as to who will sing first and where, one reads in lines 8-9: *Me. Montibus in nostris solus tibi certat Amyntas./Mo. Quid, si idem certet Phoebum superare canendo?* (Menalcas: In our hills only Amyntas vies with you. Mopsus: What then, likewise if he competes with Apollo to excel him in singing?).

Mopsus is different and appears to feel rather superior to Menalcas. In the words of Clausen (2003, 151): "Menalcas tactfully changes the subject and invites Mopsus to begin." The younger one starts with a song about Daphnis' death. One can read a reference to the state of the countryside in Mopsus' song. Putnam (1970, 172-173) makes this point discussing lines 20-44, especially the opening lines: *Mo.Exstinctum Nymphae crudeli funere Daphnin/flebant [...],/cum complexa sui corpus miserabile nati/atque deos atque astra uocat crudelia mater* (Mopsus: The Nymphs lamented over Daphnis, cut off by a cruel death, [...], when his mother holding tight her son's piteous body calls upon both gods and stars for their cruelty). According to Putnam (1970, 172): "To sing of death in a sylvan setting is ominous enough; the elegiac tone is not consonant with the pastoral world's assumed idealism. But to mourn for the 'cruel' demise of Daphnis, bucolic hero par excellence, is to hint at the ruin of the landscape." Later in the same passage (lines 34-39) Mopsus complains again of the destruction of the pastoral paradise. Lines 38-39: *Mo.pro molli uiola, pro purpureo narcisso/carduus et spinis surgit paliurus acutis* (Mopsus: Instead of the soft violet, instead of the brilliant narcissus, the thistle springs up and the thorn with its sharp prickles).

It is time for Menalcas' reply. Daphnis has been deified and in *Ecl.*5.56-61 Menalcas sings that Daphnis looks down from the Olympus and sees Mopsus' dead landscape come alive again. Menalcas twice exalts Daphnis to the stars (lines 51-52) and thus to immortality: *Daphninque tuum tollemus ad astra;/Daphnin ad astra feremus* (and we will lift up your Daphnis to the stars. Daphnis we will lift up to the stars). Mopsus, however, only sings of Daphnis' fame reaching the stars (line 43), emphasizing instead his death: *Daphnis ego in siluis, hinc usque ad sidera notus* (I was Daphnis amid the woods, from here to the stars known)[80]. Vergil displays the different attitudes of Menalcas and Mopsus: on the one hand Menalcas, the native rural man, who expresses his hope that his beloved country will be restored, and on the other Mopsus, the arrogant young newcomer, who cannot see further than his immediate gain and who grumbles about the poor condition of his land. The poet points out that Daphnis, "bucolic hero par excellence" (see above), is now far away among the gods, and that the indigenous farming population cannot rely on him to restore normality. Daphnis looks down from heaven and sees the ruined land achieve peace as if the

---

80 Lowrie (2009, 145-150) stresses the performative aspects of poetry and Vergil's view on its power. She interprets political issues, such as the land appropriations, as only contingent.

Golden Age had returned. Lines 60-61 say: *nec lupus insidias pecori, nec retia ceruis/ ulla dolum meditantur: amat bonus otia Daphnis* (Neither does the wolf design an ambush against the flock nor nets a trap against the deer: kind Daphnis loves peaceful calm). However, this was not to materialize immediately. Vergil, observing the ravages of a political strife which was still raging when he wrote this poem (about 40 B.C.), describes a future with peace and stability as still distant. When it finally arrives, farmers will be able to work their fields again and offer their prayers to Bacchus and Ceres as of old (lines 78-80).

The sixth *Eclogue* starts as a *recusatio*, as Vergil declines to write about the military successes of Alfenus Varus, a most undistinguished soldier. Vergil pays him a compliment (lines 11-12), however, as he knows that he needs the goodwill of the land commission, or perhaps of Varus himself, as he may have been in charge of land confiscations in the region at a time when many of the Mantuan people stood the possibility of losing their property. Vergil affirms that, instead of writing a panegyric poem for Alfenus Varus, he will write pastoral poems. In *Ecl.6.6-8* he notes that there are enough poets willing to sing Varus' praises, but that he *agrestem tenui meditabor harundine Musam* (now I will exercise myself in the rustic Muse on a fine reed). Although the poem is addressed to Varus, the central figures are Silenus and C. Cornelius Gallus; the latter is introduced in line 64. In his commentary on *Ecl.6.64* (Thilo, 1887, 77), Servius states that Gallus was in charge of taxing the townships in Northern Italia (*qui [Gallus] a triumviris praepositus fuit ad exigendas pecunias ab his municipiis*). In his *Commentarii Vergiliani*.13 (on *Ecl.9*), Donatus says also that Gallus was involved in the land distributions in Gallia Cis-alpina in 42-40 B.C.: *sed postea et per Maecenatem et per triumviros agris dividendis Varum, Pollionem et Cornelium Gallum [...] agros recepit* (but later he [Vergil] got his land back through [the agency of] Maecenas, and the three joint commissioners for the land division Varus, Pollio and Cornelius Gallus). As stated in the introductory section above (3.1.1), it is doubtful that Varus and Gallus were in fact involved in the expropriations in the Mantua region. In the same section, I also explained that it is feasible that Vergil used their names to symbolise the actual involvement of high-ranking officials: I will interpret the references to Varus and Gallus in the present poem along these lines. Gallus' role will be examined more extensively in our discussion of *Ecl.9* and *Ecl.10*[81].

Two young shepherds find Silenus, drunk as usual, asleep in a cave and awaken him, aided by the beautiful Naiad Aegle. They make him sing. In lines 31-42, Silenus first sings a cosmogony, about the creation of order, - *et rerum paulatim sumere formas* (and gradually to take up the forms of things) (line 36) –, the repopulation of the earth after the flood (Pyrrha, line 41), and Prometheus' gift of fire to mankind (line

---

[81] For Alfenus Varus' and Gallus' involvement, see Bowersock (1971, 75-76); Clausen (2003, 181) and my notes 69 and 91. The text of Donatus is at: www.intratext.com. See also Patterson (1987, 31-34); Ruikes (1966, 67, note 43); Wilkinson (1966, 320-324). See for Gallus: Gibson, 2012.

42). This is followed by a passage (lines 43- 73) in which Silenus sings four short references to mythological figures, comprising one or two lines, and two stories: that of the mythological Pasiphaë (lines 46-60), and that of the living poet Gallus (lines 64-73). Vergil cuts Silenus short – *quid loquar aut [...] ut narrauerit?* (why tell that he sang either of [...]?) – and he finishes Silenus' song in lines 74-81 with the stories of Scylla and Philomela. Many different interpretations of Silenus' song have been given, generally from the perspective of literary history and literary model[82].

Before interpreting *Ecl*.6, the structure of Silenus' song needs considering. After Silenus has opened with the cosmogony, the second part of his song presents three themes within a specific structure. This contains an opening with a short reference to Hylas, followed by the more extensive passage about Pasiphaë (15 lines). Next, there are again two short references, to Atalanta and to Phaëthon's sisters, after which follows the passage about Gallus (10 lines). Finally, the song finishes with two short references, to Scylla and to Philomela. Each pair of characters represents a theme: (1) Hylas' and Pasiphaë's theme is uncontrolled passion, (2) references to Atalanta and Phaëton are about fateful ambition and recklessness, and (3) Scylla and Philomena refer to murder, either of passing Homeric sailors or their next of kin. Towards the end of the song, Vergil's friend Gallus appears abruptly amidst this gathering of mythological figures to meet Linus, "a shepherd of divine song" (*diuino carmine pastor*), on Mount Helicon. In lines 69-70, Linus gives Gallus Hesiod's reed pipes: *dixerit: 'hos tibi dant calamos (en accipe) Musae,/Ascraeo quos ante seni* (he said: "these pipes give you the Muses (see take them), which once they gave to old [Hesiod] of Ascra)[83].

Two aspects of the poem are significant for an interpretation from a functional point of view: firstly, the meaning of Silenus' song, particularly the passages about the cosmogony and Pasiphaë; secondly, the roles of Alfenus Varus, Silenus and Gallus. In Silenus' song, Vergil refers to the actual political and social state of affairs in the countryside near Mantua. The song evolves from picturing a situation of order and concord in the cosmogony, to several cases of disorder, confusion and discord, such as uncontrolled passion, fateful ambition and murder, all of which Vergil encountered in his own time. The myth of Pasiphaë's impossible and unhappy love for a bull alludes to this. The bull lives in a perfect, pastoral environment enjoying himself with a heifer (lines 53-54). The woman lacks these happy blessings when she roams through the countryside (line 52): *a! uirgo infelix, tu nunc in montibus erras* (Ah! unhappy girl, you

---

[82] Clausen (2003, 175-178); Coleman (1981, 203-206); Harrison (2007c, 48-56). See also note 11 in section 1.2.3.
[83] Clausen (2003, 203): "giving the pipes of a dead singer to a worthy successor was a pastoral tradition." Nauta (2006, 320-321) states: "Although Gallus receives *calamos* [pipes] (l.69) from *Linus.... pastor* (l.67), it is not bucolic poetry that he is going to write, nor is it panegyric:" Gallus is going to write aetiological poetry. This is important with regard to the interpretation of the opening lines of *Ecl*.10 below.

now stray about the hills). Vergil is referring to the Fall of man in mythological times: Pasiphaë, possessed by madness, has lost control (line 47, *dementia cepit*), while the bull is calm. Her passion for the animal is so extreme that she wants him back and she calls upon the Nymphs to help her return the bull home (lines 55-60). It is a world upside down: the beast is lord and man has lost control. Coleman (1981, 192) observes that "the tracks of the bull, for whom *errare* is part of normal life, mock the woman who is now alienated from her own way of life," and he (1981, 205) states: "there is therefore an implicit contrast between *Amor* as a principle of creative concord in the natural world [cosmogony] and *Amor* as a discordant and destructive force in human affairs – Pasiphae, Scylla etc." Thus, this mythological reference may allude to the ravages caused by the destruction of nature through human aberrations, such as Vergil experienced in his own part of Italia.

As I explained above Varus, Silenus and Gallus also symbolise this unhappy state of affairs. In expressing the ruin of traditional country-life, Silenus, the boisterous man blessed with down-to-earth wisdom, voices the views of the common farmer. Vergil's contemporaries Varus and Gallus typify the involvement of high-ranking Romans in the expropriations near Mantua, with an unreasonably harsh Varus in charge and Gallus attempting to mediate. This is most likely also the reason behind the different treatment of the two men in the poem. Varus is refused a panegyric, whereas Gallus is generously praised in lines 64-66: *Gallum/[...],/utque uiro Phoebi chorus adsurrexerit omnis* (Gallus, how the whole choir of Phoebus rose to the soldier and man of honour). Gallus is called *uir*, which in this context means more than simply "man". The adjacency of *uiro* and *Phoebi* has a special significance, accentuating Vergil's respect for him (Cf. Clausen, 2003, 202). In Silenus' song, Gallus typifies Vergil's hope of saving the countryside, since he is not only Vergil's friend and fellow poet, but also a general and politician and an associate of Octavian (see also Putnam, 1970, 212-215).

This interpretation of *Ecl*.6 differs substantially from that of several scholars, who are mainly concerned with Vergil's poetic orientation and/or his literary models. A few examples: Williams (1968, 249) interprets *Ecl*.6 "as a poem addressed to Varus and enclosed within two references to the inspiration of Apollo." He (1968, 249) also states: "the other relevance which the [Gallus'] passage has in the song of Silenus is that it introduces Apollo, who lies behind both Virgil's poem and the song of Silenus, as the inspirer of yet another poet [Gallus]." Coleman (1981, 206) refers to "Theocritus' literary manifesto in *Id. 7*." Martindale (2000, 111) noting the intertextuality of *Ecl*.6 in general and of Silenus' song in particular – both with respect to Vergil's predecessors and to Ovid in the *Metamorphoses* – remarks that "Eclogue 6 is now normally read metapoetically, as a poem about poem-making." He (2000, 112) sees the passage about Pasiphaë as "poetics of eros." Clausen (2003, 177) does not recognise the above interpretation of Vergil's reference to Pasiphaë, stating "that Pasiphaë's perverse passion [...] (45-60), and the literary initiation of Gallus (64-73) occupy so much of the song is indicative of contemporary taste, Virgil's and that of his friends." More specifically about the Gallus' passage, Clausen (2003, 200) states:

"the only interpretation which V[ergil]'s lines (64-73) will bear is the obvious one: [...] he [Gallus] rises, so to speak, from a lower to a higher level of poetry (Hippocrene), from love-elegy and Lycoris to aetiology and the Grynean Grove [a cult-place of Apollo]." Nauta (2006, 320-321) interprets the Gallus' passage in the same way, and sees the lines on Gallus as "praise, but praise of his poetry, and that this poetry is characterised as different from, but related to Virgil's." Gibson (2012, 179) – in his paper on Gallus – sees *Ecl.*6.64-73 as "telling us that Gallus – in a generic ascent up the mountain of poetry – must now begin writing verse in the aetiological tradition." Similarly, Raymond (2013, 65) also reads "Gallus leaving the valley of Permessus for the mountains of Helicon" as Gallus' "literary movement from love elegy to the higher level of Callimachean aetiology." None of the modern scholars concludes from the Gallus' passage that he changed to writing pastoral poetry[84].

The above interpretations all belong to the literary frame. Although part of the poem is rightly identified as Vergil's search for his poetic allegiance and literary model, Vergil also pursued a second objective. The functional references to the derangement of Pasiphaë, to other mythological figures and to Alfenus Varus, Gallus and the land confiscations may be seen as a commentary on contemporary events, expressing Vergil's anxiety about the radical changes in Italia and the destruction of the traditional social and economic relationships of the rural population, for which men close to Octavian shared the responsibility, as well as his hope that the situation may improve.

In the seventh *Eclogue* Meliboeus encounters two herdsmen, Corydon and Thyrsis, and Daphnis, the ideal pastoral poet. Although Corydon and Thyrsis are *Arcades ambo* (Arcadians both) (line 4), Vergil situates the meeting on the bank of the river Mincius (modern Mincio), near Mantua[85]. The two herdsmen are "equal in singing, ready to respond" (line 5), while Daphnis sets the standards. The serious singing begins in line 29 as the shy and gentle Corydon and the smug budding poet Thyrsis offer their praises, one to Diana and the other to Priapus, and both to Galatea, to other gods such as Bacchus and Venus, and finally to love and nature.

The poem is set against the background of pastoral life, making a sharp contrast between Corydon's positive, loving and generous attitude to nature and Thyrsis' pessimistic, crude, and arrogant attitude. For instance, lines 33-34 refer to Thyrsis'

---

84 Ross, Jr. (2008/1975, 189-215 = Ross 1975, 18-38) gives the Gallus' passage a very different interpretation within the literary frame. Quoting Volk's (2008, 14) summary, he writes: "a scene that he [Ross] suggests is based on an episode in Gallus' own writing. Ross shows how Vergil, following Gallus, constructs a 'poetic genealogy' that leads from Apollo, via Orpheus and Linus, Hesiod, and Callimachus and other Alexandrian authors, and how the poet places himself in that same tradition." I will not discuss Ross' view in this book, as it is too far removed from my focus.

85 Jenkyns (1989, 32) argues rightly that *Arcades ambo* signifies that the setting cannot be Arcadia; "if some character in a book says 'I have just met two Englismen,' we can be virtually certain that the scene is not laid in England. I would not say this in Surrey; I might well say it in Paris."

lack of interest: *T. Sinum lactis et haec te liba, Priape, quotannis/exspectare sat est: custos es pauperis horti* (Thyrsis: A bowl of milk and these cakes, Priapus, once a year, are more than you can expect; you are guarding a poor garden). In lines 46-47, we encounter the contrasting positive picture of Corydon, who praises the arbute tree for providing shade for his flock: *et quae uos rara uiridis tegit arbutus umbra,/solstitium pecori defendite* (and the green arbute that shelters you with thin shade, keep the summer heat away from my flock)[86]. Vergil shows us these contrasting attitudes in order to denounce the changes that were taking place in farming in Italia, which he considered as negative and reprehensible. The poet refers to these changes by deliberately setting the poem in his native region (river Muncius) where large-scale land appropriations were taking place. Like in *Eclogues* 5 and 8, the poet's choice of the name of one of the herdsmen, Thyrsis, who is portrayed as an outsider and as hostile to farmers' life, is significant. Many of the names of Vergil's herdsmen come from Theocritus' *Idylls* (see note 79). The name of Thyrsis is most likely derived from *Id*.1[87]. Although in this *Idyll*, Theocritus' Thyrsis is a herdsman and experienced "master poet" (*Id*.1.20), his namesake in *Ecl*.7 is the loser in the singing match. In the last line of Ecl.7 Vergil confirms the superiority of the poet and traditional herdsman Corydon over Thyrsis, the outsider: *ex illo Corydon Corydon est tempore nobis* (from that moment Corydon is the Corydon for us). In the words of Clausen (2003, 232): "the name becomes metaphorical: not simply Corydon, therefore, but Corydon the ideal singer." The supposition that Vergil portrays Thyrsis as an outsider fits in with the following: many names occur in more than one *Eclogue*, but Thyrsis appears only in this poem. The book of *Eclogues* contains only three more places where Vergil uses a particular name only once. In those instances he always portrays someone who is relatively alien to the traditional pastoral setting[88].

Thus, although the seventh *Eclogue* is wrapped in the form of a conventional pastoral poem, it also refers, on the one hand, to the genuine farmers and herdsmen of old with their love for their flocks and the countryside (Corydon), and on the other hand to uninterested outsiders and *nouveaux riches*, the new landowners (Thyrsis). Many of these had made their fortunes during and after the civil war and through land confiscations. Vergil had experienced most of the smallholders being reduced to beggary and had seen his old beloved Italian countryside disappear. It is likely that the poem was written after 40 B.C.. The poem is a critical statement by Vergil about social and political developments in his time.

---

[86] Coleman (1981, 226); Coleman (ad. loc.) classifies *exspectare sat est* as "impudent." See also Clausen (2003, 211).
[87] For *Id*.1 see Gow (1986, vol.II, 1-32) and Hunter (1999, 60-107, esp. at 61).
[88] Palaemon in *Ecl*.3.50 and 3.53, refers (acc. to Clausen, 2003, 104) to a "most immoral *grammaticus*." Stimichon in *Ecl*.5.55 cannot be traced (acc. to Clausen, 2003, 167), and Antigenes in *Ecl*.5.89 has a minor role (Clausen, 2003, 108).

Immediately after the opening lines of the eighth *Eclogue*, Vergil mentions an unnamed patron about whom Clausen (2003, 233) remarks: "were they [lines 6-13, in which the patron is mentioned] to be removed, their absence would not be felt." Although Clausen sees the lines as superfluous, he (2003, 233-237) analyses the question thoroughly and concludes that the patron is Octavian and not Pollio. His first argument is taken from history and geography: in lines 6-7 Vergil says about the patron: *seu magni superas iam saxa Timaui,/siue oram Illyrici legis aequoris* (whether you are already sailing past the rocks of the great Timavus, or passing the coast of the Illyrian sea). The Timavus, a river in North Italia, flows into the Gulf of Trieste near Aquileia. It is unlikely that these lines refer to Pollio's return to Italia after his campaign against the Parthini in 39 B.C.. A return via the Aquileia region would have entailed a rather dangerous, circuitous sea journey. Octavian, however, campaigned not far from the Timavus region in 35 B.C.. According to Clausen a second argument lies in the reference to Sophokles in lines 9-10: *en erit ut liceat totum mihi ferre per orbem/sola Sophocleo tua carmina digna coturno?* (Say, shall I ever be permitted to bring throughout the world your songs, which alone are deserving of the buskin of Sophokles?). It is thought that this may refer to Octavian who had begun composing his tragedy *Ajax*. Pollio's renown as a tragic poet was too great to receive such an expression of hope for his future. A third argument (Clausen, 2003, 237) is found in a quotation from QUINT.*Inst*.10.1.91-92, where in congratulating Domitian "on his accession to the throne, and extolling his [Domitian's] literary genius, he [Quintilian] quotes the last line of Virgil's dedication": line 13 of the eighth *Eclogue*. Clausen makes the point that Vergil's dedication must have been to Octavian, as Quintilian would not have used a dedication to the rather unknown Pollio. Finally, Clausen argues that the words of lines 11-12 – *accipe iussis/carmina coepta tuis* (accept the songs begun at your command) – refer to a possible patronage of Vergil. Clausen (2003, 236) asserts that "if Pollio ever was Virgil's patron, he has been superseded, since the First *Eclogue* effectively dedicates the Book of *Eclogues* to Octavian." In my view, Clausen presents persuasive arguments – particularly his first and third – that Octavian is the most likely dedicatee and consequently that *Ecl*.8 was written in or after 35 B.C..[89]

Apart from the opening, the poem consists of two parts, in which two herdsmen, Damon and Alphesiboeus, each sing a long song. The first song, Damon's, is about a shepherd who has lost his girl (Nysa). He had hoped to marry her, but she was given away to another man (Mopsus): *Mopso Nysa datur* (Nysa is given to Mopsus) who is told: *Mopse, nouas incide faces: tibi ducitur uxor* (Mopsus, cut new torches: your

---

[89] For the suggestion that Octavian is the dedicatee see also Bowersock (1971, 73-80); Nauta (2006, 310-316); Rudd (1976, 122, note 10). Different views are given by Coleiro (1979, 259-261); Perutelli (1995, 29-31); Putnam (1970, 255); Tarrant (2000, 174 note 14). Lowrie's interpretation of the addressee of the poem (Lowrie, 2009, 144-5, esp. at 144) differs considerably. Similarly to *Ecl*.5, she focuses on the performative aspects of Vergil's poetry and his search for the right genre.

bride is brought) (lines 26 and 29). Putnam (1970, 261-278) does not specify whether Damon's shepherd's lament is a result of having lost his girl to another shepherd. But suppose that Mopsus is not a shepherd. There are some indications for this in lines 32-33. Nysa is *digno coniuncta uiro* (wedded to a real gentleman) and she is described as *dumque tibi est odio mea fistula dumque capellae* (while you hate my pipe and my goats). One would hardly expect her to marry another shepherd if she hates his work so much. Could Mopsus, instead of a shepherd, be a newcomer, perhaps a soldier who has been given a piece of land (see note 79)? The social order has been upset and the shepherd's life has been irrevocably changed. Even nature is confused, when griffins mate with mares: *iungentur iam grypes equis, aeuoque sequenti cum canibus timidi uenient ad pocula dammae* (soon griffins shall mate with horses, and in the next age timid deer will come together with dogs to the drinking places) (lines 27-28). Strangers dictate life and what the shepherd has known and loved since childhood is lost. If Damon's song is read in this way the question of the dedication to either Octavian or Pollio is particularly meaningful. Vergil wants the addressee to be aware of the grave situation in the countryside and the destruction of traditional life. Octavian, the man who is responsible, ought to do something about it.

Vergil also refers to the destruction of life in the countryside in Alphesiboeus' song. This song concerns a woman who has lost her *coniunx*; he has left her and the countryside for the city. *Ecl*.8.64-68 depicts her predicament:

> Effer aquam et molli cinge haec altaria uitta,
> uerbenasque adole pinguis et mascula tura,
> coniugis ut magicis sanos auertere sacris
> experiar sensus; nihil hic nisi carmina desunt.
> *ducite ab urbe domum, mea carmina, ducite Daphnin.*
> (Bring out the water and crown this altar with a soft band, and set on fire herbage full of sap and vigorous frankincense, that I may try to turn around the indifferent feelings of my husband with magic rites; nothing but songs is lacking here. Bring him home from town, bring Daphnis home, my songs)

The theme of these lines resembles that of Damon's song. Just as he sings about a shepherd who has lost his girl Nysa to a man who did not belong to the shepherd's world, Alphesiboeus sings about a woman who likewise lost her man Daphnis to a girl who did not belong to her world. However, the sorrows are resolved in different ways. Damon finishes his song with *praeceps aërii specula de montis in undas/deferar* (head first I shall cast myself down from the high mountain top into the waves) (line 59-60). Alphesiboeus' woman, instead, places her trust in the power of magic and song, as lines 69-70 testify: *carmina uel caelo possunt deducere lunam,/carminibus Circe socios mutauit Vlixi* (Songs can even bring down the moon from heaven, and by songs Circe has changed Odysseus' comrades).

Ecl.8 is a poem about the destruction of the normal life of the countryside. There are two reactions: Damon's shepherd is driven to suicide, but Alphesiboeus' woman uses poetry as a healing power. The woman is the stronger personage, but both suffer from the disruptions of their lives. Both the shepherd and the woman represent the positive values of pastoral life, such as home, fidelity and genuine love, while Nysa and Daphnis represent opposite values.

At the end of the poem, when Alphesiboeus finishes his song in line 109, all seems to turn out well for the woman, as she says in a variation on the refrain: *parcite, ab urbe uenit, iam parcite carmina, Daphnis* (Stop! Daphnis comes home from town, stop now songs). Vergil testifies that the values of pastoral life, as expressed through her song, eventually triumph. This is his message of hope. Putnam's (1970, 291) closing remarks about the eighth *Eclogue* refer also to this optimism: "The first song is essentially a tragic vision, looking at the end of a pastoral dream. The second offers a renewal of happiness after a time of uncertainty." But is there really a happy ending? The penultimate line (108) is *credimus? an, qui amant, ipsi sibi somnia fingunt* (Can I believe it? Or do lovers make up their own dreams?). The woman expresses her disbelief that all is well; her feeling is that everything is still in chaos. Therefore, contrary to Putnam's (1970, 290) view, that "like *Eclogues* 6 and 7 it [*Ecl*.8] is a poem about the possibilities of bucolic verse, as form and as idea" and (1970, 292) that "the totality is once more a meditation on bucolic poetry, this time [in *Ecl*.8] specifically concerned with how love can either destroy or recreate the pastoral myth," the eighth *Eclogue* conveys primarily a different message: the uncertainty for the people of the countryside remains, as the civil war and its aftermath have destroyed the way of life in the countryside and with it the essential values of Italia. Vergil is critical of Octavian, to whom the poem was probably dedicated, and who, in his struggle for power, shares in the responsibility for the destruction of the traditional social structures of the country[90].

There is a thematic connection between the ninth *Eclogue* and the first. Both poems are concerned with the evictions of the farmers and herdsmen from their land, which, after the battle of Philippi, was, in many parts of Italia, distributed among veterans. In the present poem, the poet describes the bitter situation now arisen. The poem's opening is very direct in describing the effects of the land confiscations. One can feel the anger and embitterment of the dispossessed in the first six lines. Moeris, who is now a tenant on his own old farm, brings his payment in kind to the new owner, an urban dweller: *L. QVO te, Moeri, pedes? an, quo uia ducit, in urbem?* (Lycidas: Where to, Moeris, afoot? Perhaps, where the road leads, into town?) (line 1). Moeris is particularly aggrieved that he is ordered off his old patch: *M. [...], aduena nostri/ [...] ut possessor agelli/ diceret: ' haec mea sunt; ueteres migrate coloni'* (Moeris: that a stranger, who now owns my little field, should say: "this is mine; move, tenant (of the past") (lines 2-4).

---

[90] Contrary to Nauta (2006, 310-316). Although Nauta also considers Octavian the dedicatee, he does not mention the critical nature of the poem. I consider the criticism of Octavian the kernel of *Ecl*.8., making it less panegyric than Nauta suggests.

Next, a poet, Menalcas, whom the others know (*uestrum Menalcan*) and who is personally involved, is introduced by Lycidas. This poet is said to have saved the area from dispossession (lines 7 and 10): *L. Certe equidem audieram, [...] omnia carminibus uestrum seruasse Menalcan* (Lycidas: Of course, what I have heard was that your Menalcas has saved all with his songs). Moeris, however, a true sceptic, says in lines 11-13 that one hears so many stories which are worth nothing. Songs are no match for the *tela Martia* (the weapons of war). In the central part of the poem, from line 17 onwards, the two men try several lines of Menalcas; for instance *Ecl.*9.26-29:

> M. *Immo haec, quae Varo necdum perfecta canebat:*
> '*Vare, tuum nomen, superet modo Mantua nobis,*
> *Mantua uae miserae nimium uicina Cremonae,*
> (Moeris: rather these, not yet finished, which he sang to Varus: "Varus, your name, let but Mantua remain for us, Mantua, alas, too much in the vicinity of unfortunate Cremona)

Who is Menalcas? Is he in *Ecl.*9.7-29 a reference to a living poet, perhaps Vergil himself? It is unclear whether this passage concerns Vergil. On the one hand the region described in lines 7-9 cannot be Mantua. Coleman (1981, 258) says about this: "Although ancient and modern commentators have seen in this [portrayed landscape] a description of Vergil's own ancestral farm, *colles* and *fagos* cannot be reconciled with the terrain of Mantua." On the other hand, several scholars suggest – based upon passages by Suetonius and Servius – that these lines refer to the putative efforts of C. Cornelius Gallus, who is supposed to have mediated between Vergil and Alfenus Varus, in an attempt to exempt the entire area of Mantua from confiscation. According to Servius and Suetonius, Varus was in charge of the land confiscations[91]. Servius' commentary on *Ecl.*9.7-10 (Thilo, 1887, 109-110) refers very specifically to the fact that the Mantuan area was involved (Wilkinson, 1997, 29): *usque ad eum autem locum perticam limitarem Octavius Musa porrexerat, limitator ab Augusto datus, id est per quindecim milia passuum agri Mantuani, cum Cremonensis non sufficeret* (to this spot Octavius Musa, the boundary commissioner [*limitator*] appointed by Augustus, had extended his border-poles, that is to say, through fifteen miles of Mantuan territory, since that of Cremona was not sufficient). The evidence for supposed involvement of Gallus, however, is very slight and should be considered as rather speculative. It is only based on two sources. Firstly, on Servius' commentary on *Ecl.*9.10 (Thilo, 1887, 110), where he quotes "a passage from

---

91 See also note 81. For Gallus and Varus, see: Wilkinson (1997, 29-35, esp. 29-31); Wilkinson (1966, 320-324); and Hermes (1980, 212-257), who quotes the opinion of several scholars before 1977. For the confiscations in the Mantuan region and the speculation about the putative loss of Vergil's family farm (cf. Jenkyns, 1998, 170-171) see note 66. I offer no opinion whether Suetonius correctly records Vergil's motivation to start writing the *Eclogues*; for this see Clausen (2003, 174 note 1). Suetonius' text in *Vita Vergili*.19 is from Rostagni (1944, 84).

a speech by 'Cornelius' (presumably Gallus) against Varus" (Wilkinson, 1997, 31). There is no independent support for this identification. The passage (Thilo, 1887, 110) reads as follows: *quod Mantuanis per iniquitatem Alfeni Vari, qui agros divisit, praeter palustria nihil relictum sit, sicut ex oratione Cornelii in Alfenum ostenditur cum iussus tria milia passus a muro in diversa relinquere, vix octingentos passus aquae, quae circumdata est, admetireris, reliquisti* (because of the unreasonableness of Alfenus Varus, who divided the lands, nothing had been left for the Mantuans other than swamps, as appears from a speech by Cornelius to Alfenus stating: when you [Varus] had been ordered that you should measure out leaving three miles from the wall in every direction, you hardly left 800 paces of water which lie around it). The second source is Suetonius' (*Vita Vergili*.19) reference to Vergil being saved from loosing his land: *Mox cum res Romanas incohasset, offensus materia ad Bucolica transiit, maxime ut Asinium Pollionem, Alfenum Varum et Cornelium Gallum celebraret, quia in distributione agrorum, qui post Philippensem victoriam veteranis triumvirorum iussu trans Padum dividebantur, indemnem se praestitissent.* (Soon, when he [Vergil] began with a work about Roman history, but feeling that he made a mistake with [the choice of] the subject, he changed to the "Bucolics" particularly to praise in song Asinius Pollio, Alfenus Varus, and Cornelius Gallus, because – at the time of the distribution of the land, which beyond the Po was divided by order of the triumvirs among the veterans after the victory at Philippi – these men had saved him from the loss of his land). In this passage, it is not only Gallus who came to Vergil's rescue, but also Pollio and Varus.

Irrespective of the inconclusive evidence of Varus' and Gallus' involvement in the expropriations in the Mantuan area, Vergil testifies in the passage that efforts to exempt Mantua had been in vain, and that the town was affected by the expropriations because the force of arms, the *tela Martia* and the *aquila*, was stronger than poetry, *nostra carmina*. Vergil presumably did not refer to personal experience, but tapped into his personal knowledge to portray the general feeling among the population of the region. Vergil's frustration about the situation in the country can also be read in lines 35-36 when Lycidas, claiming to be a poet, says: *L. nam neque adhuc Vario uideor nec dicere Cinna/digna, sed argutos inter strepere anser olores* (as yet, it seems that I sing nothing worthy of Varius or Cinna, but that among tuneful swans I cackle as a goose). Both the dispelled farmers and the poets writing pastoral poetry are frustrated by the events, and feel that their poetry leads to nothing. However, Vergil's reference to cackling geese is presumably not only meant to slight the impact of Lycidas' poetry, but also as a subtle reference to geese giving warning signals.

It is likely that the present *Eclogue* was one of Vergil's first, written around 40 B.C.. Iulius Caesar had been murdered only four years earlier. In lines 46-50 Vergil makes a powerful political statement by alluding to Iulius Caesar. Lycidas sings five lines of what he still remembers hearing Moeris sing in the past:

L. 'Daphni, quid antiquos signorum suspicis ortus?
ecce Dionaei processit Caesaris astrum,
astrum quo segetes gauderent frugibus et quo
duceret apricis in collibus uua colorem.
insere, Daphni, piros: carpent tua poma nepotes.'
(Lycidas: "Daphnis, why are you looking up at the new rising of old signs in heaven? See, the star of Caesar, of Dione's lineage, came past; the star which makes the fields rejoice with corn, and makes the grape draw in its colour on the hills open to the sun. Plant your pears, Daphnis: your grandchildren will pluck the fruits you have planted")

In this passage "the star of Caesar" presumably refers to the comet which had been seen after Iulius Caesar's death. Vergil, who was sympathetic to Iulius Caesar, tells us, that his star had come and gone and that his "reign", which had brought hope to the farming population in the years before 44 B.C. was now past[92]. Vergil prays for an end to the ongoing war and power struggle, and for better times, when Daphnis' grandchildren will gather the fruits that Daphnis has sown. Eventually, coexistence between the pastoral life and Rome may be possible, as *omnia fert aetas, animum quoque* (time steals everything, even our memory) (line 51). There is a mood of resignation as the two herdsmen proceed on their journey to the town in the depths of misery. Halfway through they see the tomb of Bianor. It is likely that the tomb suggests that the land is dead. Farmers, who cannot find green food for their animals, are forced to strip the trees: *densas/agricolae stringent frondes* (the farmers strip off the thick foliage). In these lines (58-61) Vergil shows us the loss of the pastoral environment, where even the last piece of shade has disappeared. Lycidas suggests singing, but Moeris' answer leaves him feeling helpless and forsaken, as he says in the last line of the poem: *carmina tum melius, cum uenerit ipse, canemus* (we will sing our songs better, when he himself has come). Their poetry is ineffective, and they cannot achieve anything on their own[93]. The master *ipse* – Menalcas – has to come. Is Vergil indicating in this early poem that he intends to put his poetry at the service of relieving the farmers' plight by exposing their miserable life? On the whole, in this *Eclogue* – and in many to come – Vergil comments bitterly and critically on the social disruption resulting from the land appropriations and the evictions of the farmers who belonged there.

---

[92] Coleman (1981, 259). Coleman (1981, 266-267), brings up an interesting allusion in line 47: "Dione shared the cult of Dodona with Zeus, [...]. The unusual epithet for Caesar thus obliquely recalls that the Julians numbered Jove as well as Venus among their ancestors. However Dodona's prophetic doves were impotent in the face of armed force [as is referred to in line 13 of the present *Eclogue*] and *the peace and prosperity heralded by the comet may be endangered likewise*." (my emphasis).
[93] Nauta (2006, 321-324) also links the power of poetry with that of the military and the political situation of the time. Nauta (2006, 321): "As in *Ecl*. 1, the dependence of bucolic poetry on the political realities, symbolised by the city, is at issue, and, as in *Ecl*.1, these realities take the form of confiscations of land", and Nauta (2006, 323): "he [Vergil] has written a bucolic poem showing how bucolic poetry is disrupted by its dependence on the political world."

3.1.2.1 Which River Did Lycoris See In Vergil's Tenth *Eclogue*?[94]

The last *Eclogue*, the tenth, is generally seen as an expression of Vergil's friendship with Cornelius Gallus. Gallus, the soldier and writer of elegiac love poetry, is in Arcadia, probably temporarily – Clausen (2003, 288) suggests that Gallus is on leave – wasting away with unrequited love (*indigno cum Gallus amore peribat*) (line 10). Gallus seems to enjoy the commiseration and the attention from the shepherds and the presence of the flocks, and initially he wants to be part of bucolic life. In the end, however, he rejects this life and in lines 62-63 he says farewell to the pastoral lifestyle: *iam neque Hamadryades rursus nec carmina nobis/ipsa placent; ipsae rursus concedite siluae*. (Again neither Hamadryads [woodland Nymphs] nor even songs please me; farewell again, woods also). Boucher (1966, 94) states: "à notre avis l'on n'en peut conclure que Gallus ait été poète bucolique" (in our opinion, one cannot conclude that Gallus was a bucolic poet). As Putnam (1970, 378) remarks: "Gallus may pretend to embrace the pastoral spirit but his final decision is to renounce its aloofness and return to the battleground of love and war." It is difficult to know whether the poem is concerned with Gallus' poetical orientation because we don't have much work of his to establish what his choice of genre or genres was. However, it is unlikely that he changed to writing pastoral poetry[95]. At the end of the poem (lines 73-74) Vergil expresses his love and friendship for Gallus: *Gallo, cuius amor tantum mihi crescit in horas/quantum uere nouo uiridis se subicit alnus* (for Gallus, for whom my love grows hour by hour, as much as the green alder shoots up in a new spring).

---

94 The section on *Ecl.*10 was written in conjunction with Marc van der Poel, professor of Latin at Radboud Universiteit Nijmegen. Citations of this section should be as: Weeda, L. & van der Poel, M.G.M. (2014). Which river did Lycoris see in Vergil's tenth Eclogue? In L. Weeda. Vergil's Political Commentary in the Eclogues, Georgics and Aeneid (pp.76-83). Berlin/Warsaw: De Gruyter Open. This section, with some minor adaptations, will also be submitted as a paper to a journal of classical studies.
95 For general commentary on *Ecl.*10, see: Boucher (1966, 16-26; 87-94); Clausen (2003, 288-292); Coleiro (1979, 268-280); Conte (1986, 100-129), reprinted in: Volk (2008, 216-244); Raymond (2013, 59-67); Williams (1968, 233-239). For Gallus' poetical orientation in Ecl.10 see Boucher (1966, 18; 25-26). Bessone (2013, 44-45) states: "In the family album put together by the Augustan elegists, [...] it is the line of succession Gallus-Tibullus-Propertius-Ovid that constitutes the canon of the elegists." Coleiro (1979, 269-271), with a discussion of much of the secondary literature on the subject. Gibson (2012, 172-186; esp. at 179-180) suggests that Gallus also wrote other poetry than the elegies for Lycoris, namely erotic poems with personal inclinations. This is far removed from the pastoral genre. Whitaker (1988, 454-458) concludes that Gallus did not write pastoral elegies. A similar problem of determining Gallus' poetical orientation due to the paucity of his extant work arises in the case of *Ecl.*6.64-73. In this passage Gallus is described as rising to Mount Helicon and receiving Hesiod's pipes. Clausen (2003, 200) and Raymond (2013, 65) interpret this as Gallus moving away from love-elegy to Callimachean aetiology. None of the modern scholars conclude from this passage that Gallus changed to pastoral poetry. See also discussion of *Ecl.*6 above.

The above considerations are within the literary frame. Examining the *Eclogues* from a functional (political) point of view, I concluded that Vergil refers to aspects of the contemporary political situation in all the *Eclogues* (see the summary in section 3.1.3). In *Ecl.*10 Vergil does not only pay homage to his friend Gallus, but also gives his commentary on the contemporary political situation. This can be deduced from two passages: *Ecl.*10.14-17 and *Ecl.*10. 21-49. I will discuss lines 21-49 first, in particular the reference to the *Rhenus* in line 47. Vergil uses the word *Rhenus* only twice in his oeuvre, the other being in *A.*8.727 in his description of Aeneas' shield, where *Rhenus* refers to the river Rhine[96]. Contrary to all other commentators, who assume that in *Ecl.*10 he also refers to the Rhine, I intend to demonstrate that in the present poem Vergil describes a different river, the *Rhenus* (modern Reno) in Northern Italia. I will also assert that my functional interpretation of the name of the river gives the poem a very significant political content and meaning.

The poem as a whole is concerned with Gallus' unhappiness for his girlfriend Lycoris' departure. In lines 2-3 Vergil writes *pauca meo Gallo, sed quae legat ipsa Lycoris,/carmina sunt dicenda* (a few verses for my Gallus should be sung, but which Lycoris herself may also read). Vergil obviously hopes that she may change her mind after reading this *Eclogue*. Her very absconding, however, also refers to contemporary events. Lines 46-49, spoken by Gallus, give some clues.

> *tu procul a patria (nec sit mihi credere tantum)*
> *Alpinas, a! dura niues et frigora Rheni*
> *me sine sola uides. a, te ne frigora laedant!*
> *a, tibi ne teneras glacies secet aspera plantas!*
> (you, unfeeling [Lycoris], far from your homeland – I would rather not believe that – ah!, you look, alone without me at the Alpine snow and cold *Rhenus*. Ah, may the cold weather not harm you! Ah, may the rough ice not cut your tender soles!)

In his Commentary on *Ecl.*10.1-2, Servius identifies Lycoris, Gallus' love, with Cytheris, Mark Antony's mistress from 49-45 B.C. Ovid mentions Lycoris three times (*Am.*1.15.30, *Ars* 3.527, *Tr.*2.445), of which two refer directly to Gallus and Lycoris, but Cytheris does not feature in Ovid's work[97]. Cytheris was a popular and attractive actress. Whether the identification is correct or not, Vergil shows Gallus suffering when Lycoris (or Cytheris) runs off with another soldier. Apollo himself had told him

---

[96] I scanned all Vergil's texts by means of Brepols' digital *Library of Latin Texts*. For *Rhenus* referring to the Rhine, see: section 4.1.1, and Weeda & van der Poel, 2014.
[97] Anderson, Parsons & Nisbet (1979, 152-153); Boucher (1966, 16-26); Clausen (2003, 294); Gibson (2012, 175; 177-178); Raymond (2013, 60). Servius' text is from Thilo (1887, 118-119). Antony's relationship with Cytheris did not finish when he married Fulvia in 47 B.C. Plutarch (*Antony.*9.4) also mentions Cytheris as Antony's mistress. Syme (1978, 200-201) states however: "Cytheris as Lycoris, the notion is highly plausible. Yet gentle dubitation intrudes. The scholiasts in late Antiquity are capable of any fantasy or folly."

in lines 22-23: *'Galle, quid insanis?' inquit. 'tua cura Lycoris/perque niues alium perque horrida castra secuta est'* ("Gallus", he [Apollo] said, "what are you raving about? Your beloved Lycoris followed another man through the snow and in rough camps"). According to Servius, it was Mark Antony whom Cytheris/Lycoris followed when she went to the *Alpinas niues et frigora Rheni* (Alpine snow and cold Rhenus) (line 47); this is generally interpreted as referring to the snowcapped Alps and the cold river Rhine. In the unlikely case that Cytheris joined Antony in Gallia, the reference to the river Rhine suggests that she went to the north-eastern part of Gallia. However, it is not plausible that she ever joined Antony in Gallia at all. After 49 B.C., when the two were lovers, Antony spent most of his time in Rome, where he was appointed by Iulius Caesar in different posts, among others, as *magister equitum*. The relationship between Antony and Cytheris finished in 45 B.C., and it was only after June 44 B.C. that Antony became governor (*imperium proconsulare*) of both Gallia Trans-alpina and Gallia Cis-alpina from 44-43 and of Trans-alpina only from 43-40 B.C. Anderson, Parsons & Nisbet (1979, 125-155), in their discussion of the Gallus Fragment, found in 1978 in Qaṣr Ibrĭm in Egypt, also mention this incongruity. They (1979, 153) write: "When Servius says that the other man is Antony (*Ecl*.10.1), the story *does not easily fit his* [Antony's] *career*"[98]. They subsequently consider a number of other men. According to Page (1960, 172-173) Lycoris is Cytheris, who "seems to have deserted Gallus for some officer on the staff of Agrippa, who led an expedition into Gaul and across the Rhine 37 B.C. (cf. lines 23, 46) while Gallus was on military service elsewhere (lines 44, 45)." Page simply assumed that *Rhenus* in line 47 is the river Rhine, without considering another option. Further, Gallus' military activities were not necessarily elsewhere, but could just as well have been in the Mantua region when he was in the area in 41/40 B.C.. Of course, it may be possible that Cytheris joined her ex-lover Antony in Gallia in 43 B.C., when, after his defeat at Forum Gallorum and Mutina (modern Modena) in April 43, he went to Gallia. In that case, the identification of the river Rhine is an anomaly, as Antony met with Lepidus who was staying in Gallia Narbonensis.

I submit that Servius' identification may be incorrect, and a woman named Lycoris was indeed Gallus' mistress, or that Lycoris is the name of the *domina* in his poems, like for instance Cynthia in Propertius' elegies (see Raymond 2013, 60). It is unlikely that Lycoris was a pseudonym for Cytheris. The only worthwhile extant fragment of Gallus' poetry begins with Gallus' lament of the wickedness of his mistress, named Lycoris. This fragment of one of Gallus' elegies is by far the oldest manuscript of Latin poetry. The archaeological site in Qaṣr Ibrĭm has probably been occupied since 50-20 B.C.. The text of the relevant part of the Gallus Fragment is as follows:

---

[98] My emphasis.

tristia nequit[ia...]a Lycori tua [...]
fata mihi, Caesar, tum erunt mea dulcia, quom tu
maxima Romanae pars eri<s> historiae
postque tuum reditum multorum templa deorum
fixa legam spolieis deivitiora tueis. etc.
(Lycoris, sad by your wickedness [...]
Caesar, my fate will then be kind to me, when you will have the largest share in Roman history, and I will read that after your return the temples of many gods are enriched being hung with your trophies)

Contrary to the view of Anderson, Parsons & Nisbet (1979, 151-152), I suggest that Gallus' lines about Caesar and the "largest share in Roman history" refer most likely to Octavian[99]. Gallus expresses his confidence in the future achievements of the new man and refers to future peace and stability and his successes in foreign campaigns. He may have written these words after Philippi (October 42 B.C.) when he saw that Octavian gradually restored order. Hence, the fragment was probably not written in 45 B.C., as Anderson, Parsons & Nisbet suggest, but after 42 B.C. (Philippi), in 41 or 40 B.C.[100].

Returning to Vergil, I suggest that his functional objective was to locate *Ecl.*10 in his native area, and thus Lycoris' identity was of no importance to him. As far as I can ascertain, all commentators hold the opinion that Lycoris travelled to the river Rhine, which I – as explained above – think unlikely. Therefore, I submit that he described the river *Rhenus* (modern Reno) in Northern Italia, the very same region where, in 41-40 B.C., after Philippi, Gallus was engaged in his duties[101]. This would also indicate that *Ecl.*10 was written in 41 or 40 B.C., at about the same time as *Eclogues* 1 and 9, which fits in with the three poems referring to the process of land expropriations in

---

[99] Contrary to Tarrant (2000, 172). See also the discussion of the fragment in Raymond (2013, 62-64)..
[100] Contrary to Gibson (2012, 184) who writes: "imagine a Roman love elegy [by Gallus] in the middle 40s B.C." Anderson, Parsons & Nisbet (1979, 153-154) considered also the likely dating of *Ecl.*10, and argue (1979, 153) that "the eclogue itself can hardly have been written later than 39 B.C." If *Ecl.*10 describes the presumed desertion of Lycoris with an officer in Agrippa's army, the date of writing has to be later than 39 B.C., as Agrippa campaigned in Gallia in 37 B.C.. See also Boucher (1966, 19), who argues that "la dixième Eglogue, [...] doit dater vraisemblablement de 40-39" (the dating of the tenth Eclogue, [...] should probably be 40-39 [B.C.]).
[101] *Rhenus* (modern Reno) in Northern Italia flows from the Apennines into the Po. The river passes *Bononia* (modern Bologna) and *Mutina* (modern Modena). *Forum Gallorum* and indeed *Mantua* (modern Mantova) are near. Pliny the Elder mentions the Reno in PLIN.3.118 and also in PLIN.16.161 (Mayhoff, 1967, 41) when he praises the reed of the Reno because none is more suitable for arrows (*quando nullus sagittis aptior calamus quam in Rheno Bononiensi amne*). Silius Italicus (Bauer, 1890, 193) writes about the Reno in his catalogue of the consuls' troops against Hannibal in SIL.8.590-599 *Vos etiam [...] parvique Bononia Rheni* (You also, [people] of *Bononia* of the little Reno). Cf. Spalten¬stein (1986, 552)..

Northern Italia[102]. It is likely that Vergil and Gallus met at that time and that this was the start of their friendship.

Thus the literal interpretation that the words of *Ecl.*10.22-23 (*tua cura Lycoris/ perque niues alium perque horrida castra secuta est*), and of *Ecl.*10.47 (*Alpinas, a! dura niues et frigora Rheni*) refer to Gallus' mistress – whose real name was Lycoris – should be seriously considered as expressing Vergil's intention. This Lycoris did not run off with a soldier to Gallia Trans-alpina, but she saw and probably crossed the river *Rhenus* (Reno), leaving an agreeable area for the inhospitable and snowy southern Alps. Romans considered Gallia Cis-alpina a civilized region, contrary to, for instance, Northern Gallia, or, even worse, Germania. The recognition of Gallia Cis-alpina as a relatively advanced part of Italia also appears from the unofficial name of the province, *togata,* a reference to the Roman dress and as such a sign of Roman citizenship and adoption of the Roman lifestyle. This was very unlike the name of Gallia Trans-alpina, *comata* (long-haired), expressing the lasting barbarous habits of the inhabitants. Indeed, in 44-43 B.C., Cicero (*Phil.*3.13) called Gallia Cis-alpina *flos Italiae, illud firmamentum imperi populi Romani* (the flower of Italy, that support of the empire of the Roman people); these words suggest that the province is regarded by Cicero as part of Italy. However, according to Jenkyns (1998, 104; cf. Manuwald, 2007, 367) the people beyond the river Po (the *Transpadani*) "were at the margin of Italy in a literal sense; and though other Italians were as far from Rome, they alone were on a frontier, with barbarous and as yet unsubdued tribes perilously close in the mountains above." It is likely that Vergil describes Lycoris leaving hospitable and civilized Cis-alpina, and going north towards these "mountains above," the Alpine region. In lines 48-49, he describes Gallus' anxiety that Lycoris might have to endure the cold, or might cut her soles on the rocks of the Southern Alps, not those of the Northern Alps, as many scholars assume[103]. Who the soldier of lines 22-23, probably an officer, was remains a mystery.

The references to Gallus are an expression of Vergil's feelings of friendship and of his concern for his friend, who seems to perish as a result of his unrequited love. Vergil's regard of Gallus as a friend is the focus of this last *Eclogue*. But why are the poet's reference to Lycoris, her desertion of Gallus and the latter's loneliness so important? I will argue that Vergil is not just expressing his feelings of brotherly friendship, but also making a political point like in the other *Eclogues*.

---

102 In *Ecl.*6 Vergil is also concerned with the expropriations in his native area, but the dating of *Ecl.*6 is problematic. For the problems of chronology, see Perutelli (1995, 28-31, esp at 31), who states: "on the evidence that we have (not all cited here), a possible order of composition would be: 2, 3, 5, 4, 8, 7, 6, 9, 1, 10. But it would be presumptuous to defend to the end such a claim." Anyhow, he places *Ecl.*6, 9, 1 and 10 as written last. Clausen (2003, xxii); Coleman (1981, 14-21).

103 Contrary to Jenkyns (1998, 185-186, esp. note 157) I "indulge the pleasing supposition that the elegiacs found at Qasr Ibrim were the work of Gallus himself." Thus, Lycoris and her fate are important elements of the interpretation of *Ecl.*10.

In this respect, lines 14-17, where Vergil locates Gallus in wild Arcadia with lonely crags and mountains – one of which is "icy cold Lycaeus" in line 15, the birthplace of Pan – may be relevant. In lines 14-15 Vergil describes hapless Gallus in a very "un-pastoral" landscape: *pinifer illum etiam sola sub rupe iacentem/Maenalus et gelidi fleuerunt saxa Lycaei* (Maenalus [mountain of Arcadia] with his pines and the rocks of icy cold Lycaeus shed tears for him as he lay beneath a lonely crag). According to Jenkyns (1989, 27), "there is is no sign of anyone in the ancient world realizing that Virgil had discovered a spiritual Arcadia symbolic of pastoral," and (Jenkyns, 1989, 35) there is "no cause to regard the Arcadia of the tenth *Eclogue* as standing for the pastoral world"[104]. Why should Vergil place Gallus in an un-pastoral Arcadia? To show that Gallus gives up his ambition to write pastoral poetry? Coleman (1981, 295) argues in this way, stating (in the literary frame) that Vergil regards Gallus' predicament a result of Gallus' failed efforts to escape from misery by writing pastoral poetry. As mentioned above (note 95), it is very unlikely that Gallus ever wrote any pastoral poetry. He either stayed with his old genre, the love-elegy – *omnia vincit Amor: et nos cedamus A mori*. (Love conquers all: and let us all yield to Love) (line 69) – or changed to aetiological poetry. Or was Arcadia chosen (as Clausen, 2003, 288 hints at) because a pastoral setting could no longer be found in destroyed Italia or war-torn Sicily, even though Vergil invokes the Sicilian nymph Arethusa in the first line?

I suggest a different interpretation: in spite of Vergil's friendship for Gallus, the latter could not be shown as belonging to the pastoral world and as feeling comfortable in it, because he had been working as an official in Northern Italia at the time of the land expropriations. As stated in sections 3.1.1 and 3.1.2 (*Ecl.9*) above it is doubtful that Varus and Gallus were involved with the actual expropriations in the Mantua region. However, it is feasible that Vergil used their names to symbolise the actual involvement of high-ranking officials, without specifying exactly who was involved where[105]. It is also doubtful that Gallus made an effort to mediate between Vergil and Alfenus Varus in an attempt to exempt the entire area of Mantua, and that Vergil may have felt indebted to him[106]. Gallus worked at the time in some official capacity in the Mantuan area, and this may have been the cause that he was seen as someone who was closely associated with the men

---

104 Jenkyns (1989, 26-39, esp. at 27 and 34-36); Jenkyns (1998, 157-167). Paraphrasing Jenkyns (1989, 26-27): Arcadia as a pastoral landscape is not Vergilian, but was introduced around A.D. 1500. Clausen (2003, 288-290, note 4); Schmidt (2008, 16-47; reprint of original 1975 paper in Volk, 2008). Contrary to Gibson (2012, 178): "here Gallus is dying from the effects of love in the *pastoral landscape of Arcadia.*" (my emphasis).
105 For Alfenus Varus' and Gallus' involvement, see notes 69, 81, and 91. Gold (2012a, 305) makes a similar point writing about patronage and the dramatis personae in a poem: "Is Propertius [for instance] describing an historical figure when he addresses Maecenas at some length in poems 2.1 and 3.9, [...], or is Maecenas transmuted into a symbol of important ideas in Propertius' poetry?"
106 For the supposed loss of Vergil's farm and attempt to mediate, see notes 66 and 91.

who carried out the expulsions of the farmers, and had contributed indirectly to the destruction of the countryside. Thus, locating Gallus in Arcadia is Vergil's poetic act to symbolise Gallus' frustration and loneliness in a harsh and possibly hostile environment, and it is not a historic reality[107]. Boucher (1966, 94) hints at this when he suggests that *Ecl*.10 "nous donne un écho d'un poème de Gallus, le προπεμπτικόν pour Lycoris"[108] (gives us an echo of a poem by Gallus, the προπεμπτικόν for Lycoris). Boucher (1966, 93) states also: "L'hommage de Virgile est donc un hommage littéraire, rendu aux élégies de Gallus, constatant leur célébrité, le fait qu'elles sont devenues un modèle" (Therefore, Vergil's homage is a literary one, paid to Gallus' elegies, of which Vergil established their fame, and the fact that they became a model).

Boucher analysed the poem within a literary frame. However, approaching the poem within the functional frame, I suggest that Vergil pursued a different objective than just paying literary homage to Gallus. His loneliness is a result of the misfortunes of war: instead of Gallus enjoying the love of Lycoris, he stays behind alone as she is taken away by a soldier in the war. Gallus' fate is similar to that of the shepherd in *Ecl*.8.26 who has lost his girl (Nysa) to Mopsus (*Mopso Nysa datur*), whose name symbolizes a newcomer in the countryside, most likely a veteran soldier[109]. Like in *Ecl*.9.11-3, where Vergil wrote that poetry is no match for the *tela Martia* (the weapons of war), soldiers have won again both in Gallus' and Vergil's life. *Ecl*.10 shows an interesting ambivalence. By referring to the river Reno and Gallus, Vergil locates the narrative in his native area, and thus portrays the social and economic destruction caused by men like Gallus. At the same time, however, Gallus himself is the victim of a soldier, who steals his love. In *Ecl*.10 Vergil used Gallus' experience to voice his own concern about the continuing civil war having no prospect of being resolved. The evictions had destroyed the old social and economic structures, and the traditional farming population was impoverished. Instead of working their small farms, the crofters became virtually serfs to newcomers[110]. Like in *Eclogues* 1, 6 and 9, here too

---

107 Boucher (1966, 93) remarks that "Virgile place Gallus dans ce paysage arcadien au moment même où il lui fait déclarer qu'il est aux armées. *Il s'agit là d'une logique toute bucolique qui permet de superposer à la réalité historique une autre forme*" (Vergil locates Gallus in this arcadian landscape at the very moment that he lets him say that he is in the army. *Here, it concerns a very bucolic logic, which permits to superpose on the historic reality another form*). (emphasis is mine).
108 Boucher (1966, 93) contends that Lycoris leaving Gallus may have been a few years earlier, and (referring to PROP.1.8.7-8) that it is "ni certain, ni nécessaire que ce départ ait marqué la fin des amours de Gallus et de Lycoris" (neither certain nor necessary, that this leaving should have signified the end of the relationship of Gallus and Lycoris). It is nothing more than "an accident." Propertius text reads: *tu pedibus teneris positas calcare pruinas,/tu potes insolitas, Cynthia, ferre niues?* (can you tread with your tender feet upon the rime on the ground, can you, Cynthia, put up with the unaccustomed snow?). Heyworth (2007, 31-32) states that this fits in with *Ecl*.10.46-49.
109 See note 79 and the discussion of *Eclogues* 5 and 8.
110 Martindale (2000, 114), who in his interpretation of *Ecl*.10 focuses on the intertextuality rather than on the contextuality, reaches a different conclusion: "But none of this means that Virgil is solemnly debating

Vergil gives his view on the expropriations and the expulsions in the Mantua region as well as on the involvement of a number of high-ranking officials to whom he alluded (Octavian in *Ecl.*1) or whom he mentioned by name (Varus in *Ecl.*6 and 9), thus denouncing the destruction and social upheaval caused by the civil war and its aftermath.

3.1.3 Summary Of The Section About The *Eclogues*

In two of the ten poems (*Eclogues* 2 and 3) Vergil touches only slightly upon the problems in the countryside, but in eight of them (*Eclogues* 1, 4, 5, 6, 7, 8, 9 and 10) he shows concern with major contemporary political matters. These eight are true bucolic poems, presenting a pastoral world where nature and man can be in harmony and where poetry can possess healing power worth more than political power or status. But Vergil also showed other, more sinister aspects: his pastoral world was threatened or had already disappeared, not through mismanagement or indifference of the farmers, but through forces from outside. Exploring the relationship of Vergil's political stance on the one hand and the poetic nature of the *Eclogues* on the other, Tarrant (2000, 173) states: "The *Eclogues* are paradoxically both the work in which contemporary events are most pervasively present and the one in which they are most thoroughly transformed to subordinate them to a poetic context." He (2000, 173-174) also contends that the historic events mentioned in the poems, such as the land confiscations, Philippi, the consulship of Pollio and the pact of Brundisium, "are translated into pastoral terms that soften and distance their topical quality, and that defeat efforts to see direct equivalents between pastoral figures and historic persons" (Tarrant 2000, 173-174). I argue however, that many ostensible "pastoral figures" and events are deliberate functional references to contemporary topics, and thus assume a political significance: for instance, Tityrus and Meliboeus in *Ecl.*1, Mopsus in *Ecl.*5 and *Ecl.*8, Pasiphaë in *Ecl.*6, Thyrsis in *Ecl.*7 and the tomb of Bianor in *Ecl.*9. The significance of the *Eclogues* is that Vergil wrote from his personal knowledge, referring not just to an unnamed general threat, but to a very specific one, namely the land confiscations. These were not vague confiscations somewhere in Italia, but occurred in his own region, near Mantua. For instance, the poet refers to the expropriations and the expulsions in the Mantua region and the involvement of well-known men (who probably also symbolize high-ranking officials in general) in *Eclogues* 1, 6, 9 and

---

the merits and demerits of different genres, let alone acknowledging the failure of his own bucolic art," (with this I agree fully). He continues: "We could say that Virgil is expressing poetic and erotic solidarity with Gallus, with consummate art is helping him court his *docta puella*." I would add: and commiserates Gallus, who is suffering from the vicissitudes caused by war, as so many others. Harrison (2007, 74) notes the: "generic enrichment" showing the duality between a "guest" love-elegiac embedded in a "host" pastoral poem.

10. In particular, he mentions: Alfenus Varus (*Ecl.*6.6-12 and *Ecl.*9.26-29) and Gallus (*Ecl.*6.64 and *Ecl.*10.1-10, *Ecl.*10.22-23 and *Ecl.*10.72-73) and indirectly even Octavian (*Ecl.*1.42-43). Of course, Vergil also pointed out the effects of the expropriations in general. Four poems contain a description of the indifference of, and exploitation by, the new owners (*Eclogues* 5, 7, 8 and 9). The threat to the pastoral life (*Eclogues* 2, 3 and 9), the destruction of rural communities (*Eclogues* 6, 8 and 9), and the disappearance of essential values (*Eclogues* 3 and 8) are also described. Finally, in *Ecl.*4 – a poem expressing the poet's hope for peace and for the return of order to the farming lands of Italia – Vergil looks to the future, when stability will be achieved as Antony – and not Octavian – brings peace to Italia. In *Ecl.*4, he introduces in his view on the preferred constitutional arrangements when the war is over, namely a hereditary form of non-elected political authority and one-man rule.

Vergil gives his commentary on contemporary political and social matters in many more *Eclogues* than is generally recognised. Boyle's interpretation of the book from the perspective of human psychology is an interesting supplement to our argument which is from the perspective of Vergil's political views[111]. Boyle (1986,33) argues that Vergil's

> hopes for a better, a less misshapen world, his hopes that urban man might relearn the Theocritean values he has forsaken and, embodying the pastoral ethic in thought and action, bring a just, fecund and joyous society once more into existence, are hopes the poet expects to remain unfulfilled. [...] But, as Virgil clearly perceives, the power of the artist to teach requires man's willingness or even ability to learn, his ability to subjugate and to control the potentially despotic forces in his psychology which drive out rational thought – sexual passion, ambition, greed, the lust for power, wealth or war – forces which are a kind of psychological madness, which deform, derange and destroy.

As he harboured great love for "old Italia", the land of farmers, Vergil was embittered and very concerned about the way the traditional social structures were being destroyed, and the way smallholders were being expelled from their farms. Vergil had personal knowledge of lawlessness, which he regarded as being a result of the long period of never-ending civil war, for which he held the leaders of the different factions responsible. At the time he wrote the *Eclogues* (between 42 B.C and 35 B.C) he kept his distance from Octavian and showed himself to be critical of his actions in *Eclogues* 1, 6, 7, 8 and 9[112].

---

111 See also Martindale (2000, 110).
112 See also note 70. Contrary to Nauta (2006, 301-332), who considers "panegyric as a central component of his *Bucolics*," I see Vergil's critical attitude towards Octavian and some of his associates as central. A brief summary of our differences follows. *Ecl.*1. Nauta: praise of Octavian; my view: praise of Octavian (*deus*), but critical of Octavian as responsible for expropriations. *Ecl.*3. Nauta: praise of Pollio's poetry; my view: praise of Pollio indeed, but critical of the destruction of traditional values. *Ecl.*4. Nauta: praise of unborn boy; my view: praise of kingship. *Ecl.*5. Nauta: praise of Iulius Caesar; my view: critical of political strife and arrogance of new owners. *Ecl.*6. Nauta: praise of Gallus' poetry; my view: poem is about Vergil's political orientation and is critical of Octavian's officials. *Ecl.*7. Nauta: not mentioned; my view: critical of new landowners and social developments. *Ecl.*8. Nauta: praise of

3.2 The *Georgics*: A Didactic Poem With Political Views

In the previous section I examined each *Eclogue* separately. This is possible as the book consists of discrete poems which can be studied as individual entities. This is not the case for the *Georgics*, the subject of this section, and for the *Aeneid*, which will be explored in the next chapter. Therefore, I will select from the *Georgics* and the *Aeneid* only the passages that in my view are relevant for the study of Vergil's political opinions.

Vergil wrote the *Georgics* between 35 B.C. and 29 B.C., having been invited to join Maecenas' circle of friends a few years before. As the opening lines show, the four books were dedicated to Maecenas: QUID *faciat laetas segetes, quo sidere terram/uertere, Maecenas, [...]/ conueniat [...],/hinc canere incipiam.* (What makes the crops full of joy, in which season, Maecenas, it is right to turn the soil, hence I shall begin my song)[113].

It is a truism to say that the *Georgics* is more than a didactic poem about land, trees, cattle and bees. It also has a very visible socio-political content, as the opening passage and the final lines exemplify. After addressing several of the gods, Vergil wrote in (*G*.1.24-28):

tuque adeo, quem mox quae sint habitura deorum
concilia incertum est, urbisne inuisere, Caesar,
terrarumque uelis curam, et te maximus orbis
auctorem frugum tempestatumque potentem
accipiat;
(and especially you, Caesar, of whom it is not known yet which councils of the gods shall soon require you, whether you wish to govern cities and look after our lands, and that the great circle of lands may receive you as the provider of the fruits of the earth and master of the seasons)

More than two thousand lines later (559-562), in what is almost the closure of the book of Georgics, he writes:

Haec super aruorum cultu pecorumque canebam
et super arboribus, Caesar dum magnus ad altum
fulminat Euphraten bello uictorque uolentis
per populos dat iura uiamque adfectat Olympo.
(These lines about the care of fields, of cattle, and of trees I sang, while great Caesar thundered in war as far as the deep Euphrates and as victor gave laws to willing nations, and entered on the path to the Olympus)

Octavian; my view: critical of Octavian for the destruction of traditional social structure. *Ecl*.9. Nauta: praise of Varus and poetry disrupted by political world; my view: critical of social disruption. *Ecl*.10. Nauta: entire poem devoted to Gallus, praise not clear; my view: Vergil commiserates Gallus. For the arguments in support of my view see the appropriate discussions in section 3.1.2.
113 Harrison (2007c, 136-167); Mynors, 2003; Thomas, 1988a; Wilkinson, 1997.

Immediately after the opening lines there is a reference to Caesar, Octavian, in lines 24-28. After he has announced in lines 1-5 that he will sing (*canere incipiam*) about agriculture, Vergil praises Caesar and places him among the gods of the future. Many lines later, he closes his didactic poem by saying that he has sung (*canebam*) about "the care of fields, of cattle and of trees." However "he has been taking it easy in a cultured resort with a Greek name [Parthenope, Naples; *G*.4.563-564]. Caesar, on the other hand, has been working wonders....[...]. Virgil is concerned with the relationship of poetry and the traditional Roman values, as, on the view here put forward, he has been all through the poem" (Griffin, 1979, 72). In many ways, in the *Georgics*, Vergil offers views on the state of affairs in Rome. Wilkinson (1997, 56-68) discusses the relationship between the *Georgics* and Vergil's literary predecessors, among others, Hesiod and his *Works and Days*. Although it is likely that Vergil owes a literary debt to Hesiod, I agree with Wilkinson's (1997, 60) assessment of the relationship[114]:

> The *Works and Days* is far from being a Georgic. [...] What it could teach Virgil was that a didactic treatise could be a vehicle for moral, religious and philosophic ideas, and at least intermittently for poetry. [...] Even if he began with the idea of following Hesiod, Virgil soon came to realise that he was engaged on something larger and warmer, a panorama of rural life in Italy, *with all its social and philosophical implications*.

This raises the question of whom the book of *Georgics* was written for and what kind of farmer Vergil had in mind. It is evident that only a highly sophisticated man could have appreciated the poem. This was probably not the crofter, who, together with his family, worked a small plot of land, but rather the absentee landlord or the owner of the large estate who lived in Rome or another city. These men were generally no active farmers themselves, but they were sufficiently knowledgeable and did not need to be taught the basics of farming. Italia at large was an agricultural society and many people had ties with the land (Schrijvers, 2004, 7-15; Wilkinson, 1997, 49-55, 67-68). Although Vergil shows that he knows the technical side of farming on a smallholding, the *Georgics* is not a handbook for farmers as the *De agricultura* of M. Porcius Cato (234-149 B.C.) or the work in twelve books *Rei rusticae libri* of Iunius Moderatus Columella (first century A.D.). It is not as comprehensive as the *De Re Rustica* of M. Terentius Varro 'Reatinus' (116-27 B.C.), which presumably exerted a great influence on the *Georgics*. Vergil himself remarks at different occasions that he has no wish to be complete. In the second proem to book 2 (42-44) he writes: *non ego*

---

114 Thomas (1988a, 4-11) and Wilkinson (1997, 3-19, 56-68) give an impressive list of Vergil's literary predecessors. Apart from Hesiod, Aratus, Theocritus, Callimachus, Lucretius, and Varro (Wilkinson), Thomas mentions also Aratus, Theophrastus, Nicander, Eratosthenes, Catullus, Gallus, Varius Rufus and some self-reference to his *Eclogues*. Mynors (2003, 325-333) gives the Greek texts of relevant passages by Eratosthenes, Aratus and Aristoteles. Wilkinson presents a relevant choice of secondary literature. (*italics* in the quotation of Wilkinson are mine). See also Harrison (2007c, 136-137).

cuncta meis amplecti uersibus opto,/non, mihi si linguae centum sint oraque centum,/ ferrea uox. (I myself do not wish to consider everything within my verses, even if I had hundred tongues and hundred mouths, and a voice of steel). And in book 4, 147-148 he says: *uerum haec ipse equidem spatiis exclusus iniquis/praetereo atque aliis post me memoranda relinquo.* (But these matters I for my part pass by due to lack of space, and I leave these to others after me to record). Vergil expresses a desire for brevity not for the sake of restricting his agricultural teaching, but because he wants to send out a different message. According to Wilkinson (1997, 3) the didactic is the book's "ostensible genre: it was deceptive and has abundantly deceived." The didactic is but a background to his description of his love for the countryside and his political and social views, which will be discussed below.

The limitations of his agricultural lessons also show in another aspect. In book 1, which deals with field crops Vergil concentrates on cereals only, in book 2, which is about trees he writes only about vine, with a few lines on olives. Book 3 is about cattle, horses, sheep and goats and no other animals are mentioned. Finally, book 4 is only on bees.

The first book begins with a proem to the whole work in which Vergil presents the contents of the four books and addresses Maecenas (Mynors, 2003, 1-99). He invokes the twelve divinities of agriculture and from line 24 onwards he asks Octavian, already deified, to give his assent to his bold enterprise (line 40: *audacibus adnue coeptis*) and to share Vergil's pity on the poor farmers (line 41; *mecum miseratus agrestis*). Vergil refers here to the desolate state of the free farmers on their smallholdings, and asks Octavian to work towards an improvement of their fate.

In the following part of book 1 (121-146) Vergil voices his belief that good husbandry is hard work, which the Father (Iuppiter) himself has desired. In Vergil's view "men depend on their own efforts, though under the aegis of helpful gods like Ceres (1.147)" (Galinsky, 1996, 95). It is not as easy as in the mythical Golden Age: however hard one toils one has to cope with weeds and insects, and man must learn to use tools. In G.1.121-123 he writes:

> *pater ipse colendi*
> *haud facilem esse uiam uoluit, primusque per artem*
> *mouit agros, curis acuens mortalia corda*
> (The Father himself has desired that the path of taking care of fields should not be easy; and he was first to begin the art of farming, sharpening men's minds by caring)

In this passage, Vergil weaves his Hesiodic inspiration in his teaching about farming. I use the words "Hesiodic inspiration" advisedly. In the *Works and Days* man's hard labour is a punishment for Prometheus' theft and puts an end to the mythical Golden Age. Vergil's belief is different from Hesiod's. Vergil sees human toil as a god given necessity, and the new Golden Age is the result of this labour. The section about good husbandry is then followed by the farmer's calendar. Vergil explains the influence of the stellar constellations on the weather, as well as Eratosthenes' five zones of the earth and the need to observe the seasons for reaping and sowing. The devastation caused by a heavy storm is described. After this follows a section about the weather signs and the need to watch out for these in order not to be caught unawares.

In the finale of the first book (from line 461 onwards) Vergil changes the subject abruptly to contemporary political matters, namely the death of Iulius Caesar and the future of Italia, the horror of war, and the ensuing destruction of the land. First, we hear of the portents after Iulius Caesar's death, but after line 489 the picture changes to the ravages of the civil war at Philippi and other places. It is generally assumed that book 1 was completed at the end of 36 B.C. or early in 35 B.C.. Wilkinson presents a coherent argument that the finale was written at the same time[115]. The political situation at that time was that Antony was far away on the Eastern front and that Octavian had just defeated Sextus Pompeius and entered Rome in triumph. In those heady days Vergil described the destructions of the civil war in lines 489-497, in a scene which a war poet could have applied to Northern France or to Ypres in World War I. Vergil prays that Octavian will restore peace and that the land can be farmed again. I will quote two passages from the finale. Firstly, the passage about the ravages at Philippi and the surrounding area, G.1.489-497 (Mynors, 2003, 94-99). Vergil probably refers to the second battle of Philippi of 23rd October 42 B.C., three weeks after the indecisive first:

> *ergo inter sese paribus concurrere telis*
> *Romanas acies iterum uidere Philippi;*
> *nec fuit indignum superis bis sanguine nostro*
> *Emathiam et latos Haemi pinguescere campos.*
> *scilicet et tempus ueniet, cum finibus illis*
> *agricola incuruo terram molitus aratro*
> *exesa inueniet scabra robigine pila,*
> *aut grauibus rastris galeas pulsabit inanis*
> *grandiaque effossis mirabitur ossa sepulcris.*

(no surprise that Philippi saw again Roman armies fight each other with equal arms; and the gods did not think it monstrous that Macedonia and the wide plains of the Haemon grew twice fat with the blood of our men. To be sure, a time will come when a farmer in those lands, as he works the ground with his curved plough, will find javelins corroded with rough rust, or with heavy hoes will strike against empty helmets, and will be astonished by great bones when graves have been dug up)

---

[115] Wilkinson (1997, 161). His argument is: "The finale follows quite naturally and embodies the emotions of the day. Virgil would not feel called upon to modify it later. I much prefer this conception to the idea [Fraenkel's idea in his book entitled *Horace*, 287-288] that the lines about Caesar were inserted after Actium."

The second passage is the prayer in G.1.498-514 that Octavian will restore order:

> *di patrii, [...]*
> *hunc saltem euerso iuuenem succurrere saeclo*
> *ne prohibete. [...]*
> *iam pridem nobis caeli te regia, Caesar,*
> *inuidet atque hominum queritur curare triumphos,*
> *quippe ubi fas uersum atque nefas: tot bella per orbem,*
> *tam multae scelerum facies, non ullus aratro*
> *dignus honos, squalent abductis arua colonis,*
> *et curuae rigidum falces conflantur in ensem.*
> *[...]; saeuit toto Mars impius orbe,*
> (Gods of my country, at least do not hinder this young prince from helping a ruined world. Long enough, Caesar, the heavenly court begrudges you to us, and complains that you trouble yourself about human triumphs, and right and wrong are here reversed: so many wars over the world, so many forms of wickedness, not any proper respect for the plough, our lands, where the farmers have been removed, are neglected, and curved pruning hooks are melted into a hard sword; unholy Mars rages throughout the world)

Dominik (2009, 126) says this about this dramatic closure of the first book:

> As Vergil specifically observes, war destroys respect for the plough: the lands lie in waste and pruning hooks are forged into straight blades (G.1.506-8). The *Georgics* is actually more of a poem about the frenzied proclivity for battle and the intrusion of politico-militaristic values into the agrarian landscape than it is an example of the delicate pastoral aesthetic.

Book 2 is about trees, especially about the vine (Mynors, 2003, 101-177). After having addressed Bacchus and Maecenas and made the point that he has no desire to be complete (line 42), Vergil describes the art of propagation and again briefly mentions, in lines 61-62, one of his favourite themes, hard labour: *scilicet omnibus est labor impendendus, et omnes/cogendae in sulcum ac multa mercede domandae* (of course, one has to work on all this, and all must be brought together into a trench, and tamed at great cost). This is followed by a catalogue of wines and of riches from Arabia, India and China, such as incense, ebony and silk. Then, Vergil sings the praises of his homeland in the passage called *laudes Italiae* (lines 136-176). He uses in G.2.140-143 a functional model referring to the peaceful nature of Italia. According to Harrison (2007c, 142): "This [passage, lines 140-142] can be taken as more than simple praise of Italian agriculture as free from mythological horrors." He reads the lines in a literary frame, namely that "the rejection of Jason's mythological ploughing in favour of Italian agriculture is also a rejection of traditional mythological epic for the *Georgic*" (Harrison 2007c, 143). I read the passage as a functional reference to the peace of Italia: never was Italia's land, unlike Colchis, ploughed by Jason's fierce bulls harvesting soldiers carrying lances (*uirum seges horruit hastis*). Instead, serene and untroubled Italia was ploughed by gentle oxen. In the preceding lines (G.2.136-138), the poet also tells us that there is no land like Italia:

> *Sed neque Medorum siluae ditissima terra*
> *nec pulcher Ganges atque auro turbidus Hermus*
> *laudibus Italiae certent,*
> (But neither the land of the Medes, very rich with forests, nor the beautiful Ganges, nor the Hermus, thick with gold, may vie with Italia's glories)

According to Harrison (2007c, 140), "the collection of place names gives a generally Oriental atmosphere, as commentators note, but he conjunction of Medes, [etc] recall the campaigns of Alexander the Great." Harrison also states that from this follows that "the poetic praises of territories associated with Alexander in Choerilus and other poets of Alexander-epics are inferior to the praises of Italy and Caesar/Augustus in the *Georgics* itself" (Harrison 2007c, 141). However, Vergil also makes a political point in his reference to Alexander: Italia needs a strong military and political leader – as great as Alexander was – who will resolve the internal and foreign stalemate and restore Rome's glory. I suggest that Vergil had Octavian in mind, and not Antony, who had been engaged in the East, as he mentions Caesar in lines 170-172: *et te, maxime Caesar,/qui nunc extremis Asiae iam uictor in oris/imbellem auertis Romanis arcibus Indum* (and you, almighty Caesar, who, already victorious on Asia's farthest borders, you just now drive the unheroic Easterling from the Roman heights). The *laudes Italiae* (lines 136-176) were presumably written in 30 B.C. as can be deduced from the above lines 170-172 referring to the time immediately after Actium when Octavian went to Alexandria and after the deaths of Antony and Cleopatra campaigned in Syria. In 30 B.C. the worst of the civil war was over, and Vergil expresses his hope and confidence that the glory of a unified Italia will finally arrive. Contrary to Harrison's (2007c, 138) view, I contend that Vergil is not "firmly rooted [...] in the anti-Oriental and pro-Italian propaganda of the period surrounding the battle of Actium." Rather, he is stating his belief that Octavian might be the right man to repulse the Parthian danger. If this happened, the land would be restored and people would enjoy peace and tranquillity again. This stability, however, had to be founded on military strength. The passage contains many lines which, on the one hand, praise Italia as a fertile land with many riches, and on the other refer to her as having bred a *genus acre uirum* (a fierce race), two sides of the same coin.

In the next part, the poet turns to the different soils of Italia and its suitability for different trees. The planting, manuring and caring of vines are discussed. Naturally, the theme of hard labour is explored again. A short section on trees that require less care concludes this part.

In the final part of the second book (lines 458-542), Vergil approaches a major political issue. In the first thirty-seven lines (458-494) Vergil portrays farmers, of whom Mynors (2003, 162) says: "*Agricolae* are indeed much blessed. They are not what the world calls rich, but they live in peace and in pleasant places among honourable neighbours." In *G*.2.458-460 Vergil writes:

> *O fortunatos nimium, sua si bona norint,*
> *agricolas! quibus ipsa procul discordibus armis*
> *fundit humo facilem uictum iustissima tellus;*
> (o farmers, exceedingly fortunate, if they just know their blessings, for whom, far from the arms of disagreeing men, the most righteous earth, brings forth from her soil an easy nourishment)

According to Mynors (2003, 162), the words *iustissima tellus* can be interpreted as a functional reference to "a traditional view," namely that "your ground will always repay what you have entrusted to it, and more." This view is expressed by, among others, Aristotle. Although many farmers may have thought differently, Vergil presumably wants to capture the age-old traditions still to be found in farmer's work. In *G.*2.490-494, Vergil summarizes this happy state of the farming population:

> *felix qui potuit rerum cognoscere causas*
> *atque metus omnis et inexorabile fatum*
> *subiecit pedibus strepitumque Acherontis auari:*
> *fortunatus et ille deos qui nouit agrestis*
> *Panaque Siluanumque senem Nymphasque sorores.*
> (fortunate is the man who has been able to understand the causes of events, and who has crushed under his feet all fear and rigorous fate, and the noise of greedy Acheron: fortunate also is the man who knows the gods of the country, Pan and old Silvanus and the sisterhood of the Nymphs)

Pan, Silvanus and the Nymphs together are a functional model for the country life. Mynors (2003, 169) puts it rightly: "If the deities were to be taken to represent a literary genre, it would be bucolic rather than didactic poetry, for all that they appear in the proem to Book 1; they stand for the idyllic country life of which a description follows, rather than for vigorous farming activity."

From line 495 onwards Vergil recounts the pursuits of the man in the city, and through these introduces political issues. The city is where the political action is, resulting in war and civil strife and destroying the peace of the farmers' life. In *G.*2.495-498 one reads:

> *illum non populi fasces, non purpura regum*
> *flexit et infidos agitans discordia fratres,*
> *aut coniurato descendens Dacus ab Histro,*
> *non res Romanae perituraque regna;*
> (people's high office has not influenced the man, nor the purple of kings, and dissension troubling treacherous brothers, nor the Dacians coming down from the conspiring Danube, nor Roman activities and kingdoms which will be destroyed)

These lines describe the contemporary political troubles. The *discordia fratres* refers most likely not to domestic strife, but, as Mynors (2003, 170) states, to the situation in Parthia (Tiridates and Phraates IV), "whose dissensions were dealt with by Octavian in 30 B.C.". Dacus refers to the Dacians who "had sided with M. Antonius against Octavian, and continued to cause trouble after Actium".

Through these examples Vergil contrasts the world of high office with that of the harmonious farmer's life described in the previous and also in the following lines. Horace expresses similar feelings in the Ode to Maecenas (*Carm.*3.29), where he urges the latter to forget Roman politics and come to his estate near Tibur to relax with a good wine (see section 2.3). The farmer's life, as Vergil portrays this in G.2.498-503, is different. A man of the country does not suffer from pity for the needy, as there are no poor. He also does not envy the rich, as he has enough. He is neither immune to pity and envy nor does he stand above it: these feelings simply do not arise when one lives in the blessed country.

> neque ille
> aut doluit miserans inopem aut inuidit habenti.
> quos rami fructus, quos ipsa uolentia rura
> sponte tulere sua, carpsit, nec ferrea iura
> insanumque forum aut populi tabularia uidit
> (the man has not felt pity for the needy, nor envy of the rich. He plucked the fruits, which his branches and his own fields have voluntarily and freely born; and he did not see the iron laws, the raving Forum, or the public record office)

This is followed by yet more praises of country life, culminating in G.2.523-531, especially in lines 524-527, which contain, according to Mynors (2003, 174), "two good tests, to see if farm animals prosper."

> ubera uaccae
> lactea demittunt, pinguesque in gramine laeto
> inter se aduersis luctantur cornibus haedi.
> ipse dies agitat festos
> (cows droop udders full of milk, and on the rich pasture fat young goats tussle, horns facing horns. The farmer himself has a day off)

The proofs of a well-managed farm are when cows produce plenty of milk, the goats are healthy and the farmer has time for a day off.

In the last eleven lines (G.2.532-542) of the book, Vergil concentrates on Rome. G.2.532-534 and 538-540 say:

> hanc olim ueteres uitam coluere Sabini,
> hanc Remus et frater; sic fortis Etruria creuit
> scilicet et rerum facta est pulcherrima Roma, [...]
> aureus hanc uitam in terris Saturnus agebat;
> necdum etiam audierant inflari classica, necdum
> impositos duris crepitare incudibus ensis.
> (the old Sabines lived such a life once, and Remus and his brother; thus, indeed, Etruria grew strong, and Rome was made the most beautiful place to be
> [...] golden Saturn lived such a life on earth; and not yet had one heard the war trumpets blare, not yet the clanging of the swords, as they were laid upon the hard anvils)

Mynors (2003, 175-177) argues that *Sabini*, *Remus et frater*, and *Etruria* portray the foundation of Rome. Vergil points out that in the era just before and after the foundation, when Saturn lived on earth (line 538), Rome herself was the most beautiful place to be. This was also the time of the king of Latium, with whom Saturn was identified and whose sole surviving descendants are those who till the ground. Thus the farmers in the country uphold the real Roman *mores* and form the backbone of society. What has gone wrong? Vergil's answer is in lines 539-540: the war trumpets and the forging of the sword.

Although the poet devotes the greater part of the second book describing agricultural practices, something like one fifth of the book is concerned with the praise of Italia (lines 136-170), and – particularly towards the end – the ideal country life and the differences between the country and the city (lines 458-540). These differences do not just represent the antithesis of peaceful country life versus the stress of city life, but go deeper. Vergil uses them to refer to the contemporary political situation. Wilkinson (1997, 92) interprets the passage as follows: "to relieve its length the finale is presented as a triple contrast: between city luxury (460-6) and country sufficiency (467-74); between scientific philosophy (475-82, 490-2) and knowing the gods of the country (483-9; 493-502); and between worldly ambition (503-12) and innocent country pursuits (513-40)." However, the contraposition in this lengthy passage goes much deeper and is, in essence, political. The contrast is not between the hectic life of the city dwellers and the happiness of rural life, but between centralized power and armed conflict on the one hand, and stability and self-sufficiency on the other (Mynors, 2003, 162-177). Vergil deplores not only the destruction of the traditional country life, like he did in the *Eclogues*, but he also points out that the responsibility for this lies with the political elite, which has been waging a civil war and fighting for power for decades.

Book 3 is concerned with animals: horses and cattle in the first part and sheep and goats in the second (Mynors, 2003, 178-257; Wilkinson, 1997, 92-99, 165-170, 323-324). Apart from the proem (lines 1-48) and a short transition to the second part (lines 284-294), the whole of the third book consists of a "didactic" exposé about the care of animals. Vergil provides the political context in the proem. The proem shows Pindaric influences, and the poet says in lines 12-16 that he will erect an imaginary temple (Mynors, 2003, 181). The temple will be built beside the Mincius, Mantua's river. In line 16 Vergil says: *in medio mihi Caesar erit* (in the middle [of the temple] I will have Caesar). The poet will offer his verses to Octavian: verses, which he, in Pindaric fashion, describes as a hundred horse-drawn chariots (lines 17-18): *illi uictor ego et Tyrio conspectus in ostro/centum quadriiugos agitabo ad flumina currus* (In his [Octavian's] honour I, a victor striking in Tyrian purple, will drive a hundred chariots drawn by four horses beside the river [Mincius]). Mynors (2003, 181) suggests that either these verses, modelled on Pindar's epinikian poetry, are not referring to victories in athletic festivals, but to the "victory of Roman poetry over Greek," or that Vergil "may also have been thinking of the latest foundation in the Greek series [of games], the *Actia* instituted by Octavian when he refounded the temple of Apollo at Actium/ Nicopolis after his victory on 2 September 31 B.C." (Mynors, 2003, 181-182). My own interpretation of these lines is much closer to this second suggestion. This Pindaric setting is a suitable background to praise Octavian. Through the functional reference to Mantua, Vergil poetically links the future emperor with his beloved part of rural Italia. This also fits in with the last part of the proem describing the carvings in gold and ebony on the temple doors: a celebration of the triumphs of the Romans under Octavian. Lines 26-29 tell part of the story, that of Actium and Antony and Cleopatra.

> in foribus pugnam ex auro solidoque elephanto
> Gangaridum faciam uictorisque arma Quirini,
> atque hic undantem bello magnumque fluentem
> Nilum ac nauali surgentis aere columnas.
> (I will engrave on the doors in solid gold and ivory the battle of the people of the Ganges and the army of conquering Quirinus [Octavian], and there also the great Nile flowing and swelling with war, and towering columns made of the brass [from the beaks of captured] ships)

This passage concerns the final defeat of Octavian's last adversaries, Antony and Cleopatra. The *Gangaridum* represent the Oriental forces that fought under Antony at Actium, and *uictoris Quirini* refers to Octavian (Harrison, 2007c, 149-156; Mynors, 2003, 184). At the time there was much talk of giving him that name in honour of his achievements; eventually this became Augustus. The "columns made of the brass from the beaks of captured ships" came from the captured Egyptian fleet. Some were set up in the Capitol, some in the temple of Divus Iulius (Wilkinson, 1997, 169). In the following lines, other triumphs of Octavian are mentioned, both in the East and in the West. In the proem, Vergil expresses the possible return to normality with Octavian as the bringer of peace and prosperity, which are the conditions necessary for the farmer to once again concentrate on the care of his animals. The latter is described from line 49 onwards. In lines 40-48, Vergil introduces a hunting scene which forms a somewhat curious interlude to the care of horses, cattle and sheep. Harrison's (2007c, 156) literary interpretation that "here as elsewhere in the *Georgics* we find a strong sense of impending literary ascent, with the promised military epic [the *Aeneid*?] looming large" is plausible: it may be one of the poet's reaffirmations that he will write an epic. Yet, in passage as a whole Vergil focuses on Actium and its aftermath, as Octavian's victory has removed the most significant threat. This is a statement of Vergil's relief that the future looked better.

From *G*.3.49, Vergil continues with cattle and horses and their breeding. In line 103, he refers to the animals' sexuality, their grief at defeat and their pride in victory. After this, a lengthy passage (lines 157-283) follows about the rearing and training of calves and foals, and about the danger of the sexual preoccupation of cattle and horses, which is a threat to their efficiency. In the second half of book 3 (lines 284-566) Vergil is concerned with sheep and goats and their care in winter and in summer. Sheep and goats provide men with wool and milk. But dangers also loom: thieves, wolves and snakes. Man has to look after his sheepdogs to protect the animals and the poet gives more good advice for the safety of the flocks. Vergil finishes book 3 with the horrible deaths of animals due to an epidemic plague in Northern Italia.

Vergil's commentary on political issues in the third book is limited, the leading theme being the effort required for the breeding and care of horses, cattle and sheep. However, Vergil does make a political point, which is his hope that normality returns, and that the farmer can farm again. If Italia wants to regain its traditional values and rebuild some economic order, peace has to be reinstated.

Book 4 of the *Georgics* has three parts (Mynors, 2003, 258-324; Wilkinson, 1997, 100-120): in the first (lines 1-280), Vergil is concerned with beekeeping: in the second (lines 281-314), he gives a short interlude about what to do when a swarm falls ill and dies: in the third (lines 315-558), he relates the *Aristaeus epyllion* proper. At first sight this epyllion seems a rather strange closure of the *Georgics*, and there has been much speculation about Vergil's motives for including it. In his commentary on G.4.1, Servius says: *sane sciendum, ut supra diximus, ultimam partem huius libri esse mutatam: nam laudes Galli habuit locus ille, qui nunc Orphei continet fabulam, quae inserta est, postquam irato Augusto Gallus occisus est* (It is known of course that, as I said above, the final part of this book was altered: for the praises of Gallus stood there where now the story of Orpheus is, which was put in after Gallus was killed by an angry Augustus). Cornelius Gallus, the first prefect in Egypt, had become too ambitious, had fallen from favour, was forced to commit suicide in 27 B.C., and suffered a posthumous *damnatio memoriae*. Gallus' downfall happened in 30-29 B.C., just around the time that Vergil finished the *Georgics*. This was obviously not the right time to sing Gallus' praises. Hermes (1980, 298) concludes that Servius' notes about "laudes Galli" should be considered unworthy of belief. However, it is no longer possible to check Servius' story. It is feasible that Vergil intended from the start for the epyllion to close the poem. Whatever happened to the end of the poem, as they stand, the *Aristaeus epyllion* and the interlude (lines 281-558) form an organic part of the whole, and show a clear expression of Vergil's views. Before I analyse it, however, I will discuss the first part of book 4[116].

---

116 Hermes' (1980) dissertation about the issue of Vergil's putative change of book 4 contains a wide ranging discussion of the secondary literature until 1977. Hermes' (1980, 298) final conclusion is: "Die vollkommene Komposition des Epyllions, seine enge Verzahnung mit dem Gesamtwerk, die Unwahrscheinlichkeit von Servius' bericht über das Verfahren gegen Gallus, der fehlende Nachweis einer vorsuetonischen biographischen Tradition über Vergil als möglicher Quelle für Servius, die aufgezeigten Parallelen zu ähnlichen Berichten, all dies widerlegt die Argumentation, daß die Eigenheiten des Epyllions nur durch spätere Eingriffe, das Entstehen der Nachricht nur durch eine fundierte Quelle erklärt werden können. Solange keine neuen Indizien entgegenstehen, sind die Servius-Notizen über 'laudes Galli' als Frucht der Erschließungstätigkeit über Leben und Werk Vergils und damit als unglaubwürdig anzusehen." (The argument, that the characteristics of the *epyllion* can only be explained by later interference, or that the origin of the information can only be explained by a source

The first part of book 4 contains not just good and practical advice about beekeeping, but also interesting observations about the life of the bees. The proem is short and sets out the structure of the book in a very compact form. In the first lines (G.4.1-2), Vergil writes that the fourth book will not concern only bees and honey: *PROTINUS aërii mellis caelestia dona/exsequar* (Forthwith, I will describe the celestial gift of honey from heaven). The book will also concern the bees as a "nation," G.4.3-5: *admiranda tibi leuium spectacula rerum/magnanimosque duces totiusque ordine gentis/mores et studia et populos et proelia dicam* (in the right order I will sing of wonderful displays of tiny acts, and charitable leaders, and the character and endeavor of a whole nation, the peoples and battles). The swarm of bees, with its many human traits, is symbolic of Vergil's "nation", enabling him to give his commentary on a number of very contemporary political issues.

The bee colony has one leader that governs the other bees and directs the work of building the hives and gathering the honey. It is interesting to see which words Vergil uses to describe the leader. In line 4 of the proem the leader is a *dux*; in line 21 the word *rex* is used for the first time, is then repeated eight times in the first part of book 4, that is, until line 315[117]. However, there are also times when two king bees struggle for power. This is described by the poet in G.4.67-103. In G.4.67-68 we read *Sin autem ad pugnam exierint – nam saepe duobus/regibus incessit magno discordia motu* (If however, they have gone out for battle – for discord with great commotion has often seized two kings). Naturally, one of the two bees is the stronger one, and Vergil remarks in G.4.89-90 *deterior qui uisus, eum, ne prodigus obsit,/dede neci; melior uacua sine regnet in aula* (he who looked inferior, let him be killed, that he is not a burden; let the better reign in the palace without hindrance). These passages refer to the civil war: the battle described is between two king bees from one and the same beehive. The passage in the lines 89-90 refers to Octavian (*melior*) as the rightful victor with a justified claim for the leadership over Antony (*deterior uisus*). Vergil hopes that Octavian may be able to realise this claim and to create peace and order.

In the first part of the book Vergil devotes some eighty lines (149-227) to the hard work of the bees and their propagation. He refers to contemporary issues again in G.4.210-218; I interpret the passage as referring to the nature of absolute despotism

---

which is well founded, is contradicted by the following qualities of the *epyllion*: its complete composition, its close connection with the total work, the improbability of Servius' information concerning the action against Gallus, the lack of evidence of a biographical tradition before Suetonius suggesting Vergil as a possible source of Servius, and the recorded parallels with similar information. As long as no new indications emerge which would contradict the above, Servius' commentary on the 'laudes Galli' should be considered a result of fabrications of Vergil's life and work, and thus unworthy of belief). See also Thomas (1988a, 13-16).

117 Not counting *caeli regem* in line 152.

in Egypt and the East[118]. Their king is the leader of the people and "overseer of their toils" (*ille operum custos*), but his authority is so weak that when he is away disorder is rife *amisso rupere fidem, constructaque mella/diripuere ipsae et cratis soluere fauorum* (when he has gone away, they break their fealty, and break to pieces the honey they have gathered together and take apart their honey-combs).

Thus, according to Vergil, bees are like a nation living under the authority of a strong leader. Griffin (1979, 68) remarks that "the bees presented him with a powerful image for the traditional Roman state, in its impersonal and collective character." The bees in the allegory present indeed many traits of collectivism, but this can just as well be interpreted as the collectivism of the people at large, common in all lands around the Mediterranean. I am inclined to read the whole passage about bee life (lines 1-227) as describing *any nation* and not just Roman society. Further in his essay Griffin (1979, 69) says: "The bees, then, with their collective virtues and their lack of individuality and art, serve as a counter-part to the old Roman character. Their patriotism and self-denial (and devotion to their 'king' is only devotion to the state and to authority, not an encouragement to emperor-worship) are admirable." Vergil is indeed not encouraging "emperor-worship," but he is expressing the view that for the Roman people (with or without "their collective virtues") the problems have become so serious that times have come to fundamentally change the status quo. He suggests that time is ripe for a strong leader, perhaps even for a monarch, and that "the traditional Roman state" has come to an end. Octavian may be a suitable candidate. In the words of Griffin (1979, 70):

> Only Caesar can rescue the world turned upside down, and Virgil prays desperately for his success. The reconstruction longed for in the first *Georgic* is, we may feel, under way by the fourth; order is being restored, and the poet becomes aware of the cost – a society efficient and admirable, but impersonal and dispassionate.

Next, we are introduced to the *Aristaeus epyllion* (*G*.4.281-558)[119]. First, Vergil deals with the possible disappearance or death of one's bees, and how to get a new stock in *G*.4.281-314. The great Arcadian master is introduced in *G*.4.283. His identity is revealed in line 317 as the beekeeper Aristaeus, who has lost his bees as a consequence of the anger of the gods for his attempted rape of Orpheus' wife Eurydice. After he is reconciled with the gods in lines 301-302 he is shown how to make a new swarm of bees out of a bullock. The animal is "finished off by blows, the pounded flesh decomposes

---

118 Cf. Harrison (2007c, 139, note 14): "The other passage at *Georg*. 4.211 *Medus Hydaspes* clearly shows similar contemporary connections given the presence of Egypt and Parthia in the same context and the topic of the absolute nature of Eastern kingship."
119 Nadeau (1984, 59-82) pointed at the similarities between the narrative in the *Aeneid* and the Aristaeus epyllion. See also Conte (1986, 130-140); Harrison (2007c, 161-166); Mynors (2003, 293-323); Wilkin¬son (1997, 108-120).

in the unhurt hide" (*plagisque perempto/tunsa per integram soluuntur uiscera pellem*). When the carcass is left with thyme and fresh lavender (*casia*) in a damp and warm environment, bees will grow out of the cadaver. This is the art of "bougonia" (born of an ox) practiced in Egypt.

The myth of Aristaeus is not just the end to a great didactic poem, but also an allegory for Octavian and Antony, whose struggle for power had reached its height in September 31 B.C.; Vergil finished the *Georgics* two years later. The narrative is a functional reference to Octavian (the beekeeper), and to his adversaries Antony and Cleopatra, and perhaps also to Sextus Pompeius. The story oscillates, as it were, between Aristaeus who reminds us of Octavian and the same Aristaeus who is Antony. At the end of the story 'Octavian-Aristaeus' is the winner of the struggle for power when he assumes control over the bees, that is, the Roman state. Nadeau (1984, 59) follows a similar line of interpretation: "My intention is to show that the Aristaeus epyllion is an allegory for Augustus, Antony and Cleopatra, and Actium. [...], the contrast between the Statesman and the Lover: between, that is, Augustus and Antony." However, there is an important difference between his view and mine. The main contrast is not that between the statesman and the lover. The story oscillates between, on the one hand, the sense of duty of Octavian to restore order and bring peace and, on the other hand, the destructive alliance of Antony and Cleopatra[120]. The view that in an allegory one *persona* (Aristaeus) or one object may, at the same time, represent opposite qualities, or portray two different persons (Octavian's duty and Antony's passion), may strike as being rather fanciful. However, this can be found in other places too, for instance in the story of Pallas' sword belt (*A*.10.480-505), which Turnus takes after he killed Pallas and which symbolises his cruel exultation (*A*.10.500): *quo nunc Turnus ouat spolio gaudetque potitus* (now Turnus rejoices in the spoils, and is delighted having got possession of it). The same belt is later the cause of cruelty, when Turnus is slaughtered by Aeneas (*A*.12.941-949) after pleading for his life. The sword belt (the object) is a functional reference to both Turnus' emotions of elation when having killed Pallas as well as Aeneas' fury killing Turnus (*A*.12.947-948): *tune hinc spoliis indute meorum/eripiare mihi?* (you, adorned with the spoils of one of mine, you to be snatched away from me?). In other words: Turnus takes possession of the belt and is elated, but then Turnus wears the belt and is killed.

Mynors (2003, 293), discussing "the production of a fresh stock of bees from the putrefying carcass of an ox or bullock," argues (2003, 293-294) that the subject "demanded inclusion as being remarkable in itself and recognized normally in the technical literature. It was also apparently well known to the reading public, for there are frequent references to it in the poetry from the third century BC onwards." Mynors

---

[120] Harrison (2007c, 164-167) argues that Aristaeus represents a parallel between Octavian's military career through his military victories and Vergil's poetic career "through military and nationalistic epic."

gives several examples. I suggest that Vergil included the subject of the production of a new stock not only for the reasons Mynors mentions, but also because Vergil wants to refer to the political theme of the contrast between the sense of duty of Octavian to restore order on the one hand, and the alliance of Antony and Cleopatra on the other. In my view, a number of features of the passage from line 281 onwards suggests that Vergil was also considering contemporary issues. For instance, locating the art of "bougonia" in Egypt and the East (*G.*4.287-288, 290) may refer to the recent war against Antony and Cleopatra and the still unresolved military problems with the Parthians (cf. Nadeau, 1984, 72-73; see also Mynors, 2003, 297). In addition, Vergil's choice of the beekeeper is significant. Mynors (2003, 294) argues that "the discoverer of the new method [of producing a new swarm] must fulfil certain conditions: he must (1) be a beekeeper," and adds the attributes this man must have. I suggest that Vergil chose a beekeeper for different reasons. It is not by chance that *pastor Aristaeus*, in line 317, is the answer to the question posed in line 315: *Quis deus hanc, Musae, quis nobis extudit artem?* (What god, Muses, found out this skill for us?). Aristaeus is Vergil's functional model for Octavian. Aristaeus, the beekeeper, is responsible for his bees in the same way as Octavian is responsible for his people: the bees symbolize the nation. The contrast Octavian-Antony can further be deduced from the following passages: *G.*4.317-332 (Octavian's claim to restore order), *G.*4.351-356 (attacks on Octavian's heritage), *G.*4.360 (*iuvenis* as a reference to Octavian), *G.*4.453-459 (Antony's passion for Cleopatra and her death) and *G.*4.554-558 (Octavian's victory). I will now focus on each passage in turn.

In *G.*4.317-332 Aristaeus complains bitterly to his mother Cyrene about the loss of his bees and tells her to let the rest of his work be destroyed as well. Lines 317-321 and 326-328 say:

pastor Aristaeus fugiens Peneia Tempe,
amissis, ut fama, apibus morboque fameque,
tristis ad extremi sacrum caput astitit amnis
multa querens, atque hac adfatus uoce parentem:
'mater, Cyrene mater, [...]
en etiam hunc ipsum uitae mortalis honorem,
quem mihi uix frugum et pecudum custodia sollers
omnia temptanti extuderat, te matre relinquo.
(The shepherd Aristaeus, fleeing from Peneian Tempe, when, as the story goes, his bees had been lost through sickness and hunger, sorrowfully stood at the sacred source of the river, and with loud lament addressed his mother with these words: "mother, mother Cyrene, [...] look, even this honour of my mortal life, that the expert care of crops and cattle had with difficulty squeezed out for me for all my endeavour, I have lost, although you are my mother)

In the *Georgics* the bees stand for the Roman state, and *G.*4.317-332 can be understood as referring to Octavian fighting for political control in Rome. Aristaeus' complaint, in lines 326-328, that his entire endeavour was of no avail refers to Octavian's claim that he be allowed to continue and to finish the work of establishing peace and order.

After Vergil has given the names and the pursuits of the sea nymphs who are in the company of mother Cyrene, the nymph Arethusa appears in a following passage (G.4.351-354). She hears Aristaeus' "loud lament" and calls on Cyrene to pay attention.

> *sed ante alias Arethusa sorores*
> *prospiciens summa flauum caput extulit unda,*
> *et procul: 'o gemitu non frustra exterrita tanto,*
> *Cyrene soror,*
> (But, before the other sisters, Arethusa with her golden head above the waves looked into the distance, and cried from afar: "o sister Cyrene, it was not without reason that you were frightened by such lament)

It is no coincidence that Vergil gave this role to Arethusa. She is a Sicilian nymph and her presence reminds readers of Octavian's shipwreck off the Sicilian coast in the war against Sextus Pompeius. The nymphs bring Aristaeus to his mother Cyrene's underwater palace. In line 360 Aristaeus is called *iuvenis*, a name by which Octavian was often referred to. The beekeeper duly enters the palace and is looked after by the nymphs. Cyrene decides that Proteus should be consulted. Mother and son thus depart to the cave of Proteus and watch him return home. When the seer has settled, Aristaeus approaches him to ask him why he has lost his bees. Proteus tries to avoid replying, but the pastor overwhelms him and in G.4.448-449 says to him: *deum praecepta secuti/uenimus hinc lassis quaesitum oracula rebus* (by the orders of the gods, we have come here to seek an oracle for my flagging circumstances). Proteus answers in G.4.453-459:

> 'Non te nullius exercent numinis irae;
> magna luis commissa: tibi has miserabilis Orpheus
> haudquaquam ob meritum poenas, ni fata resistant,
> suscitat, et rapta grauiter pro coniuge saeuit.
> illa quidem, dum te fugeret per flumina praeceps,
> immanem ante pedes hydrum moritura puella
> seruantem ripas alta non uidit in herba.
> ("Nothing less than the anger of a god troubles you; you pay for great crimes: unhappy Orpheus evokes these punishments – by no means up to your deserts – against you, if Fate did not oppose, and he is severely angry as his wife is torn from him. She, when she rushed away from you in headlong flight along the river, she, the ill-fated girl, did not see the enormous snake amid the deep grass at her feet that inhabited the banks)[121]

Aristaeus is told that the gods are angry because he attempted to rape Eurydice, who died by snakebite when she ran away from him. In line 457, the story swings to a reference to Cleopatra who was believed to have died from snakebites and to "Antony-

---

[121] In G.4.455, the OCT gives *haudquaquam ob meritum poenas*. As *ob* makes no sense, I follow the suggestion of Mynors (ad.loc.) to read *ad*.

Aristaeus," who is reproached (line 454: *magna luis commissa*) for his illicit affair with Cleopatra. Vergil continues in *G*.4.460-527 with the story of Orpheus and Eurydice and the former's attempt to rescue her from the underworld. I interpret 4.460-527 as also alluding to Antony and Cleopatra, as their love affair was also destined to fail. The narrative continues as Proteus suddenly disappears and Cyrene tells her son to expiate himself with the gods, the nymphs and Eurydice. Aristaeus does as his mother bids him, and on the ninth day he offers his funeral dues to Orpheus. After this his bees are returned to him. In *G*.4.554-558 the poem reads:

> hic uero subitum ac dictu mirabile monstrum
> aspiciunt, liquefacta boum per uiscera toto
> stridere apes utero et ruptis efferuere costis,
> immensasque trahi nubes, iamque arbore summa
> confluere et lentis uuam demittere ramis.
> (but there they see an unexpected portent, wonderful to be told: everywhere in the belly on the putrefied flesh of the oxen, bees are buzzing and they swarm forth from the burst sides, they haul in enormous clouds, and then crowd together in a treetop hanging down in a bunch from the tough branches)

Aristaeus' new swarm of bees is the result of bougonia. If one accepts the interpretation that the bees refer to a nation of people, the bougonia symbolizes the resurrection of the nation: the new state (the new swarm of bees) rises from a corpse (ravages of the civil war). This passage expresses the cost with which Octavian attained control of the Roman state. Therefore, these lines show Vergil's concern regarding the way the Principate had been established and the havoc it has created. The lines contain an obvious criticism. "Octavian-Aristaeus" is the eventual victor and one can see Vergil's hope that perhaps an end to the war and slaughter is in sight.

The book closes with a σφραγίς (lines 559-566), in which the poet gives his name (line 563, *Vergilium*), an indication of the date (lines 560-561, *Caesar fulminat ad Euphraten*) and the place where he wrote the poem (line 564, *Parthenope*). Vergil was in Naples where he was enjoying life at the time that Octavian travelled through the East after Actium. The reference to Octavian is significant. Mynors (2003, 323-324) says about the epilogue:

> The dating provides the excuse for a final tribute to the hero and benefactor [Octavian], who has not merely made it possible for him [Vergil] to be a poet, but by the restoration of peace and good order has given back its true meaning to the good life, the country life, of which the poem treats. And the mention of himself, modest though it purports to be, is so aptly balanced, quatrain for quatrain, against that tribute to Octavian as to take on something of the quality of a manifesto.

I agree with Mynors' view that the *Georgics* shows more optimism than the *Eclogues*. The book has indeed the character of a manifesto, but in my view a manifesto of hope and not of achievement. When Vergil finished the book in 31 or 30 B.C., peace was only just beginning. The very last line of the book – *Tityre, te patulae cecini sub tegmine fagi* (of you I sang, Tityrus, under the cover of a spreading beech) – refers to the very first line of the book of *Eclogues*. Vergil's self-reference expresses that the problems described in *Ecl*.1 have not been resolved yet[122]. My view differs from that of Harrison (2007c, 166) who argues that "the effect of citing the first line of the *Eclogues* at the end of the *Georgics* seems to be that of ending a phase in the Vergilian poetic career, and in the teleological transition of the *Georgics* towards military epic." I consider Harrison's interpretation within the literary frame as supplementary to mine, in the sense that Vergil is making at the same time a literary and political statement: Vergil expects that in his future epic Octavian's achievements will show that many of the problems have been resolved and that a new society is emerging.

3.2.1 Summary Of The Section About The *Georgics*

The *Georgics* is divided into two parts, the first consisting of books 1 and 2 and the second of books 3 and 4. Book 1 is sombre in tone, emphasises hard work and ends with a catastrophe, the death of Iulius Caesar and the horror of the war which followed. Book 2 is lively and deals with lighter work. This pattern is repeated in the second part, books 3 and 4. Book 3 begins with a factual description of the care of cattle, horses and sheep, but ends with the disaster of animals dying of the plague. The last book teaches about bees and deals with the loss of the whole swarm, but ends with the positive climax of their resurrection through bougonia. The first two books are about immovables, fields and trees, while books 3 and 4 deal with animals and bees.

The proem to book 1 deals with the desolate state of farming and the sufferings of the farmers, and asks Octavian for his pity. The finale of book 2 picks up this theme and, after praising the beauty of Italia, Vergil portrays the peaceful country life of old versus the stress of modern city life. In a reference to the contemporary political situation, he deplores the destruction of traditional country life. A pattern of related themes repeats itself in the last two books. The proem of book 3 praises Caesar Octavian and his victories, among others the defeat of Cleopatra, and links the future *princeps* with Mantua, the poet's favourite part of Italia. In the epilogue to the whole book of the *Georgics* at the end of book 4 Vergil returns to this subject and lauds Octavian for his victories. He expresses his hope that the problems he set out in the very first lines of book 1 will be resolved by Octavian. Thus, Vergil places his main themes at the crucial points of the structure of the whole book: the poverty of the free farmers in Italia (proem to 1), the destruction of traditional country life (finale of 2), Octavian's victories (proem to 3), and his hope that Octavian can restore peace and

---

122 For a different view see Theodorakopoulos (2000, 161). See my commentary on *Ecl*.1 in section 3.1.2.

order (finale of 4). The *Georgics* ends with virtually the same line as that which opens the book of *Eclogues*, subtly symbolizing the continuity of his concern about the state of the countryside: *Ecl.*1.1 *Tityre, tu patulae recubans sub tegmine fagi*, and *G.*4.566 *Tityre, te patulae cecini sub tegmine fagi*.

The teaching about the bees in *G.*4.1-314 also contains a powerful political message: Vergil supports Octavian's claim of the leadership over Antony's, suggesting that the Republic has come to an end, and that a monarchy should be contemplated, with Octavian as a suitable candidate. This is confirmed in the Aristaeus epyllion which refers to Antony as the man who neglected his duty and to Octavian as the future *rex* who can restore peace and order.

4 The *Aeneid*: An Epic With A Commentary On Contemporary Affairs

In this chapter I consider Vergil's commentary on social and political issues in the *Aeneid*. My supposition is that the poet's commentary will not only be found in direct or indirect references, but also by Vergil using models, literary and/or functional. Therefore, the chapter is divided into two parts. The first part (section 4.1) is about references, particularly those to Augustus (section 4.1.1), Cleopatra (section 4.1.2) – and often to Mark Antony[123]. As it is not possible to discuss the whole *Aeneid* in a book like this, I will present only a selection of representative examples. The presentation of the results of the analyses of the *Aeneid* is different from the presentation of the *Eclogues*. This is because the *Aeneid* – an unbroken and continuous narrative – cannot be subdivided into distinct individual poems.

The second part (section 4.2) will be concerned with the question whether Vergil used a model for Dido and Aeneas, either a literary or a functional model or both. In particular, I will discuss models in the *Aeneid* in general (section 4.2.1), the question whether Dido was a historical character and the early myths about her (section 4.2.2), Dido in the *Aeneid* (section 4.2.3), options of models for Dido (section 4.2.4), and the question whether Cleopatra was a functional model for Dido (section 4.2.5). Finally, I will argue (section 4.2.6) that in some cases Vergil used Augustus as a functional model for Aeneas. At the end of the chapter a short summary will be given in section 4.3.

In the last chapter 5 I will discuss Vergil's political views bringing together the evidence from the *Eclogues*, the *Georgics* and the *Aeneid*.

4.1 References In The *Aeneid*

I mentioned in section 2.1 that the references found in the *Aeneid* can be traced in all forms of visual art in the Augustan era. They were understood by the Romans and Galinsky (1996, 141-224) has presented many examples, such as the *Ara Pacis*, the statue of Augustus of Prima Porta, the portraits of Augustus, wall frescoes, the Forum of Augustus and the temple of Apollo at the Palatine. About the *Ara Pacis*, which he considers to be the most important monument of the Augustan age, he (Galinsky 1996, 141) says: "In its combination of experimentation, deliberate multiplicity of associations and inspirations, and a clear overall meaning, it is a splendid example of the culture in general"[124]. In Galinsky's opinion the same holds for poetry and thus

---

123 In this chapter I will use the name of Augustus that was given to Octavian in 27 B.C..
124 See also the discussions about the *Ara Pacis* in Kleiner (2005a, 212-225; 2005b, 219-229).

literature is a continuous interplay of images and associations. (Galinsky, 1996, 225-287). In this section I will examine not only the texts where Augustus, Cleopatra, and other leading persons from Vergil's time are mentioned in the *Aeneid* by name, but also the indirect references to them.

4.1.1 References To Augustus

The *Aeneid* has several direct or quasi-direct references to Augustus. Shortly after a brief reference to the house of the Iulii (*A*.1.267-268), the first reference to Augustus is found in *A*.1.286-291, where Venus complains to Iuppiter about the fate of Aeneas caused by the wrath of Iuno. Although in this passage Augustus is not mentioned by name, the words *nascetur pulchra Troianus origine Caesar* (from this illustrious origin shall be born the Trojan Caesar), in line 286, refer to him: the Iulii claimed to be descendants of Aeneas and, as Iulius Caesar's adoptive son, Augustus had joined this clan. The words which follow a few lines later in *A*.1.294-296, (*claudentur Belli portae; Furor impius intus/saeua sedens super arma* (the gates of war shall be closed; within unholy Furor, sitting on savage arms), refer to the end of the civil wars, the coming of peace and the role of Augustus in bringing this about.

Other well-known passages are *A*.6.789-795 (Augustus will extend the empire beyond the Garamantes (in Africa) and the Indians) and *A*.8.675-728 (Octavian's fight against Mark Antony and Cleopatra, ending with his great triple triumph). The mention of the coming of the Golden Age, which Anchises foretells in *A*.6.792-794, *Augustus Caesar, diui genus, aurea condet/saecula qui rur sus Latio regnata per arua/Saturno quondam* (Caesar Augustus, descendant of a god, who will again found a Golden Age in Latium in the middle of fields once reigned by Saturn) reflects Vergil's high expectations for Augustus' reign. The civil war will end, reconciliation between the warring factions will be achieved and order will be restored[125]. In *A*.6.794 Augustus is linked to Saturn, the founder of the Roman citadel. The foundation of Rome by Saturn is described in *A*.8.357: *hanc Ianus pater, hanc Saturnus condidit arcem* (father Janus built this fort, Saturn the other). Saturn is not only a founder, but also a lawgiver (*A*.8.319-322: *Saturnus [...], legesque dedit* (Saturn, and gave them laws), a typical royal prerogative. Linking Augustus to Saturn in the above passage refers to the future kingship of Augustus[126].

---

[125] The theme of the arrival of the Golden Age and the reconciliation has been discussed comprehensively by Nadeau (2004, 249-267 and 2010a, 226-230).
[126] Contrary to Lowrie (2009, 172), who does not conclude that the passage refers to future kingship.

In *A.8.626-731*, Vergil describes Aeneas' shield. The poet tells us what the shield represents in line 626: *res Italas Romanorumque triumphos* (the story of Italy and the triumphs of Rome). In lines 671-713, he describes the sea battle near Actium and its immediate aftermath. In this passage the poet shows the contrast between Augustus, who has not only the Senate and the people of Rome, but also the gods at his side, and Mark Antony who is supported by the Egyptian forces and by Cleopatra. The latter is fighting under the threat of imminent death and is aided only by her Egyptian divine evil omens (*deum monstra*) and not by powerful gods. The role of Cleopatra in the battle of Actium (*A.8.671-713*) will be discussed in more detail in section 4.1.2. Augustus is mentioned again in *A.8.675-681*:

> in medio classis aeratas, Actia bella,
> cernere erat, totumque instructo Marte uideres
> feruere Leucaten auroque effulgere fluctus.
> hinc Augustus agens Italos in proelia Caesar
> cum patribus populoque, penatibus et magnis dis,
> stans celsa in puppi, geminas cui tempora flammas
> laeta uomunt patriumque aperitur uertice sidus.
> (in the middle it was possible to see the ships covered with bronze, the battle of Actium, and you could see the whole of Leucate swarming with numbers in Mars' order of battle, and the waves glowing with gold. Here Caesar Augustus standing on the high stern leads the Italians into battle, together with Senate and people, the Penates and the mighty gods; his cheerful face pours out double flames, and on his head his father's star is revealed)

Whether Octavian played such a heroic part at Actium is a moot question, but fortunately Agrippa, his loyal general and admiral, was there: *parte alia uentis et dis Agrippa secundis/arduus agmen agens:* (Elsewhere, with favourable winds and with the help of the gods, mighty Agrippa leads his force) (*A.8.682-683*)[127]. Vergil's description of Aeneas' shield ends with a jubilant prophecy of the greatness of the new ruler. In *A.8.714-728*, he tells us of Octavian's triple triumph in 29 B.C. when he celebrated his victories in the Illyrian campaign, in the sea battle of Actium and the final surrender of Antony and Cleopatra at Alexandria. Lines 714-715, and 720-728 say:

> at Caesar, triplici inuectus Romana triumpho
> moenia, [...].
> ipse sedens niueo candentis limine Phoebi
> dona recognoscit populorum aptatque superbis
> postibus; incedunt uictae longo ordine gentes,
> quam uariae linguis, habitu tam uestis et armis.
> hic Nomadum genus et discinctos Mulciber Afros,
> hic Lelegas Carasque sagittiferosque Gelonos

---

127 In *Epod.9* Horace also refers to Octavian's lack of courage.

finxerat; Euphrates ibat iam mollior undis,
extremique hominum Morini, Rhenusque bicornis,
indomitique Dahae, et pontem indignatus Araxes.
(But Caesar, who had entered the walls of Rome in triple triumph. He himself, seated at the white marble entrance of shining Phoebus, surveys the gifts of nations and fastens them on the high doors; the conquered peoples pass along in a long column, as diverse in languages as in fashion of dress and arms. Here Mulciber had arranged the Nomad race and the ungirt Africans, there the Leleges and Carians and the Gelonians, armed with arrows; the Euphrates moved now with calmer waves, and the Morini, remotest of man, passed along, and the Rhine with double horn, the untamed Dahae, and the Araxes indignant at his bridge)

In this passage Vergil uses his poetic licence to the full. Octavian could not have been seated *niueo candentis limine Phoebi* (at the white marble entrance of shining Phoebus) as the temple of Apollo was not ready before 28 B.C.. According to Miller (2009, 65) this is a "famous anachronism" and the temple of Apollo is a substitute for that of Iuppiter Capitolinus (McKay, 1998, 211; Miller, 2009, 54-94, esp. at 65, 75 and 208). Moreover, Vergil mentions a pot-pourri of peoples that cannot have been present at Octavian's actual triumph, as he mixes adversaries of Octavian at Actium with those of later dates. Some peoples are referred to by their names, while other peoples are represented by the rivers which border on their territories (Euphrates, Rhine, Araxes). Some came from Africa, such as the Nomads, who had come with Bogudes, king of Mauretania and ally of Antony. Others came from the East: the Leleges and the Carians from the southwest of Asia Minor, the Gelonians all the way from the Dnepr, and the Dahae, a people from Scythia. From the West came the Morini, from the region of modern Calais.

Vergil presents three categories of peoples. Firstly, there are conquered peoples (*uictae gentes*), who, after military defeat, were placed under Roman rule. Secondly, there are peoples who had been conquered, but who for strategic or economic reasons received special attention from the Roman authorities in order to be rehabilitated, as was the case with the Leleges and Carians. However, not all of the peoples which are identified or represented by rivers had been conquered and pacified, and Vergil's third category consists of the peoples which had not been subjugated yet (*indomiti*) and for whose members the Romans had a healthy respect. This is the case of the Dahae, who indicate the formidable force of the Parthian cavalry, and the Armenians, represented by the Araxes. The latter were initially allied to Rome, but soon after the battle of Carrhae a Parthian army invaded Armenia, and the Armenian king Artavasdes joined the Parthians, thus revoking the treaty with Rome. In line 727, Vergil also mentions the *Rhenus bicornis* (the Rhine of double horn), a reference to the point near Nijmegen, where the river divides in Rhine and Waal. This represents the inhabitants of the region, the Batavians[128]. Writing some years

---

[128] Eden (1975, 190-191); Fordyce & Christie (1977, 287); Miller (2009, 208-210); Page (1962b, 249-250). For the Eastern peoples, see Bivar (1983, 48-56, esp. at 55). For the Leleges and Cares, see Fordyce & Christie (1977, 286). A detailed discussion of this passage is given in: Weeda & van der Poel (2014,

after the triumph, Vergil used his mythical prophecy of the peoples in the triumphal procession not only to symbolize the extent of the empire, but also as a functional reference to his vision of a stable and peaceful future under Octavian's leadership. The three categories of peoples indicate the political astuteness that is required to manage the empire: the political and military relations with the conquered peoples differ greatly from those with the peoples at the Eastern and Western borders. In the latter situations the leadership in Rome must make decisions which are tailor-made for the particular threat in a specific border region. It is also interesting to note what Vergil has omitted. For example, he does not mention that Cleopatra's effigy was paraded in the procession, and the Egyptians do not feature among the peoples displayed in the triumph. These omissions show the poet's charitable attitude towards the queen.

Aeneas' shield shows not only the glory of war, but also the horrors, such as the rape of the Sabine women in *A.*8.635-637, the dismemberment of the traitor and coward Mettus Fuffetius in *A.*8.642-645 and the more recent history and civil strife represented by Catilina in *A.*8.668-669. The horrors of civil war had preoccupied Vergil for a long time and he had often vented his sorrow and indignation in the *Eclogues* and the *Georgics*. However, Iuppiter's promises in the first book of the *Aeneid* (1.254-296) were being kept and Vergil's description of Aeneas' shield voices his hopes of better times, gradually turning into expectations of better times.

The *Aeneid* also contains many indirect references to Augustus, for example *A.*6.69-70. The passage describes the temple which Aeneas had promised Apollo, which probably refers to the temple on the Palatine dedicated by Augustus in 28 B.C., as well as to the Apollonian Games set up in 212 B.C.. The passage reads: *tum Phoebo et Triuiae solido de marmore templum/instituam festosque dies de nomine Phoebi* (I will then found a temple of solid marble to Phoebus and Trivia, and institute festal days in Phoebus' name). Vergil also refers indirectly to Augustus in his description of Aeneas visiting the Hades where he meets young Marcellus, in *A.*6.860-886. The poet portrays the grief felt in Rome after Marcellus' death, and his interment in Augustus' new-built mausoleum. The connection of Marcellus, who as the son of Octavia and husband of Julia the Elder was being groomed as Augustus' successor, with Augustus' tomb signifies, on the one hand, the fragility of the hereditary system, and on the other Vergil mourning the death of a promising young man, and deploring the loss of a worthy potential successor to the *princeps*[129]. There are many more references to Augustus in the ways in which Vergil depicts Aeneas, and this raises the question

---

588-612). In this paper, it is argued that Vergil's use of the words *Rhenus bicornis* in line 727 and the manner in which he places these words within the context of lines 722-728 mean that the poet refers to the inhabitants of the Nijmegen region.
129 Hardie (2000, 317-318); Page (1962a, 500-504); Williams (2006a, 513-516). See also Shackleton Bailey (1986, 199-205) on *A.*6.882-883: *tu Marcellus eris*.

whether Augustus was a functional model for Aeneas in the same way as Cleopatra was for Dido. This is very likely, and I will discuss this in more detail in section 4.2.6.

There is not just praise for Augustus in the *Aeneid*. Vergil underwent a development in his attitude towards Augustus, and this is visible in the *Aeneid*. He extolled the virtues of Augustus, as the right man to bring peace and stability, but privately his sympathy was with the suffering and sorrow of many of the characters in the poem[130]. Vergil held a positive view of Aeneas, and consequently of Augustus, which is particularly visible in the first books. This positive view can be seen, for example, in Iuppiter's revelation of Rome's future in *A*.1.254-296 and in the prophecy of Anchises in *A*.6.789-795. However, in the same book (*A*.6.847-853), Vergil expressed a concern about the price of imperial success, which amounts to criticism of the new era. He felt that, as imperial conquerors, the Romans paid a high price. This is expressed the famous passages in which the Romans are given their marching orders, namely *parcere subiectis et debellare superbos* (to pardon the vanquished and to vanquish the proud). As Griffin (1979, 65-66) says: "This unrivalled speech [*A*.6.847-853] is at once a boast and a lament, a proud claim by a conqueror and a sigh of regret for the cost." Vergil is not anti-Augustan, but he is clearly unhappy with the way things are going. The passage says:

> excudent alii spirantia mollius aera
> (credo equidem), uiuos ducent de marmore uultus,
> orabunt causas melius, caelique meatus
> describent radio et surgentia sidera dicent:
> tu regere imperio populos, Romane, memento
> (hae tibi erunt artes), pacique imponere morem,
> parcere subiectis et debellare superbos.
> (Others, I trust, shall forge the bronze more easily to breathing, bring in the marble lifelike features, plead cases better, and with a rod sketch off heaven's motions and predict the rising of the stars: you, Roman, do not fail to rule the nations (that will be your skill) and to add civilisation to peace, to pardon the vanquished and to vanquish the proud)

The *alii* are the Greek, the masters of art. For the Romans there remain the hard arts of conquest and dominion. This passage contains explicit criticism of the new age. According to Griffin (1979, 68) this criticism is that:

---

130 Stahl (1993, 174-211) quotes a number of scholars, among others, Quinn, 1968 and R.D. Williams, 2006, who wrote in the sixties of the last century about the public and private voices of Vergil. He quotes Williams (2006a, xxi): "But side by side with his [Vergil's] public voice is the private voice, expressing deep concern for the lonely individual who does not fit into these cosmic schemes."

> In the Aeneid Virgil has succeeded in devising ways of bringing out this complex of ideas, central to his vision of Rome and of history: of Roman destiny as an austere and self-denying one, restraining *furor* and *superbia*, and imposing peace and civilization on the world; at the cost of turning away, with tears but with unshakable resolution, from the life of pleasure, of art, and of love.

In the *Aeneid*, there is also much violence brought about by Aeneas and his men. Dominik (2009, 127) gives a detailed list, from which I select here some of the acts of violence which are Aeneas' responsibility. In: *A*.10.310-311, *primus turmas inuasit agrestis/Aeneas* (first Aeneas attacked the crowds of peasants), we see Aeneas in the battle against Turnus, perhaps referring to Octavian's expropriations after Philippi. One also reads about violence in *A*.11.100-105, for instance in line 102 *corpora, per campos ferro quae fusa iacebant* (bodies that lay dead by the sword spread all over the plain), and in *A*.11.372-373, *inhumata infletaque turba,/sternamur campis* (let us be scattered over the fields, a mob unburied and unlamented). In *A*.12.35-36, we read Latinus' words that *recalent nostro Thybrina fluenta/sanguine adhuc campique ingentes ossibus albent* (until now Tiber's streams remain warm with our blood, and the vast plains are still white with our bones). Dominik (2009, 127) summarises this as "the intrusion of the politico-military world of the Trojans into the life of the Italian countryside and its inhabitants precipitates violence, war, and death on an unprecedented scale." I interpret Vergil's aversion to and condemnation of the violence of Aeneas as a reference to Octavian's line of conduct in the civil war. Just as Aeneas did his duty and founded Rome, Octavian did his by establishing order by military force. Nonetheless, the poet condemns the unnecessary destruction and cruelty.

The finale of a poem has a special significance: the poet has a last opportunity to make his point[131]. Vergil does just that when he describes the death of Turnus and the events preceding it, such as the felling of a sacred olive tree by Aeneas' troops in *A*.12.770-771: *sed stirpem Teucri nullo discrimine sacrum/sustulerant, puro ut possent concurrere campo* (but the Teucrians had cut down without respect the sacred tree, so that they could fight on open ground). Although the perpetrator of the violation is Aeneas, *A*.12.766-771 can be interpreted as an indirect reference to Octavian's violation of the Italian countryside at the end of the civil war, a theme which we often encounter in the *Eclogues*.

Aeneas has to fulfil his duty and cannot allow his adversary Turnus to continue to challenge him. He has been charged by the gods with establishing his new realm and Turnus has to submit. The power of arms will decide. When, in the final clash between the two, Turnus is forced down on his knees and begs Aeneas for mercy, the latter notices the belt of young Pallas on Turnus' shoulders. In the last eight lines of the epic (*A*.12.945-952) Aeneas changes into a merciless victor. These last lines are:

---

[131] Horsfall (1995, 192-216); Putnam (2011, 101-117); Rijser (2011, 135-150); Tarrant (2012, 16-30, 327-341).

> *ille, oculis postquam saeui monimenta doloris*
> *exuuiasque hausit, furiis accensus et ira*
> *terribilis: 'tune hinc spoliis indute meorum*
> *eripiare mihi? Pallas te hoc uulnere, Pallas*
> *immolat et poenam scelerato ex sanguine sumit.'*
> *hoc dicens ferrum aduerso sub pectore condit*
> *feruidus. ast illi soluuntur frigore membra*
> *uitaque cum gemitu fugit indignata sub umbras.*
>
> (as soon as Aeneas absorbed with his eyes the spoils, reminder of cruel grief, he cried out, inflamed with fury and terrible in wrath: "you, decked out in the spoils of one of mine, escape me? Pallas sacrifices you with this blow, Pallas repays you for your guilty blood!" That is what he said, and in burning rage he sank his sword deep in the breast before him. His [Turnus'] limbs gave way by the cold; his life fled indignantly with a sigh to the shadows of death)

A much discussed question is whether it is necessary to kill Turnus in such a brutal way, *feruidus et ira terribilis* (inflamed with fury and terrible in wrath). Is Aeneas' action lawful or does Aeneas shed too much blood? Galinsky discusses in detail the question of permissible anger. He examines the views in Rome at the time of Augustus and the philosophical origins of permissible anger in Aristotle, Plato, the Epicureans and the Stoics. He (1988, 331) states that "later Roman law incorporated many of Aristotle's ideas on the responsibility for acts committed during emotion."[132] In the *Nicomachean Ethics* 1149a25-1149b27, Aristotle gave four reasons why a lack of restraint due to anger is less to blame than lack of restraint due to other emotions. Galinsky (1988, 331-332) summarises:

> first, anger is based on a judgement, [...]. Secondly, anger is more "natural" than a desire for excessive and unnecessary pleasures. Nobody would argue that Aeneas engages in a pleasurable act. Thirdly, anger is an open response, and not crafty and dissimulating. It is good to keep this in mind when one reads critics who insist that Aeneas, if he needs to kill Turnus, at least should do it with less emotion. And fourth, anger is accompanied by pain (e.g., due to the provocation) and is not engaged in simply for the pleasure of it.

Galinsky (1988, 339) also remarks that "in sum, so far from finding Aeneas' anger repugnant, most of the ancient ethical tradition would find it entirely appropriate and even praiseworthy. After the breach of the *foedus* earlier in Book 12, Aeneas has every reason to respond with anger."

I have reservations about Galinsky's arguments. Vergil uses very specific words to describe Aeneas' state of mind, which suggest that Aeneas has temporarily lost his faculty of judgement. Firstly, in lines 946-947 the words *furiis accensus et ira terribilis* (inflamed with fury and terrible in wrath) are applied to Aeneas. Putnam (2011, 109) pointing out the similarities between Dido in book 4 (*A.*4.376 *furiis incensa*, set on fire

---

[132] For the anger of Aeneas, see: Galinsky, 1988; Lowrie (2009, 163); Putnam (2011, 102-117); Tarrant (2012, 9-30).

by fury) and Aeneas in the last lines of the book (*A.*12.946, *furiis accensus*, inflamed with fury), states that:

> as we look at the end of the *Aeneid* through the prism of the emotional world that Virgil creates for Dido and which stays with us throughout the epic, Aeneas both becomes her and kills her as he slays Turnus, but with one major difference. Dido is the passive victim of furies who opts for self-slaughter. Aeneas is equally a prey to madness but turns its violent manifestation onto his suppliant opponent.

I will argue in section 4.2.3 (see note 156) that, by loosing self-control, Dido – like Aeneas in the passage above – did not act as a good queen should. This shows "the humanness of heroes" (Putnam, 2011), both for Aeneas and for Dido. Tarrant (2012, 337) observes that "Virgil's language contains no overt condemnation of Aeneas, but the image of him 'inflamed with furious rage' is undeniably disturbing. [...] Neither *furiae* nor *accendere* is elsewhere applied to Aeneas in Virgil's own voice." Vergil uses words like *furia* at other places, even twice in *A.*12.680 when Turnus tells his sister that he is ready to meet Aeneas for the final confrontation: *hunc, oro, sine me furere ante furorem* (pray, allow me first to be furious in this madness). The poet portrays Turnus' uncontrolled fury in the following lines (681-696), comparing the raging Turnus to a rock coming loose from a mountaintop. Vergil did not condemn *furia* as such. He used the word *furia* to describe justified anger in, for instance, *A.*8.494, when king Euander describes how Etruria rose in *furiis iustis* (righteous fury) against their cruel despot Mezentius, who found shelter with Turnus, his friend. Aeneas' *ira* is characterised by the poet as *ira terribilis*. Although Vergil understood Aeneas' anger, the specific qualification of the anger as *terribilis* suggests that it was excessive, as his victim Turnus was lying wounded before him.

According to Tarrant (2012, 19) Vergil "highlights the intense emotional state into which Aeneas is thrown by the sight of Pallas' belt." The poet makes the point that Aeneas has lost his self-control, and thus is no longer able to act on judgement: Aeneas does not meet Aristotle's first requirement. Vergil levels his criticism not at the killing of Turnus, but specifically at the brutal manner in which it is carried out. Stahl (1993, 210) states: "my conclusion then would be not only that Vergil fully agrees (and wishes to guide his reader to the same position) with Aeneas' act of killing Turnus, but views it as the only morally justified solution to his epic." I concur with his view that Vergil agrees with the killing of Turnus, but Vergil suggests that the moral justification is tainted by the brutality of the killing. This corresponds with the poet's view that war is a messy business, in which men – Augustus and Aeneas alike when involved in war – show their weakness, and which always results in cruelty and violence. As Quinn (1979, 67-68) points out when he discusses the final passage of the *Aeneid*:

> True, Turnus must be got rid of: however humane the gesture if Aeneas had spared his life, it would be dramatically and poetically intolerable for Turnus to survive to fight another day. Aeneas' victory leaves no place for Turnus. But Aeneas does not have to kill his enemy in a *mad*

> *blaze of anger.* He kills Turnus in revenge, as the agent of a personal vendetta, not as the agent of the destined victory of his people. [...] Instead of asking them [the critics, the students of Greek tragedy, the philosophers in that original audience, [...] and others less sophisticated] to criticize Aeneas, was not Virgil asking his audience to admit to themselves that by the time final victory comes, *no man, least of all perhaps the leader of the winning side, can hope to count his hands or his conscience clean?*[133]

Quinn suggests that Vergil depicts good king-Aeneas as a human being with his ugly sides. Tarrant (2012, 27), however, sees the final scene of the *Aeneid* as "typical of Virgil's double-sided outlook to remind his readers of the bloody past of their *princeps* while also looking to him as the author of peace."

Losing self-control turns Aeneas from a good king into a bad king, similar to Dido losing self-control in her fury when she inveighs against Aeneas at his departure from Carthage (see section 4.2.3). The view which Vergil takes of Aeneas at the end of the epic also reflects badly on Augustus. Indeed, I interpret this passage as an allusive reference to Augustus, implying criticism of him. As mentioned above, Anchises impressed upon his son the moral attitude of an honourable and just Roman leader in *A.*6.851-853:

> *tu regere imperio populos, Romane, memento*
> *(hae tibi erunt artes), pacique imponere morem,*
> *parcere subiectis et debellare superbos.*
> (you, Roman, do not fail to rule the nations (that will be your skill) and to add civilisation to peace, to pardon the vanquished and to vanquish the proud)

In lines *A.*12.933-934, Turnus, reminding Aeneas of his father's words, threw himself on his mercy in vain; Aeneas ignored his father's words and plunged his sword into Turnus' chest. *Romane* means that Anchises especially urged the modern Romans who were busy building the empire to show compassion. *Romane* makes these lines a functional reference to Augustus' lack of compassion. As Putnam (2011, 116-117) puts it in his elucidating chapter on the ending (of the *Aeneid*):

> What would Aeneas's disobedient, furious killing have meant to the *princeps* himself? How does it complement the expected glory of Rome, present and to come? [...] At his epic's finale the poet does not put before us someone literally, or figuratively, throwing away his weapons, as Anchises asks of Pompey and, above all, of Caesar in book 6. Rather, he presents us with a vivid illustration of anger-driven vengeance at work, [...]. This account is not to the liking of those who wish to see Aeneas as a paradigm for the just and noble ruler, as a model for Roman leaders to come.

Rijser (2011, 139-147) also addresses the question of the meaning of the closure of the *Aeneid*. Citing Putnam's "What would Aeneas's disobedient, furious killing have meant to the *princeps* himself?" question, he (2011, 141) states:

---

133 My emphasis.

if we trust the antique *testimonia*, the *Aeneid* was indeed what the *princeps* wanted; and yet that same *Aeneid* contains the open and painful questions about Roman rule that Putnam has shown to be there without doubt. In that case, what Augustus wanted must have been exactly that: not a simple panegyrical text, but a layered, multi-vocal one that explained the tribulations he had sought to end, the blood of which was still damp on his hands. Such a work might include tragic conflict, even the suggestion of guilt. To accommodate that suggestion, we must of course discard or at least modify the idea of Augustus the tyrant, and move toward a more civilized, perhaps even sensitive and certainly very intelligent Augustus.

In other words: Augustus could live with such criticism. I will argue in the fifth chapter that Vergil was a commentator who was both critical and supportive.

Augustus had also been accused of cruelty in the civil war, for instance in the case of the farmers' evictions from their land, which had caused many casualties, and even worse in the slaughter at the surrender of Perusia. The *Aeneid* contains many ambivalent passages in which Vergil both lauds and criticises Augustus. This shows that the poet's objective was probably not only to write an epic about the mythical foundation of Rome, but also to give his commentary on contemporary issues. One finds in the *Aeneid* many direct and indirect references to politically significant events, such as the war with Cleopatra and Antony, the emergence of the Principate, the sufferings caused by the civil war and Augustus' conduct in war. This "double-sided outlook" caused Tarrant (2012, 27, note 111) to suggest that "it seems possible that even as early as 19 [B.C.] Virgil could have felt that the tone of the *Aeneid* was now too dark for the times; might that have been a factor in his dying impulse to destroy it ?" I agree with Putnam's suggestion that – if Vergil had in fact ever felt any wish to have the manuscript of the *Aeneid* destroyed – this wish "would more likely arise from his worry about the moral quality of that empire's headship and therefore of the Roman Empire itself, or of any empire" (Putnam, 2011, 116). Vergil felt that the necessary fundamental changes should not be achieved at the cost of great suffering by some or result in the loss of traditional moral values. His involvement was more than mere concern. It is unlikely that on his deathbed Vergil would have changed his beliefs, which he held during his whole writing career and which we read in the *Eclogues* and the *Georgics* as much as in the closing lines of the *Aeneid*. Why should the latter be destroyed – after his death – when his views had been there for all to read for the last decades?

At the end of the book (section 5.1), I will discuss his political views in more detail.

4.1.2 References To Cleopatra

Many direct references to Cleopatra can also be found in the *Aeneid*[134]. The best known passage is in *A*.8.608-731. This is: the story of the new shield made by Vulcan which Aeneas received from his mother Venus. Although Cleopatra remains unnamed in this passage, there is no doubt that Vergil is writing about her. Antony is mentioned by name (line 685) and Cleopatra is connected with him in line 688. In the course of his description of the history of Rome, which takes up virtually the remainder of book 8 (*A*.8.626-728), Vergil relates the important events up until his own days. The Egyptian queen appears three times in *A*.8.671-713, a passage which deals with Actium and its aftermath. Cleopatra is referred to for the first time in *A*.8.685-688: *Antonius [...], sequiturque (nefas) Aegyptia coniunx* (Antony, and there follows him (disgrace) his Egyptian wife) (*A*.8.688)[135]. According to Harrison Cleopatra is a *nefas* (abomination): "Cleopatra herself, attempting to do the unspeakable in overcoming Augustus and becoming mistress of Rome as Antony's wife" (Harrison1998, 235). However, like Binder (1971, 235), I interpret *nefas* as referring to Antony's liaison, because it was for Romans not a legitimate marriage, and particularly to his acquiescence to the queen's command of Roman soldiers at Actium. Cleopatra appears again in *A*.8.696-700:

> *regina in mediis patrio uocat agmina sistro,*
> *necdum etiam geminos a tergo respicit anguis.*
> *omnigenumque deum monstra et latrator Anubis*
> *contra Neptunum et Venerem contraque Mineruam*
> *tela tenent. [...]*
> (In the middle of this the queen calls upon her troops with her native rattle; she does still not look back at the twin snakes behind. Divine portents of every kind and the dog Anubis, the shadow of death, hold weapons against Neptune and Venus and against Minerva)

This passage is often quoted by many modern scholars as an example of the low regard in which Vergil held Cleopatra[136]. Reinhold (1981/1982, 97), who refers not only to *A*.8.696-700, but also to HOR.*Carm*.1.37.6-14 (Horace's "Cleopatra Ode"), and to PROP.3.11.30-58, states: "The savage propaganda campaign unleashed [by Octavian in 32 B.C.] against Cleopatra poured out a flood of extravagant indictments

---

[134] Parts of this section and sections 4.2.3-4.2.5 were originally written as a paper entitled "Vergil and Cleopatra" together with professor Marc van der Poel (Radboud Universiteit Nijmegen).
[135] On Aeneas' shield see: Hardie (1989, 97-109, 120-125, 336-376); McKay, 1998. Chaudhuri, 2012 presents an interesting view on Vergil's concealment of the name of Cleopatra by wordplay. It is unlikely that Vergil used this instrument here, as he refers rather directly to Cleopatra.
[136] On Vergil's views of Cleopatra see: Kleiner (2005b, 191); Schäfer (2006, 11-12, 229-230); Syed, 2005; Williams (2006b, 273); Wyke (2004, 104-105). For the propaganda against Cleopatra by Augustus and the poets see: Kleiner (2005b, 112, 136-137, 274); Oliensis (2007, 226); Pomeroy (1984, 24-28); Wyke (2004, 98-140).

and recriminations (lust, whoring, incest, use of magic and drugs, drunkenness, animal worship, rampant luxury) that have echoed down through the ages in history, literature, and the popular image of her." According to Wyke (2004, 104):

> Neither daughter, wife nor mother, Cleopatra has scarcely any physical presence at all in the Horatian and Virgilian narratives. At best the queen is drunk with sweet success (*Ode* 1.37.11-12) or pale with fear of her coming death (*Aen.*8.709). Only barking Anubis and the rattling *sistrum* which, in the *Aeneid*, accompany the queen into battle might suggest the dissonance of barbarian speech.

Kleiner (2005b, 191) writes about this passage: "In the *Aeneid*, for example, Virgil describes Cleopatra trailed by a motley array of Egyptian deities with an animalistic nature – a strong contrast to the august stature of the core Roman divinities." Syed (2005, 181), focusing on gender and ethnicity and arguing ethnic differences, asserts that this passage "articulates the profound otherness of Octavian's enemies in ethnic and national terms, [albeit] an articulation that is overdetermined precisely because it has to overcome the taint of civil strife inherent in a battle between two Roman generals." Schäfer (2006, 229-230), quoting large parts of *A.*8.671-710, states:

> Und jetzt ging es natürlich erst einmal an die Verherrlichung des Sieges, [...]. Aber wie so oft, entscheidend ist nicht, was passiert, sondern wie man darüber redet. Und in dieser Hinsicht konnte sich der spätere Augustus auf die römischen Dichter verlassen. Horaz widmete Actium eine euphorische Ode. In Vergils Epos wurde sogar eine Darstellung beschrieben, die auf dem Schild des Aeneas zu sehen gewesen sei und den Charakter einer Prophezeiung besaß[137].

Significantly, Schäfer omits lines 698-701 about the Egyptian and Roman gods: two lines which can be interpreted as casting Cleopatra in a more positive light[138].

Hardie (1989, 336-376) argued rightly that Vergil's focus in this part of book 8 is on the history of Rome. Hardie (1989, 348) states: "the *ecphrasis* (like the whole of book eight) is essentially concerned with Roman, not Italian, history, and with the growth of the city of Rome to become the world-power." I agree with Hardie's analysis of Vergil's motives and I read the same focus in this part of the *Aeneid*. However, Vergil's portrayal of the sea battle has fewer supernatural Gigantomachic aspects than Hardie sees. In

---

[137] And yet, the emphasis was of course firstly on the glorification of the victory, [...]. As often, what happened is not the point, but rather the way one talks about it. In this respect, Augustus could afterwards rely on the Roman poets. Horace dedicated a euphoric Ode to Actium. Vergil's epic contained even a description with features of a prophecy, which was to be seen on Aeneas' shield.

[138] Schäfer (2006, 248) refers also to *A.*8.697, suggesting that this line describes Cleopatra's effigy in the procession of Octavian's Triple Triumph in 29 B.C.. Schäfer states: "indem er bei seinem Triumph über Ägypten ein Bild Kleopatras mit zwei angelegten Uräusschlangen mittragen ließ." (because he [Octavian] carried in the procession after his triumph over Egypt a statue of Cleopatra with two cobras laid against her). However, the *anguis* in line 697 symbolizes the threat of death for Cleopatra during the battle of Actium.

essence, it is a narrative in which the poet describes the events rather realistically. Thus, I do not share Hardie's and other scholars' interpretation of, for example *A.8.696-700*, according to which Vergil describes in this passage the clash of two worlds, the evil East and the superior West. In my opinion it is much less complicated.

So how to interpret *A.8.696-700*? Firstly, although *omnigenumque deum monstra* in line 698 is generally rendered as "monstrous gods of every form" (Loeb), *monstrum* also originally means a divine omen indicating misfortune, an evil omen, or a portent, which is the meaning in for example *A.3.59* (*monstra deum refero* (I bring the divine portents)[139]. Secondly, Anubis' presence concurs with these evil omens. Anubis, the Egyptian god, represented with a dog's head, is a god of the realm of the dead and in particular the accuser of souls at the final judgement after death. Therefore, I prefer to render *A.8.697-700* as: "she does still not look back at the twin snakes behind. Divine portents of every kind and the dog Anubis, the shadow of death, hold weapons against Neptune and Venus and against Minerva." Accordingly, the lines express that Cleopatra at that stage of the battle is not yet aware that she is fighting under the threat of imminent death, aided only by her Egyptian divine evil omens and not by powerful gods. The Egyptians fought against superior Roman forces who were aided by their gods: "Neptune, the god of the sea where the battle takes place, Venus, the mother of the Roman race, Minerva the goddess of wisdom." (R.D. Williams, 2006, 273). Thus, I interpret the symbolism of lines 697-698 as expressing Vergil's compassion for the approaching death of a courageous Cleopatra, and not "the conflict of religious attitudes between East and West." (R.D. Williams, 2006, 273). Gurval (1998, 237) hints at this interpretation by pointing out that Vergil alludes to Dido, when he states that there is some reminiscence with Dido: "like Dido [...], the Egyptian queen is also fated to die." In the next passage there is also textual similarity with Dido (Gurval, 1998, 240). In *A.8.709* we read that Cleopatra was *pallentem morte futura* (pale at the coming of her death) and in *A.4.644* Dido is described as *pallida morte futura*. Gurval, however, does not suggest that Vergil used Cleopatra as a model for Dido.

---

139 For "the monstrous gods" see for example: Conington & Nettleship (1963, 154): "expressing a Roman's contempt for the heterogeneous assemblies of deities"; Fordyce & Christie (1977, 283): "in the language of familiar abuse"; Gransden (1976, 179): "The monstrous and barbarous deities of Egypt are here arrayed"; Page (1962, 248): "for the 'monstrous gods' of Egypt see Juv. 15 ad in"; Pease (1967, 26-27): "monsters described as worshipped by the Egyptian queen". Fordyce & Christie refer for the use of *monstrum* in *A.7.21*, where they interpret *monstrum* rightly as "originally a religious term used of a supernatural phenomenon which conveys a portent or an omen", and give five places in the *Aeneid* and two in the *Georgics* where Vergil used *monstrum* meaning portent/omen (Fordyce & Christie, 1977, 58). Contrary to our opinion, they do not suggest that the latter meaning of *monstrum* also applies to the present passage; Hardie (1989, 98): "The Virgilian battle [Actium] is between two quite separate races of gods, the Roman Olympians and the alien Egytian divinities, monstrous and non-anthropomorphic (*Aen.8.698*)." Hardie (1989, 104) repeats "the monstrous forces"; Williams (2006b [orig. 1996], 273): "Anubis [...] who exemplifies the various monstrous shapes in which their [Egyptian] gods were visualized." Finally, McKay (1998, 210) is rather neutral: "bestial, barking Anubis."

The culmination of all this is found in a third passage where Cleopatra's flight to Egypt is described (in *A*.8.707-713):

> *ipsa uidebatur uentis regina uocatis*
> *uela dare et laxos iam iamque immittere funis.*
> *illam inter caedes pallentem morte futura*
> *fecerat ignipotens undis et Iapyge ferri,*
> *contra autem magno maerentem corpore Nilum*
> *pandentemque sinus et tota ueste uocantem*
> *caeruleum in gremium latebrosaque flumina uictos.*
>
> (The queen herself was depicted challenging the winds, spread sail, and now, yes now, slacken and let go the ropes. Amid the slaughter, pale at the coming of her death, the Ruler of fire had represented that great queen, carried off by waves and by the wind that blows from the South of Italia; he had made in front of her the mourning Nile with his great body, spreading open the folds of his gown and welcoming with the whole of his garment the defeated to his blue lap and sheltering streams, full of coverts)

Modern commentators argue that in his account of the battle at Actium (lines 671-713), Vergil – compelled by Octavian's propaganda – presents Cleopatra as worshipping animalistic deities (Kleiner, 2005b, 191; Reinhold, 1981/1982, 97), as being a barbarian (Wyke, 2004, 104), or as having a shameful liaison with Antony (Binder, 1971, 235; Harrison, 1998, 235). On the contrary, I suggest that in this passage, Vergil presents Cleopatra with restraint. His words show kindness, awareness of her emotions and compassion with her fear, even panic, particularly when he portrays her pallor and the shadow of death hanging over her. Particularly impressive is the image of the mourning Nile, standing for Egypt, and of its streams giving shelter to the great queen in her defeat. It is unlikely that these lines are the fruits of Octavian's propaganda. The latter is supposed to have presented the final stages of the civil war (after 35 B.C.) as a conflict with an external foe, Cleopatra. It is abundantly clear, however, that, in line 685, it is Antony who leads the forces against Octavian at Actium, *hinc ope barbarica uariisque Antonius armis* (on the other side Antony with his foreign might and his mix of troops), and that Cleopatra takes second place in line 688, *sequiturque Aegyptia coniunx* (follows him his Egyptian wife). Syed (2005, 179) emphasizes the "orientalization of his [Antony's] entourage." In her opinion, the oriental nature of Antony's (and Cleopatra's) army had "a powerful impact on the ideological polarization of the two enemies represented here." This "otherness" of Antony's forces is part of her (2005, 180) argument that "otherness is stressed [by Vergil] in national terms, which in turn have a defining force for the Romanness constructed in this passage." Syed (2005, 179) is right in arguing that Vergil's representation of Antony's forces at Actium "has little or no basis in historical fact." His description of the presence of oriental forces is indeed exaggerated. I would suggest, however, that Vergil used this caricature for a very different purpose, that is to ridicule Antony's position in Alexandria and his failed Eastern ambitions.

The afore mentioned passages contain direct references to Cleopatra. The story of Pallas' sword-belt in *A*.10.495-498 can be interpreted as an allusive reference to the queen:

et laeuo pressit pede talia fatus
exanimem rapiens immania pondera baltei
impressumque nefas: una sub nocte iugali
caesa manus iuuenum foede thalamique cruenti,
(And while he [Turnus] said this, he stood with his left foot upon the lifeless body [of Pallas], seizing the belt with it's enormous weight and the crime engraved on it: the group of young men slaughtered cruelly on one wedding night, and the bridal-chambers stained with blood)

On this belt is depicted the myth of the Danaids: the fifty daughters of the Egypto-Greek king Danaus who were married to their cousins and who – with one exception – slaughtered their newly-wed husbands on their wedding night. Clearly, the myth is symbolic here, and there has been much discussion about the nature of the symbolism. In Kellum's (1985, 172-175) opinion, the above lines demonstrate that the poet portrays the darker side of Cleopatra. She argues that the Danaids represent the evil forces of oriental barbarism, defeated at Actium. According to Harrison (1998, 234) the spouse-murdering Danaids of Egypto-Greek origin "are surely an appropriate mythological representation of Cleopatra, the official enemy at Actium, defeated through Apollo's help in the Augustan accounts of the battle." This refers to Cleopatra, who had murdered two of her younger brothers, who were also her husbands: the first Ptolemy XIII in 51 and the second Ptolemy XIV in 44 B.C.[140]. Obviously, Vergil does not paint a flattering picture of Cleopatra in this passage. However, he probably interpreted these murders within the contemporary context. First, Cleopatra acted in the true fashion of Hellenistic monarchs. Second, many opponents of the political leadership in Rome were also murdered, in particular during the proscriptions. Third, Cleopatra, by eliminating her political rivals, does not differ essentially from Octavian, who had both Antyllus, Fulvia's elder son by Marc Antony, and Caesarion murdered, and who had forced Gallus to commit suicide, to mention only a few examples (cf. Pomeroy, 1975, 124, 186-187).

---

[140] Harrison (1998, 223-242) gives an extensive discussion of the different views on the meaning of the symbolism. A discussion of Roman attitudes towards other peoples is given in Isaac (2004, 359, 369-370). One can also interpret this passage as a reference to Dido. In preceding book 10 Vergil refers to similar negative traits of Dido, for example in *A*.4.584-629, when she threatens to murder Ascanius, curses Aeneas, and prays for ongoing hostility between her people and Aeneas' descendants.

4.2 Models In The *Aeneid*

In section 1.2.3 I introduced the notions of the literary frame and the functional frame, and the concept of the functional model. In this section, I will argue that in the *Aeneid* Vergil used both literary and functional models. However, I will focus on the latter, as the literary model – in general and also in particular in the *Aeneid* – has been researched sufficiently and in great detail in many scholarly papers. In successive sections I will discuss the subject of models in the *Aeneid* in general (section 4.2.1), the question whether there ever was a Carthaginian queen Dido, who she was and the early myths (section 4.2.2), Dido in the *Aeneid* (section 4.2.3), models for Dido (section 4.2.4), the question whether Cleopatra was a functional model for Dido (section 4.2.5), and finally whether Augustus was a model for Aeneas (section 4.2.6).

4.2.1 A General Introduction

The leading characters in the *Aeneid* have acted as models for many others over a period of more than two thousand years. Did Vergil perhaps use models too? He was certainly inspired by Homer. But whether he had in mind models for his main characters is a different question. And if this is the case who was or were his model or models? Was Aeneas sufficiently known through mythical stories? Did Vergil use a model for Dido? Or was Dido a known figure? Did he perhaps use models for both? Other questions can be raised as well, such as: if Vergil used models, did he only choose them in order to present Augustus in a favourable light and through Aeneas foreshadow Augustus, or is the choice also a commentary on the social and political situation of his time?

In section 1.2.3 a distinction between the literary frame and the functional frame was introduced. Consequently, I distinguish between two forms of models: the literary model and the functional model. In both models the author describing a *persona* has a person in mind whose "parallel" in character, social position or physical appearance he uses. Similarly, when he depicts an event, the author uses what he considers an analogue.

I will use the term literary model when the author refers to a predecessor or an admired colleague-author. In that case, the poet's main objective is to create a literary continuity with his paragon by referring or alluding to the latter's work. In a functional model the author does not primarily have a literary objective. His main purpose is to deliver either a specific statement or a functional description of persons or events. These statements often concern political or social issues, and/or the actors in those fields. In a functional description the author intends to portray the nature of an issue, and/or the manner in which his *persona* acts. A functional description may also suggest the impact of the *persona*'s actions. In the case of both persons and events the author may select a model generally renowned for the characteristics he wants to illustrate. Hence, the choice of a model for persons is often either a contemporary, a mythical or a well-known historical person who becomes the origin of associations in the readers' minds. As a consequence, when the model is an illustrious contemporary person, the author by implication alludes to this contemporary person. Explaining the major characters of the *Aeneid* and their actions, Binder (1971, 2) uses the words "typologische Auslegung" (typological interpretation), which is not synonymous but similar to my definition of functional models. With this he (Binder, 1971, 3) means that the personae in the *Aeneid* are like their models: "He [Augustus] *is* not Hercules or Aeneas, but he is *as* they are, their historical portrait." Therefore, in the epic there are poetic connections between the myth and the present which refer the reader to contemporary events.

Most modern scholars hold the view that Vergil employed a model when he described the mythical Dido and in the extensive literature on the subject much has been written about the different options, some of which mention Cleopatra[141]. It is likely that Vergil had two objectives. The first was the writing of an epic about the founding of Rome and its (mythical) history. For this purpose he found his inspiration in either Homer, the Greek tragedians, Apollonius Rhodos, or Ennius, or all four. Their work or works formed the literary model for the *Aeneid*, both for the architecture and for the *personae* and events[142]. The *Aeneid* contains numerous examples of literary models: I choose at random. Firstly, in *A*.1.496–504, where Aeneas meets Dido for the first time, Vergil likens her to Diana and her company. According to Nelis (2001, 82-86) Vergil refers to both Artemis/Nausicaä (by means of the Homeric simile) in HOM. *Od*.6.102-108, and to Artemis/Medea in *Argonautica*.3.876, where Apollonius imitates Homer. Knauer (1979, 155), whose book is concerned with Homer as a model for the *Aeneid*, points out rightly that "Vergil konnte sie [Nausikaa] schwerlich als Gestalt in die Aeneis übernehmen, den Didos Gestalt hat andere Voraussetzungen[143]." Still, both references can be considered literary models for Dido, as Vergil creates a literary continuity with either Homer or Apollonius, or both[144]. A second example is the episode of the wounding of Dido in *A*.4.66-73. In Nelis' (2001, 25-180, esp. at 131-132) view this refers to Apollonius' depiction of Medea wounded by the arrow of Eros in the third book of the *Argonautica*. Nelis (2001, 5-21) refers to Vergil's literary debt to both Apollonius and Homer as "a pattern of two-tier allusion linking Vergil, Apollonius

---

141 In chronological order: Crees and Wordsworth (1927, xi); Pease (1967/1935, 24–28); Knauer (1964, 155, 209); Otis (1966, 62-96); Jones (1971, 118); La Penna (1985, 48-63, esp. at 54); Cairns (1989, 57); Easterling and Knox (1993, 58); Farron (1993, 61-62); Horsfall (1995, 133-134); Galinsky (2003, 17-23); Nelis, 2001; Griffin (2004, 183-197).
142 Hardie (2000, 312-326) and Tarrant (2012, 28-30), among other scholars, have pointed out that Vergil was not only inspired with respect to form, but that there was also much tragic influence.
143 Vergil could hardly adopt her [Nausikaa] as a model (Gestalt) in the *Aeneid*, as Dido's persona has different requirements.
144 See also Page (1962a, 188 [at *A*.1.498]), who mentions only Homer's text.

and Homer." Nelis (2001, 7) states that he "will attempt to demonstrate that Vergil's epic is built out of a consistent, structured pattern of imitation based on awareness of Apollonius' imitation of the *Iliad* and *Odyssey*." In his book (2001, 5-9) he gives a wide selection of secondary literature on the use of models and references in Latin poetry. I will discuss Nelis' views about Medea as a model for Dido in more detail in section 4.2.4[145]. Otis (1966, 71-76) also discusses the wounding of Dido: "There can thus be no doubt that Virgil is primarily indebted to Apollonius" (Otis 1966, 73).

I intend to demonstrate that it is likely that Vergil had an overriding second objective, which was political. This objective was to foreshadow and portray in his epic Augustus, whom he believed to be the leader who could bring peace and stability. For this purpose Vergil used for his *personae* (Dido, Aeneas) functional models of his time. Thus, in the readers' minds his *personae* could be associated with living persons. Vergil created mythical characters, setting them back more than a thousand years in time, combining myth and reality in order to interpret his own period. As Pease (1967, 24-28) pointed out, a number of scholars link Aeneas, Dido, and perhaps even the minor characters in the *Aeneid* with Augustus, Cleopatra, and their contemporaries. I will discuss the views of Pease more fully in section 4.2.5. It is likely that, when Vergil created the *persona* of Dido, he used the most unique and visible characteristics from his functional model without making Dido – the heroine of the first half of his epic – an identical copy of her model in each and every detail. My proposition is that Cleopatra served as the functional model for Dido and that the portrayal of Dido in turn reflects Vergil's appreciation of the Egyptian queen. The use of Cleopatra and Augustus as functional models for Dido and Aeneas respectively becomes the origin of associations with contemporary persons or events in his readers' minds. For example, when Aeneas followed his destiny and deserted Dido, the reader is reminded of Antony who – unlike Octavian – shirked his responsibility and stayed with Cleopatra. The *Aeneid* provided Vergil with an opportunity to deliver his commentary on the social and political situation of his time.

Virtually all scholars who identified a model for Dido, considered only the option of a literary model, and did not examine the possibility of a functional model. To my knowledge, it is only Otis (1966, 62-96) who hints at the latter. He (1966, 76) outlines Vergil's use of the literary model when he says:

> Virgil in short has taken Apollonian, Homeric, and even tragic materials to form the structure of a very complex and very un-Apollonian and un-Homeric epic. His similes are clearly modelled on those of Apollonius and Homer but, unlike theirs, are integrated with the whole poem in virtue of their association with *leitmotifs* that recur at pivotal moments of the action.

---

[145] See also Galinsky (1996, 229-231), who discusses a number of mythical women as possible literary models.

What Otis (1966, 76) says about "their association with *leitmotifs* at pivotal moments" can be considered representing Vergil's second (functional) objective in addition to the literary. However, this is only my conjecture, as Otis does not further elaborate on this point and does not suggest the specific notion of the functional model.

Who are the favourite models in the secondary literature? Many women, generally mythical heroines and even goddesses, are paraded as possible models for Dido (Horsfall, 1995, 133-134; Muecke, 1983, 144 notes 43-50). One finds Hypsipyle, Medea, Helena, Calypso, Nausicaä, Cleopatra and many others. Horsfall (1995, 133) remarks: "In despair, attentive readers of *Aen*.4 are reduced to drawing up lengthy lists of Dido's mythical and literary analogues." In the case of Dido he (1995, 133-134) offers a useful classification by distinguishing between three categories of models: (i) "alleged allegorical comparisons, notably Cleopatra, (ii) Dido in Naevius, Varro, and Ateius Philologus, (iii) Homeric antecedents, female and male, and antecedents in Greek tragedy and Hellenistic poetry." At the end of the fourth or the beginning of the fifth century A.D. at least one attentive reader of the fourth book of the *Aeneid* made his choice of a model. Macrobius wrote in his *Saturnalia* (Macr.5.17.4): *adeo ut de Argonauticorum quarto, quorum scriptor est Apollonius, librum Aeneidos suae quartum totum paene formaverit, ad Didonem vel Aenean amatoriam incontinentiam Medeae circa Iasonem transferendo* (Willis, 1963, 315) (Thus he has modelled his fourth Book of the *Aeneid* almost entirely on the fourth Book of the *Argonautica* of Apollonius by taking the story of Medea's passionate love for Jason and applying it to the loves of Dido and Aeneas)[146]. Knauer (1979, 209) states "Die Medea des Apollonios von Rhodos wie die des Euripides haben das Bild der Dido bestimmt[147]." Farron (1993, 61-62) holds the same view: "Vergil obviously modelled the Dido episode on that [love of Jason and Medea], as was observed, with exaggeration, by Servius, in his introduction to Book 4, and by Macrobius (*Sat*.5.17.4)." I differ from Farron's (1993, 62) view that "the Dido story is completely an episode. It has no effect on the *Aeneid*'s plot or on Aeneas' moral and intellectual development." On the contrary, through Dido's episode Vergil makes Aeneas' destiny clear. In section 4.2.4, I will discuss Nelis' (2001) claim that Medea was the model for Dido. I will argue that Medea was probably one of the literary models for Dido, but that she was not Dido's functional model. Desmond (1994, 32), discussing "Virgil's Dido in the Historical Context," states that "Dido also functions as a figure for Cleopatra." However, the focus of Desmond is on the "feminine, sexualized, oriental threat to centralized Roman power" (1994, 32). I argue that Vergil offered a much more comprehensive view on the two queens (see also note 152 and section 4.2.3).

---

[146] The translation is by Davies (1969, 359); reprinted with permission of Columbia University Press.
[147] Medea of Apollonius Rhodos and of Euripides have determined the image of Dido.

In the following section (4.2.2) the question whether Vergil used stories about a mythical Dido which may have existed before his time – Horsfall's second category – will be considered.

4.2.2 Dido: Was She A Historical Character? Early Myths

Dido's history as described by Vergil was founded on the established tradition of his time, which was narrated by Timaios, a historian from Tauromenium, Sicily (ca.356–260 B.C.), and perhaps by others whose works are no longer extant (Desmond, 1994, 24-27; Monti, 1981, 20-21). Other mythical stories about Dido circulated at the time, of which some will be discussed in this section[148]. Nowadays, there is general consensus – based on modern archaeological research – that there was an earlier Phoenician trade post on the site of old Carthage and that the city was founded by Elissa (Dido) of Tyros in 814 B.C. (Moscati, 1984, 38-47).

In Phoenicia's history, the beginning of the ninth century B.C. was of crucial importance. At that time the power of Assyria increased and the independence and freedom of the Phoenician cities diminished rapidly. The annals of the Assyrian king Assurnasirpal II (883–859 B.C.) say (Moscati, 1968, 15):

> At that time I marched along the side of Mount Lebanon, and to the Great Sea [...]. The tribute of the kings of the seacoast, of the people of Tyre, Sidon, Byblos, etc [...] – silver, gold, lead copper [...], and ivory, and a *nahiru*, a creature of the sea, I received as tribute from them and they embraced my feet.

The Phoenician cities did not put up an armed resistance and gradually submitted themselves to Assyria. It is assumed that internal strife in some cities, the increasing pressure from Assyria, and the harshness of the Assyrian regime led in the ninth century B.C. to a growing emigration to other parts of the Mediterranean region. This also caused the departure of Elissa, the sister of king Pygmalion of Tyros, who was married to her uncle Acharbas (who in *A*.1.343 is called Sychaeus), and left the city after the assassination of her husband, together with a group of citizens from Tyros. The eldest source on these events is a fragment which originated from Timaios and was quoted in the *Strategemata* of Polyaenus (Jacoby, 1950, 624)[149]. The fragment says:

> Timaios says that she, who in the Phoenician language is called Elissa and who was a sister of king Pygmalion of Tyros, is reported to have founded Carthage in Libya. When her husband was murdered by Pygmalion she put her possessions in ships and fled together with some citizens.

---

148 Timaios, Fragments in: Jacoby (1950, 624); See also: Horsfall (2007, 138-144); Pease (1967, 16).
149 Polyaenus lived in the second century A.D.

After great suffering and after a long journey she arrived at Libya and was received friendly by the local people. After she had founded the afore-said city, and as she wanted to become queen of the Libyans, she was forced by the citizens to marry, but she resisted. She pretended to solemnize the ceremony which would free her from her vows, but she had a very high pyre erected near her palace, set this on fire, and threw herself from the building on the pyre.

The story in this fragment – Dido committing suicide to escape from a forced marriage – differs substantially from that in the *Aeneid*. Aeneas does not feature at all in the fragment. Noteworthy is of course that in about 300 B.C. Timaios assigned the founding of Carthage to Elissa of Tyros. Vergil may have used and perhaps modified a well-known mythical story about Dido, which has since been lost. This leads to the question of what and how much was known about Dido and the founding of Carthage in Vergil's time. Our knowledge about this is very limited due to the paucity of the extant sources about Dido from the time before Vergil.

Some fragments in which Dido is mentioned have survived. These are fragments of the *Bellum Poenicum* of Gnaeus Naevius, some of the *Annales* of Quintus Ennius, some texts in later commentaries of the fourth century A.D., such as those of Servius and Macrobius, and finally a fragment that is included in the *Anthology* of Planudes translated by Ausonius[150]. These later texts indicate that indeed more archaic stories about Dido existed which have been lost but which Vergil may have known. Whether he was guided by myths about Aeneas and Dido, which existed in his time, has given rise to much speculation in the secondary literature. I will discuss the most relevant texts.

First, in book 1 of the *Bellum Poenicum*, Naevius (ca.270–ca.200 B.C.) described the history before the First Punic War, in which he fought. Naevius went back to the flight of Anchises and Aeneas from Troy and he mentioned a great storm in which the Trojans found themselves. Dido, however, is never mentioned in the whole extant part of the *Bellum Poenicum*. Some modern authors believe that a number of fragments from the *Bellum Poenicum* 1 may refer to Dido, for example fragment 18, fragment 19 and fragment 20[151]. In addition, there exist a number of references of commentators of later centuries, which may suggest that Naevius mentioned Dido. In his commentary on *A.4.9*, Servius (Thilo & Hagen, 1923, vol. I, 462) has handed down to us: *cuius filiae fuerint Anna et Dido, Naevius dicit* (Naevius said, that Anna and Dido were his daughters). At the beginning of the fifth century A.D., Macrobius (Macr.6.2.30-31) wrote that the first book of the *Bellum Poenicum* exercised great influence on Vergil (Willis, 1963, 365; see also Horsfall, 2001, 138-144). The passage says: *Sunt alii loci plurimorum versuum quos Maro in opus suum cum paucorum immutatione verborum a veteribus transtulit. […] in primo Aeneidos tempestas describitur, et Venus apud Iovem*

---

150 Paton (1960, 248); the epigram about Dido that is cited here is by an anonymous author.
151 Horsfall (2007, 138–144); Hunink (2006b, 63-64). The indication of the fragments of the *Bellum Poenicum* is according to Morel, 1995.

queritur de periculis filii, et Iuppiter eam de futurorum prosperitate solatur. hic locus totus sumptus a Naevio est ex primo libro belli Punici. (There are other places with many verses, which Vergil has transferred from former writers to his own work, with the change of a few words. In the first book of the *Aeneid* there is a description of a storm; Venus complains to Juppiter of the dangers for her son, and Juppiter comforts her showing her the success of the future children. The whole of this place is taken from Naevius, from the first Book of his *Bellum Poenicum*).

Second, two extant fragments from the *Annales* of Ennius, in which he related the history of Italia and Rome from the mythical beginning after the fall of Troy, may refer to Dido and the founding of Carthage. These are fragment inc.27 (verse 472) from *Annales, liber 7*: *Poenos Sarra oriundos* (Phoenicians [people of Carthage] descended from Sarra [Tyros]), and fragment 8.24 (verse 297) from *Annales, liber 8*, where Ennius writes about the Second Punic War and where he warns the Romans not to underestimate the people of Carthage. The text says: *Poenos Didone oriundos* (Phoenicians descended from Dido). These two fragments are found in books 7 and 8 of the *Annales*, but Dido cannot be found in the extant fragments of book 1, where Ennius writes about Aeneas' mythical journey to Italia and the founding of Rome and where her name is to be expected[152].

Third, in Ausonius' translation from the Greek of the epigram in the *Anthology of Planudes*, it is said of Dido that she never met Aeneas and never lived in Libya at the time of the destruction of Troy, but that she committed suicide by the sword in order to escape a forced marriage to Iarbas. She asks the Muses why they made Vergil slander her honour (Paton, 1960, 248-249; part 4, epigram 151). This epigram is most likely from an anonymous author from the Hellenistic era, and may indicate that a story about Dido and Aeneas was known before Ausonius' time. But the epigram also suggests that it was considered an unlikely story.

Fourth, Servius' commentary on *A.4.682, exstinxti te meque, soror* (you have destroyed yourself and me, sister) says: *Varro ait non Didonem, sed Annam amore Aeneae impulsam se supra rogum interemisse* (Varro said that not Dido but Anna, impelled by her love for Aeneas, took her own life on the pyre) (Thilo & Hagen, 1923, vol. I, 580). This text turns the whole *Aeneid* upside down, with either both sisters taking their lives or Dido living on after Aeneas' departure.

Finally, Macrobius (*Saturnalia* 5.17.5-6) writes that Vergil has portrayed Dido's passion so beautifully that *quam falsam novit universitas, per tot tamen saecula*

---

[152] Fragment inc.27 in Hunink (2006a, 82); Skutsch (1985, 114); Warmington (1988, 84). Fragment 8.24 in Hunink (2006a, 92); Skutsch (1985, 95); Warmington (1988, 98). Hunink (2006a, 73-74) states that fragment inc.18 refers also to Dido, namely to her arrival in Africa. The problem is here that Dido is not mentioned by name and that this text can also refer to others, for instance to Punic soldiers in general. The indication of the fragments of the *Annales* in Hunink's and my text is according to Skutsch, 1985.

speciem veritatis obtineat (what everybody knows to be incorrect, still has been viewed as true during so many years). Everyone knew of the chastity of the queen, but chose to believe the poet's version (Willis, 1963, 315. See also Davies, 1969, 359).

In sum, Timaios' text about Dido and the anonymous epigram in the *Anthology of Planudes* are strikingly similar. Both texts say that Dido took her own life to avoid a forced marriage. In Timaios' text, Aeneas is not mentioned at all, and the author of the epigram even explicitly denies any relationship with Aeneas. Thus, the evidence is very conflicting and it appears that it is no longer possible to trace whether Vergil used stories about a mythical Dido – written or oral – which may have existed before his time, and which he adapted and turned into the Dido we know from the *Aeneid*. Horsfall (2007, 142) says the following about this: "But are we in a position to say anything about the function and character of Dido in the BP [*Bellum Poenicum*]? Or about the influence of Naevius' Dido on Virgil's? Any reconstruction is a mere house of cards."[153] This "house of cards" applies not only to the Dido in the *Bellum Poenicum* but also to the picture of her which could arise from other extant mythical sources. Nowadays one can only conclude with any form of certainty that a mythical Dido from Carthage was known before Vergil's time and that it is likely that someone said that a Dido committed suicide on a pyre. Vergil's Dido, however, is a "complete" woman to whom he attributed many features. Did Vergil perhaps connect the arrival of a mythical Aeneas, which Naevius had mentioned, with a semi-historical Dido and did he construct a new myth from these facts? Anyway, the answer cannot be found in our extant sources and it will remain unresolved whether Vergil used earlier myths. It is likely that Vergil's Dido and Aeneas are fiction.

4.2.3 Dido In The *Aeneid*

How does Dido come across in the *Aeneid*? Who is Dido, in her public appearances and as a private person? To find plausible answers, a number of relevant passages from books 1 and 4 of the *Aeneid* will be briefly discussed[154].

In *A*.1.338-368, Vergil relates that Dido left Tyros together with her supporters to establish a new kingdom and to rule there as their queen. *A*.1.360 reads: *his commota fugam Dido sociosque parabat* (moved by this, Dido prepared her flight and her company). In *A*.1.364, the poet says: *dux femina facti* (a woman was the leader of

---

[153] Horsfall (2007, 138-144). It is noteworthy that Horsfall (2007, 144) also states: "the influence of Naevius' Dido on Virgil's in character and function was, I suspect, vastly greater than can now be plausibly guessed, let alone proved."
[154] Quinn (1963, 48-49). Quinn discusses extensively Dido's and Aeneas' love and the inevitability of "Dido's downfall." See also: Cairns (1989, 136-145); Horsfall (1995, 123-134); Muecke (1983, 134-155); Rudd (1976, 32-53).

the venture). The last three words express that it was very unusual that a woman is the leader of the expedition. In book 1 this point is again emphasized when Aeneas cautiously enters Carthage and sees Dido at work there. In *A.1.507-508, iura dabat legesque uiris, operumque laborem/partibus aequabat iustis aut sorte trahebat* (she administered justice and made laws for her people, and she settled their tasks in fair portions or assigned these by lot), Vergil portrays Dido as a woman who acts to all intents and purposes as queen and who uses her regal powers to the benefit of her people[155]. In several other passages in book 1 Dido is portrayed as a good queen: she is *forma pulcherrima* (A.1.496, a great beauty), she is likened to Diana and has divine qualities (A.1.499), and goes *ad templum* (A.1.496) with royal piety. When a party of stranded Trojans is allowed to address her, Dido declares that the Trojans are very welcome. She invites them to stay and to build Carthage with her and her people. She emphatically includes Aeneas. Vergil suggests here that she is considering establishing a new dynasty with Aeneas if he were to arrive in Carthage. In A.1.573-574, Dido says: *urbem quam statuo, uestra est; subducite nauis; Tros Tyriusque mihi nullo discrimine agetur* (The city I founded is yours; haul up your ships on land; I will not discriminate between Trojans and Tyrians).

At the end of book 1 (A.1.748-749) things develop as the reader expects. Dido is struck by Amor: *nec non et uario noctem sermone trahebat/infelix Dido longumque bibebat amorem* (And unhappy Dido also spun out the night with varied talk and long she drank the cup of love). It is often held that Aeneas courted Dido and that she reluctantly consented. Dido certainly had her doubts, as is made clear in book 4 when she discusses her new love with her sister Anna. However, Dido also took initiatives herself as one reads in book 4. She takes the lead and decides to win over Aeneas when she shows him round the city (A.4.74-75). In A.4.129-159, Dido and her suite and Aeneas with his Trojans go hunting. A sudden thunderstorm forces them to take shelter and Dido and Aeneas find themselves in the same cave: *speluncam Dido dux et Troianus eandem/deueniunt* (Dido and the Trojan chief came to the same cave) (A.4.165-166). Juno and Venus consented to the marriage, as we read in A.4.126-127: *conubio iungam stabili propriamque dicabo./hic hymenaeus erit* (I [Juno] will link them in a lasting marriage and I will pronounce her his own. This will be their wedding). When the queen and Aeneas leave the cave Vergil tells us (A.4.170-171): *neque enim*

---

155 Syed does not have such a positive perception of Dido. Comparing Dido and Cleopatra, she (2005, 184) asserts that in the *Aeneid* "there is a series of literary allusions that link Dido to threatening images of female rule." As evidence she discusses among other things A.1.490-504 (Syed, 2005, 184-185) and A.1.507 (Syed, 2005, 185-186). I do not concur with her view that Vergil's representation of Dido's (and Cleopatra's) rule is expressed "in terms that reassert well established attitudes about women's roles in ancient societies" (Syed, 2005, 186), seeing "Dido and Cleopatra associated with the discourse of orientalism. Female rule and orientalism intersect in these two figures to create powerful images of the Other against which Romanness is defined" (Syed, 2005, 186). Vergil held Cleopatra (and Dido) in high regard and saw them as a new version of what female rule could be like.

specie famaue mouetur/nec iam furtiuum Dido meditatur amorem (For no longer Dido is guided by appearance or reputation, no more does she think of a secret love). In *A*.4.54-173, Dido is a woman who is totally engrossed in her love for Aeneas and who creates opportunities to share her love with him.

With Aeneas hanging about in Carthage, Iuppiter decides that he cannot any longer condone Aeneas' neglect of his duty, and the chief god sends Mercury to dispatch Aeneas to Italia at once. Dido is aware that Aeneas is going to leave her and she reproaches him for his departure. Dido's anger and distress are not just a result of Aeneas' choice to follow his own path and to reject her love. Something else is the matter. In *A*.4.327-330 Dido says:

> '*saltem si qua mihi de te suscepta fuisset*
> *ante fugam suboles, [...],*
> *non equidem omnino capta ac deserta uiderer.*'
> (if at least your child had been born to me before your flight, [...], I should not consider myself utterly hurt and deserted)

This is not just an expression of Dido's distress due to the loss of Aeneas' love. In this passage the childless Dido also displays her frustration over her failure to start a new dynasty with him. Aeneas leaves for Italia and Dido takes her life on the pyre. They will meet once more when Aeneas visits the underworld.

Although, in general, Vergil writes "sympathetically" about Dido, the poet does not hold unreserved affection for her. When the story develops Vergil also reveals Dido's negative traits. Dido acts without self-control and dignity when she begins to suspect Aeneas' departure (*A*.4.300-303); such fury does not befit a good queen. This is repeated a few moments later when she tells Aeneas what she thinks of him (*A*.4.365-392, esp. at 4.376: *furiis incensa*, set on fire by fury)[156]. Vergil also shows Dido in an unfavourable light in *A*.4.584-629. She sees that Aeneas' fleet is preparing to depart and for obvious reasons this arouses a deep anger within her. However, she does not voice her anger but instead is enveloped in a fierce hatred. Again, Vergil does not portray her as a queen who acts in a composed manner, as a good queen should. Although the poet – and his audience – may have felt compassion with Dido's despair, he probably wanted to point out that the responsibilities of her high office should take precedence over her private grief. Shortly before uttering her curse, Dido had wished a little baby brother for Ascanius (*A*.4.328-329) (cf. Rudd, 1976, 47-48). I do not concur with Desmond (1994, 30), who argues that Dido's change from a "good" to a "bad" queen occurs because "Dido's activities as a lover explicitly compromise her status as 'good king.'" In my opinion, Vergil portrays her genuine love for Aeneas, which she connects with her wish for a child to establish a new dynasty. This is very much

---

[156] See also section 4.1.1, where I discussed *furiis accensus* being applied to Aeneas' killing of Turnus at the final of the epic, referring to Aeneas' loss of self-control not befitting a good king.

part of Vergil's depiction of Dido as a responsible ruler. Her "activities as a lover" are no aberration, but her loss of self-control, when her plans are frustrated, is. The lines A.4.600-603 from her long tirade show the other side of Dido:

> non potui abreptum diuellere corpus et undis
> spargere? non socios, non ipsum absumere ferro
> Ascanium patriisque epulandum ponere mensis?
> (Could I not have grabbed him [Aeneas], torn his body to pieces, and scattered these on the waves? Could I not have killed his men by the sword, and Ascanius himself, and dished him up at his father's tables to feast upon?)

Her anger is not just directed against Aeneas: a few lines later she prays for an ongoing hostility between her people and Aeneas' descendants (A.4.622-626):

> tum uos, o Tyrii, stirpem et genus omne futurum
> exercete odiis, cinerique haec mittite nostro
> munera. nullus amor populis nec foedera sunto.
> exoriare aliquis nostris ex ossibus ultor
> qui face Dardanios ferroque sequare colonos,
> (Then you, Tyrians, torment with hate his offspring and all the future race, and offer to my ashes these gifts. No friendship or treaty must be between the nations. Let an unknown avenger come forth from my bones, who with his torch and sword pursues the Trojan settlers)

The above passage is a prophecy by Dido, in which she foretells that Aeneas will experience many hardships and struggles and "legend told that his reign was brief and that he met an unnatural death at the river Numicius, his body disappearing and so not given burial" (Goold, 2006, 464-465 note 6). The last two lines (*exoriare.... colonos*) refer not only to Aeneas' fate, but can also be interpreted as referring to the Punic wars and to Hannibal (*aliquis ultor*) and as an allusion to Vergil's own days.

Vergil's portrayal of Dido is subtle and shaded, showing her good and bad sides. The picture of her is that of an independent queen, superior to many men, a leader of her people, who makes decisions about the organization of the city. She possesses the ambition to establish a new empire. Dido shows courage and physical strength in her public role, and she has an elevated social position. She is the leader of the Carthaginian society, at the top of the elite. On a personal level, she openly embraces her love for a stranger and takes initiatives in her relationship with him. Initially, in her new passion she does not lose sight of her public responsibilities as she regards her new love as an opportunity to safeguard the future of her dynasty. However, the poet is not unreservedly positive about Dido. When the story develops one sees Dido's negative traits. Vergil portrays her also without self-control and dignity. Dido did not fit the model of the female member of the Roman elite of Vergil's time. Although from the second century B.C. onwards women of the Roman elite moved about more freely, they remained dependent on their husbands, their fathers-in-law or other male members of their family. Dido was not the ideal wife and mother. She stood out high above the few women who had achieved some elevated station in public life. Compared to those women she was unique[157].

In this context it is also important to note the way Vergil portrays Lavinia, as Yvan Nadeau pointed out to me: "What does the portrait of Lavinia have to tell us about Augustan politics? She is the 'female interest' of the second half of the *Aeneid* as Dido is the 'female interest' of the first half."[158] In *A*.6.763-765, Lavinia is mentioned for the first time in Anchises' prophecy: *Siluius, Albanum nomen, tua postuma proles,/ quem tibi longaeuo serum Lauinia coniunx/educet siluis* (Silvius, Alban by name, your last-born son, whom your wife Lavinia late in your life shall bear in the woods). This is rather typical of Lavinia's portrait in the *Aeneid*, as she is more often talked about than she herself speaks. In *A*.7.52-106 we learn more about her, the dutiful and self-effacing daughter of king Latinus, who is *iam matura uiro, iam plenis nubilis annis* (she was now ripe for a husband, and marriageable). Turnus woos her and this match is strongly supported by Amata, Latinus' wife. But forceful portents tell the king that *externi uenient generi* (sons-in-law shall come from foreign lands) and that their offspring will rule the world (lines 96-101). Iuno resists vehemently Lavinia's fate in marrying Aeneas and we read the foreboding of the struggle between the latter and Turnus in *A*.7.313-322: in line 321 a parallel is drawn between Paris and Aeneas. Thus, Aeneas is twice accused of landing in a foreign land and stealing women who were promised to other men: blamed by Iarbas in the case of Dido and by Iuno with respect to Lavinia. The parallel with Paris also implies a parallel between Helen and Lavinia as being the causes of war[159]. In *A*.7.318-322 we read:

> *sanguine Troiano et Rutulo dotabere, uirgo,*
> *et Bellona manet te pronuba. nec face tantum*
> *Cisseis praegnas ignis enixa iugalis;*
> *quin idem Veneri partus suus et Paris alter,*
> *funestaeque iterum recidiua in Pergama taedae.*
> (you shall be endowed with the blood of Trojan and Rutulian, maiden, and Bellona escorts you as your bridewoman. Not only Cisseus' daughter was pregnant with a firebrand and brought

---

[157] Vergil may have been aware of the position of women in Cleopatra's Ptolemaic-Egyptian society, which differed considerably from contemporary Rome: Fantham, Foley, & Kampen, et al. (1994, 140-168); Pomeroy (1984, 171-173). For general discussions of women's role and position, see: Fantham, Foley, & Kampen, et al. (1994, 260-265, 271-274, 294-329) (although in the latter section the emphasis is on women, family and sexuality, it presents a good summary of women's position in general); Oliensis (2007, 221-234); Pomeroy (1984, 115-119); Treggiari (2005, 130-147).
[158] Nadeau, 2011, private communication. See also Williams (2006b, 170-171, 190-192); Woodworth (1930, 175-194).
[159] Bellona is the sister of Mars. Cisseus' daughter is Hecuba, who dreamed that she was pregnant with a firebrand before giving birth to Paris. Nadeau (2010a, 221-222); Williams (2006b, 190-191). Vergil draws the parallel between Paris and Aeneas at an earlier occasion in *A*.4.215, when Iarbas calls Aeneas *ille Paris* (that Paris) (Williams, 2006a, 350).

forth a son [whose wedding caused] a blaze; no, Venus is the same in her own son, a second Paris, and deadly torches will come once more to rebuilt Troy)

Iuno lets the Fury Allecto strengthen Amata's resolve that Lavinia marry Turnus, and the queen hides her daughter in the woods: Lavinia only reappears in *A*.11.479. The matter is eventually settled after Aeneas has struck down Turnus in the duel, when the latter says: *tua est Lauinia coniunx* (Lavinia is your wife) (*A*.12.937). Lavinia is portrayed as the dutiful, demure girl, the ideal Roman maiden, subordinating herself to her father and to her duty. The difference between Dido and Lavinia is of course that Dido and Aeneas were passionately in love, while Aeneas is not in love with Lavinia (Woodworth, 1930, 185-187). Vergil makes this clear in an indirect way in *A*.12.192-194, when referring twice to Latinus as Aeneas' *socer* (father-in-law), and only mentioning Lavinia in line 194 within the context of the dynastic and political settlements between Aeneas and Latinus. Vergil makes the point that Aeneas did his duty both when he left Dido and again when he married Lavinia in a *mariage de raison*. Lavinia accepted this arrangement, because she had no choice, as was to be expected of a daughter. Similarly, Octavian did his duty marrying Livia Drusilla in 38 B.C., although this marriage was blemished by Livia being a wife and mother. Thus, the Aeneas/Paris parallel can be interpreted as a critical allusive reference to Octavian also stealing other people's women. Vergil's portrayal is in a sense a forerunner of Augustus' *Leges Iuliae* (Woodworth, 1930, 187). The passage about Lavinia (*A*.7.52-106) can also be interpreted as Vergil using Augustus as a functional model for Aeneas, and thus referring back to another aspect of the contemporary political situation. The parallel is that Octavian did his duty as a leader taking responsibility for restoring stability in Rome: this was in sharp contrast to Mark Antony, who enjoyed himself in a consuming love affair with Cleopatra. Woodworth (1930, 188-194) identified three relevant parallels between Lavinia/Aeneas and Livia/Augustus, which I will examine in more detail in section 4.2.6, where I discuss the possibility of Augustus being the functional model for Aeneas.

The contrast between Vergil's portrayal of Dido on the one hand and of Lavinia on the other is also significant for another theme, namely the poet's opinion about the role of women in society. Vergil held a much more "liberal" view on this than the great majority of his contemporaries[160]. This can be deduced from his choice of Cleopatra as a functional model for Dido – which I shall argue below – and the unique features that he gave his Dido and which he must have recognised in Cleopatra, such as for example their queenship, independence, role in battle and intelligence. This suggests that Vergil did not consider Cleopatra an evil woman, but that he approved

---

[160] For the role of women in Roman society see Fantham, Foley, & Kampen, et al. (1994, 260-265, 271-274, 294-329); Oliensis (2007, 221-234); Treggiari (2005, 130-147); Wyke (2004, 98-140). For the position of Cleopatra see Fantham, Foley, & Kampen, et al. (1994, 136-139); Kleiner, 2005b; Pomeroy (1984, 3-40, esp. 24-28). See further for the life of Cleopatra: Schäfer, 2006; Volkmann, 1958.

of her positive qualities. He presumably also knew of the much more prominent role of women in Ptolemaic society and I guess that by referring to Cleopatra in his portrait of Dido he showed his approval, and perhaps even his admiration of the extension of women's activities in more domains than those of the traditional Greek or Roman women[161]. His rather flat depiction of Lavinia, the paradigm of the dutiful Roman woman is in strong contrast with this and it is evident that Vergil felt more attracted to Dido than to Lavinia, or to Cleopatra than to the average Roman matron [162].

4.2.4 Models For Dido

Above (section 4.2.2), I concluded that it will remain unresolved whether Vergil used earlier myths as a model for Dido, Horsfall's (1995, 133-134) second category. In this section I will explore whether Vergil may have used a model from Horsfall's third category ("Homeric antecedents, female and male, and antecedents in Greek tragedy and Hellenistic poetry"). In examining Vergil's use of mythical or literary antecedent, Dido's unique and special features, namely her public actions as a queen, her independence and her leadership, are significant. Although Vergil could have used several models for different aspects of Dido's *persona*, and although it may be feasible that he did this for some features, it is not likely that he did so for the unique character and status of Dido. None of the mythical women, whom he may have used, founded an empire, built a city, or was the independent queen of her people, the commander of soldiers or a lawgiver. Although some of these characteristics are indeed assigned to the queens of the Amazons or Hypsipyle, they did not achieve the full measure of queenship as Dido did.

Other mythical women are also inappropriate as models, as can be seen from a comparison between Dido on the one hand and, for example, Andromache and Medea on the other. These two women have been chosen because, on the one hand, they exemplify the female role and position in their own time and, on the other their characters and actions can be adequately constructed from the extant epic literature. In the sixth book of the *Iliad* Andromache is portrayed as a woman who obviously loves her husband (*Iliad*.6.407-613), and to whom she is subservient. Her role is within

---

[161] Fantham, Foley, & Kampen, et al. (1994, 136-168) and Pomeroy (1984, 41-51) analyse the role of women of the Ptolemaic nobility in more detail.

[162] Indications of Vergil's positive attitude towards women can also be found in the *Eclogues*. In *Ecl*.1, Amaryllis enables Tityrus to purchase his freedom. In *Ecl*.8, Nysa is not given away in marriage to a shepherd, but to a newcomer who offers her a better future instead. Similarly, in *Ecl*.10, Lycoris, Gallus' love, ran away with a soldier. Vergil does not disapprove of these women, who determined their own future. The woman in Alphesiboeus' song in *Ecl*.8 loses her husband to a girl who does not belong to her world. Vergil gives the woman her own independent view on the events which have overturned her life in the countryside. See also the relevant discussions in sections 3.1 and 5.1.

the family as a wife and mother. At home she is the manager. When she ventures beyond domestic affairs, she is curtly rebuked by her husband Hector, as in the scene in which she offers him some sound military advice (*Iliad*.6.484-492). However, this is something she accepts. For her it is not possible to conceive a life without her husband as protector and bread-winner. She is thus very well in keeping with the archetype of the female member of elite within Homeric society (Loraux, 1981, 75-117; Fantham, Foley, & Kampen, et al., 1994, 33).

Medea in Apollonius Rhodius' *Argonautica* is a different story. Medea develops, from a girl with a consuming passion for the stranger Iason, into a woman. She struggles with this love and its consequences. She is portrayed as somebody who can analyze and articulate her feelings: a woman with brains and with a heart. She shows initiative, stands up for her own interests, and takes her own decisions, such as leaving her parental home in Colchis in spite of her family ties. In the end she stands up against Iason, the hero, and considers herself equal to him. Medea is much more a woman of the world than Andromache and in her case we do not hear anything about domestic chores. Apollonius was very familiar with Alexandrian high society in the third century B.C.. He was born in the city and lived and worked there for many years as Librarian of the Museum and tutor to Ptolemy III. When he wrote his epic in the middle of the third century B.C., the first signs of a broadening role for women were becoming apparent. Although it is feasible that Apollonius portrayed Medea with the position of the originally Greek female elite of Alexandria of those days in mind, she did not reach the elevated status of a Hellenistic queen. This was reserved for the female members of the Ptolemaic dynasty (Pomeroy, 1984, 41-82). Nelis (2001) argues that Medea as portrayed by Apollonius in the *Argonautica* was the model for Dido. Nelis has indeed demonstrated that there are significant references to Apollonius' Medea, and she is probably one of Dido's literary models. Nelis (2001, 85) refers briefly to "Dido's queenly status" when he writes: "Dido may be a lover in a similar mould [like Medea]. In another sense, however, the two women are quite different. Dido, when she is compared to Diana, is a queen intent on the building and organisation of a city, and her public functions are her main concern." Although Nelis acknowledges Dido's public status, he does not suggest a second (functional) model for Dido. It is unlikely that Medea was Dido's functional model as Medea did not posses Dido's unique key features: a queen who performed all the duties which queenship demanded. Nelis (2001, 184) concludes: "The sheer weight of the evidence set out in the two preceding chapters suggests that the Medea of Apollonius is the central model for the creation of Vergil's Dido." Nelis has indeed demonstrated that there is much literary continuity. In my opinion, however, the functional model is "central."

The differences between Dido, as portrayed in Vergil's *Aeneid*, on the one hand, and her mythical sisters Andromache and Medea on the other are very clear. Dido is a queen with all the ensuing characteristics, and Andromache and Medea are royal princesses and wives. In the cases of all three mythical women their decisions in matters of love have an important bearing upon the course of their lives, but with some crucial differences. Andromache is an example of self-effacing conjugal love. Medea revenges the rejection by Iason but her vengeance remains within the limits of their personal relationship, as it is played out on their sons. Dido however experiences her love for Aeneas as a woman with a public duty and sees his departure not just as a personal rejection. The decisive issue for her is the loss of authority she suffers. Her suicide is in a sense also an abdication from the throne. Dido's *persona* is unique for the time in which Vergil created her, while Andromache and Medea occupy positions which one would have expected women to hold in the societies of either Homer's or Apollonius' times.

4.2.5 Cleopatra And Dido Compared

I concluded before that it is impossible to know whether Vergil used existing myths about Dido. Neither does Horsfall's third category (models from Greek epic, tragedy or Hellenistic poetry) seem to fit. Horsfall's (1995, 133-134) first category, "the alleged allegorical comparisons," seems to be promising. In this section I will argue that Vergil had one particular woman in mind whose characteristics he applied when he created the public and private *persona* of Dido. If – as I believe – he wanted to emphasize the unique character of Dido in her public role, he was most likely to choose a model whose public appearance could be recognized by every reader, immediately and without reserve. Although some scholars mentioned similarities between Dido and Cleopatra, it was only Pease (1967, 24-25) who offered evidence of similarities between the two women, for example the point that "both women are queens," that both had a relation to an "important figure in Trojan-Roman history," and that both committed suicide. However, Pease is not wholly clear when he simply writes that Dido was a queen. He (1967, 24, note 163) asserts that "emphasis upon Dido's queenly dignity appears constantly [in the *Aeneid*]," and later in his commentary on the opening line of book 4 (*At regina*) he (1967, 83-84) says that "Virgil intended to emphasize throughout the queenliness of Dido, as Horace (*C*.1, 37, 30-32) did that of Cleopatra." Pease's choice of words – queenly dignity, queenliness – may imply that he considered Dido a woman who was as decorous and distinguished as a queen, but that he did not attribute to her the full royal status. He also does not suggest that Cleopatra was the functional model for Dido, as I do. Pease (1967, 27) holds a position in the middle when he says: "While, then, the figure of Cleopatra seems to have furnished some details for the picture of Dido, we should beware of pressing analogies where they may not exist," and (1967, 28) "If Dido is designed to suggest to some extent the figure of Cleopatra [...]." Pease (1967, 26) also points to some differences, for example the fact that Cleopatra rules a decadent society, while Dido is a pioneer, that they were of Aryan and Semitic descent respectively, and that Cleopatra "is bent upon her own licentious pleasures, while Dido is not only capable of great devotion to the memory of her dead husband but is desirous of establishing the Punic throne with a fixed succession" (Pease, 1967,26).

Other scholars also noticed parallels between Dido and Cleopatra. Quinn (1963a, 35) and Cairns discuss these only within the context of Dido's love for Aeneas and the latter's desertion of the queen. Cairns (1989, 57) refers to the "destruction through 'love'" of Antony and Cleopatra and states: "It is well understood that Virgil to some extent modelled Dido upon Cleopatra." Desmond (1994, 32) says: "Dido also functions as a figure for Cleopatra" (*sic*). All three scholars refer to Pease. Horsfall (1995, 133-134), suggesting his first category of analogues for Dido, namely "alleged allegorical comparisons, notably Cleopatra" also associates this with the tragedy of Dido's and Aeneas' love, their guilt and blame. Horsfall refers to Pease and Cairns, and to La Penna (1985, 54); the latter focused on Fama's gossip of both Aeneas' and Dido's care-free passion (*A*.4.189-197), and on Mercury's reproach to Aeneas for neglecting his duties (*A*.4.259-278). Galinsky (2003, 17) summarizes his essay as follows: "There are considerable affinities between Horace's portrayal of Cleopatra (Carm.1.37) and Virgil's of Dido. They involve verbal echoes, theme, treatment and especially tragic problemisation. [...]. Horace's Cleopatra, rather than the real Cleopatra, is one of the many models for Virgil's Dido." Syed's approach differs considerably. She (2005, 184-193) argues the specific proposition that Vergil's objective in the *Aeneid* was to (re)define Roman identity. Comparing Dido and Cleopatra, she states that Vergil did this by "projecting Cleopatra's gendered and ethnic otherness ['for the Romans of the Augustan period'] on Dido" (Syed 2005, 192), thus allowing the poet "to define Roman identity in the *Aeneid* not so much against the backdrop of the civil wars but by gesturing toward Rome's conflict with Carthage." Hardie (2006, 25-41) focuses on the erotic bond between Dido and Aeneas, and examines the consequences of their putative incestuous brother-sister relationship in the *Aeneid*. He (2006, 28) argues that this relationship reflects contemporary Roman political invective which "in the 30s B.C. was directed against an alien royal household, the Ptolemaic dynasty of Alexandria [of Cleopatra and her brother-husbands]." To sum up, some scholars quoted have a very specific focus (for instance Syed, 2005; Hardie, 2006), while others recognize only a similarity to some extent between the two women.

I suggest that Cleopatra was Vergil's functional model for Dido for the purpose of giving his views on major contemporary political issues. The functional model implies that many passages in which the poet writes about the person of Dido can be seen as references to Cleopatra. When Vergil wrote the *Aeneid* he was living and working close to the centre of power. Vergil's position near Augustus would have made him highly aware of political developments and most likely he was also well informed about the political and social events of the fifteen-year period preceding the time when he started writing the *Aeneid*. It would not be surprising therefore, that he had a clear picture of Cleopatra in mind.

Above, the most relevant passages about Dido in the *Aeneid* have been analyzed, and a summary of Vergil's portrayal of Dido has been presented. Comparing Dido and Cleopatra, striking analogies both in public and in personal appearance become visible. In their public roles both were unique. The mythical Dido, queen of Carthage, held a position in her virtual society that was exceptional for a woman. Equally, the position of the historical Cleopatra was in general unattainable for women at the close of that age. Dido and Cleopatra were both independent sovereigns: they enacted law, administered justice and commanded their troops. They ruled kingdoms on the southern coasts of the Mediterranean, and both came to power after conflicts and strife within their families. Mythical Dido was a threat to Rome for two reasons. Firstly, Rome would not have been founded if she had managed to tempt Aeneas to stay with her, and secondly Dido built Carthage, a future threat to Rome. Cleopatra formed an actual danger to Rome and in the eyes of her Roman contemporaries she was a fundamental player at an important junction in Rome's history. The continuity of their dynasties was a prime issue for both of them, as much for Dido in her relation to Aeneas as for Cleopatra in her "marriage" with Antony. Both women saw great opportunities to build a powerful empire with their new partners.

There are also several parallels with respect to their personalities. Both women were intelligent and communicative. Cleopatra was attractive, but not especially beautiful, while Dido is described as a great beauty. They knew how to charm men, with Cleopatra as the clear champion in this respect. Both felt and behaved as equal partners of their lovers: in the case of Cleopatra this developed into a dominant position over Antony, while the relation between Dido and Aeneas was too short-lived to witness any profound development. Both women committed suicide in the prime of their lives. They acted out of frustration that their designs had failed, and they refused to subordinate themselves to their male opponents: Dido felt betrayed by Aeneas and Cleopatra had lost both her empire and Antony, and did not want to subject herself to Octavian.

4.2.6 Augustus And Aeneas Compared

One of Vergil's objectives in writing the *Aeneid* was to give his views on contemporary political issues. To this end, he used – among other things – Cleopatra as a functional model for Dido. His readers could recognise in Dido's *persona* and in her actions similarities with Cleopatra and thus take cognizance of the poet's views on Cleopatra. If the argument that Vergil used a functional model for Dido is accepted, the question arises whether he used a similar design for Aeneas. There are two arguments for this point of view. First, if Vergil wished to give his commentary on the political issues at the end of the first century B.C., it is unlikely that he would have done this by using a (functional) model for Dido but not for Aeneas. Second, in the *Aeneid* much is double-sided, using Tarrant's (2012, 27) terminology. Why not a duality Aeneas/Dido and Augustus/Cleopatra?

Several scholars have already identified that there are similarities between the *persona* of Aeneas and the real Augustus. Without attempting to be complete, I will briefly consider the views of Woodworth (1930), Cairns (1989), Powell (2004), Nadeau (2007, 2009, 2010), Tarrant (2000, 2012), and others.

Woodworth (1930, 188-194) called attention to three relevant parallels between Lavinia/Aeneas and Livia/Augustus: (1) Although Lavinia was not married, as Livia was, she was betrothed to Turnus. In both cases the welfare of the state demanded a different marriage for the women than was originally foreseen or was the case. (2) Aeneas, who after all is a poor newcomer in Italia "is to found his destined race by a union with the royal blood of the native stock" (Woodworth, 1930, 192). Similarly, Augustus was a parvenu for whom a marriage in Roman aristocracy would be very advantageous. (3) The expected result of the union of Lavinia and Aeneas is male offspring, which happens with the birth of Silvius, and this "corresponds to the unfulfilled but long-cherished hope of Augustus to beget an heir and *found a dynasty*" (Woodworth, 1930, 193)[163]. To my mind, this last parallel is the most significant as it again shows (in *A*.7.96-106) Vergil advocating a hereditary kingship, which he has done consistently throughout his work even before the *Aeneid* in *Ecl*.4 and in *G*.4.

Nadeau (2004, 255; 2007, 94-98; 2009, 35-42; 2010a, 230-231) also hints at the notion of Augustus as a functional model for Aeneas. Although he does not use the words "literary or functional model," through his detailed examination of the intertextuality between the *Aeneid* on the one hand and the *Iliad* and *Odyssey* on the other, he confirms Vergil's debt to Homer. Nadeau gives this literary inspiration an additional meaning, showing that much of what Aeneas experiences in his mythical pursuits runs parallel to important events in Octavian/Augustus' life. Therefore, the question is what came first. Did Octavian re-act Aeneas, which is very unlikely, or did Vergil choose events or traits of Octavian and shaped Aeneas out of these? The latter seems more likely. I will only briefly indicate some of the similarities that Nadeau describes and I refer the reader to his work for the details. The most notable examples are Aeneas' problems in the waters around Sicily (*A*.6.162-174), which can be interpreted as a reference to Octavian's struggle with Sextus Pompeius. Nadeau (2007, 94) also interprets the passage in *A*.3.209-267 as referring to Sextus Pompeius "who caused famine in Rome, causing disturbances there, before he was defeated by the fleet newly-trained and equipped by Agrippa." Contrary to Nadeau, I think it more likely that this passage refers to the more general struggle before Octavian established his reign, because: in the prophecy of doom by the Harpy Celaeno (lines 245-257), the emphasis is on the *war* which Aeneas/Octavian has to fight (lines 245-249) and not on hunger (lines 255-257). My interpretation is supported by Williams (2006a, 286) who states that in this passage "we see the Trojans again as exiles wandering in a wilderness of sea, very far from their promised home." Nadeau (2007, 97 and 2009, 35) suggests that the *pietate grauem ac meritis [...] uirum* (a man great in his sense of duty and great in his merits) in *A*.1.148-153 can be identified as fifth-century B.C.

---

[163] My emphasis.

Menenius Agrippa (see also Morwood, 1998, 195-198) and is thus an allusion to M. Vipsanius Agrippa, the friend of Octavian, and to his victory over Sextus Pompeius. In my opinion, the identification of Menenius Agrippa is rather speculative and I prefer to interpret *A.1.151* as referring to *any man* who, in the words of Morwood (1998, 197), has the personal authority as "tamer of mob violence", and not necessarily a historical person. A further example given by Nadeau is the last stage of Aeneas' visit to Hades to reconcile with his opponents (*A.6.854-886*) which is connected to the death of Marcellus. Vergil mentions the Mausoleum of Augustus (built in 27 B.C.), and links a gloomy prediction for Aeneas with a gloomy prediction for Octavian. Nadeau (2004, 105-120, esp. at 120, and 255) thinks of the plot by Caepio and Murena in 23/22 B.C.. I discussed this passage in section 4.1.1, about references to Augustus, and I suggested there that Vergil is referring to Augustus' abortive efforts to establish a dynastic kingship. In addition, Nadeau mentions, among other things, the passage on Aeneas' wounding and recovery with the aid of Venus (*A.12.383-429*). I am sympathetic to Nadeau's (2004, 255) statement that the passage has a "sense of foreboding" of doom, relating to "Augustus' nearly-fatal illness of the same year [23 B.C.] – the which illness is symbolized, as we have seen, by the arrow-wound which nearly proves fatal to Aeneas – a matter we [Nadeau] studied in Chapter 3 [of his book]." The passage can indeed be interpreted as a functional reference to Augustus' illness and the fragility of the young Principate.

A third view is that of Tarrant (2012, 24), who argues that:

> although Aeneas is an independent character and not an allegorical substitute for Augustus, the connections between the two are so strong that the view taken of one must inevitably colour one's view of the other; as Richard Thomas has written, 'ambivalence about Aeneas and ambivalence about Augustus and contemporary Rome go hand in hand'[164]

In addition to the scholarly views above, I am putting forward that when Vergil describes Aeneas using loaded expressions such as *rex Aeneas* or *pius Aeneas*, he is in fact also referring functionally to Augustus. This matches the Roman belief that excellent traits run in aristocratic families and that, consequently, Aeneas' positive qualities of character return in Augustus (Powell, 2004, 162). Cairns (1989, 3-4) also refers to the many instances in the *Aeneid* where the word *rex* or related words are used. He compares this with the *Iliad* and the *Odyssey* and concludes that Vergil

---

[164] Tarrant (2000, 178-179; 2012, 24-30). Thomas (1988b, 261), stated: "While we can never quite say, without reducing the *Aeneid* to something less than what it is, that Aeneas *is* Augustus, at the same time to deny a general correspondence and relationship between the two would be to suggest that Virgil was isolated from the great events through which he lived – an isolation which would be at odds with his attitude in the *Eclogues* and *Georgics*, and which would in any case be intrinsically unlikely." See also Binder, 1971.

uses the term far more often[165]. The character most frequently described as king is Aeneas, which is a clear indirect link between Aeneas and Augustus. Cairns (1989, 4) formulates this as: "Of course caution must be exercised in applying things said about Aeneas to Augustus, and the pair are to be seen as analogues rather than equated. But any repeated attribute of Aeneas must to some extent have reflected on Augustus." The same holds for *pietas*. Although the number of times that the words *pius Aeneas* are used has not been counted as in the case of the word *rex*, it has been mentioned that *pietas* and Aeneas are much connected. Vergil never applied the notion *pietas* (or *pius*) in the direct sense to Augustus: the connection is by implication, as for instance in *A*.1.294-296, where Iuppiter speaks of the end of *furor impius* when Augustus closes the gates of war (Powell, 2004, 157-159, esp. at 158, and 143-149). Augustus saw *pietas* as an important value and thus I see the use of the word in the *Aeneid* as another significant reference to the *princeps* and his ideals.

Indeed, I concur with Tarrant's (2012, 24) point that the "connections between the two [Augustus and Aeneas] are so strong that the view taken of one must inevitably colour one's view of the other." I argue that this is precisely what Vergil wanted to achieve by applying the functional model. The ambivalence in the case of both Dido and Aeneas lies in the poet's use of two models at the same time, a literary and a functional. However, he did this for different purposes: the literary model had a literary objective, the functional model had a political objective. Although I argue that Augustus is the functional model for Aeneas, there are passages in the epic which seem to contradict this view, for example *A*.8.671-728, which I discussed above. In this and other passages the historic Augustus Caesar has his very own role (Actium, triple triumph). This is similar to the manner in which Cleopatra features in the *Aeneid*: both as Dido modelled on Cleopatra and in her own right as Cleopatra, queen of Egypt. However, there is no contradiction when Vergil presents the models in their own historic reality. On the contrary, Vergil reinforces the reader's association between the models (Augustus, Cleopatra) and the modelled (Aeneas, Dido): a main function of the functional model is indeed to evoke an allusion to contemporary persons or events, and readers would experience the poet's presentation of historic Augustus and Cleopatra as an affirmation of their association.

4.3 Summary

In the *Aeneid*, Vergil refers several times to both Augustus and Cleopatra. These references are either direct, or indirect, or achieved through the use of functional models for Aeneas and Dido. Vergil uses Cleopatra extensively as a functional model for Dido. Although he uses Augustus in some cases as a functional model for Aeneas,

---

[165] *Iliad* 287 times, *Odyssey* 194 times and *Aeneid* 334 times.

this is not as frequent and comprehensive as the poet's use of Cleopatra as a model for Dido.

The political themes which emerge most strongly in the *Aeneid* are in general the same as those in the *Eclogues* and the *Georgics*. For instance, the sufferings caused by the civil war and the violation of the countryside (*A*.10.310-311, 12.766-771), Vergil's expectations of better times under Augustus' reign (*A*.6.792-794, 8.626-731), and his view that a stable one-man rule is needed to establish peace and order (*A*.6.860-886, 8.319-322). The epic also has several passages that are very critical of Augustus. For example, in *A*.6.847-853 Vergil is critical of the high price to be paid for imperial success; in *A*.11.100-105 and *A*.11.372-373 he condemns the violence of the civil war; in *A*.12.945-952 he is critical of Augustus' use of violence (symbolized by the brutal killing of Turnus); and in *A*.12.35-36 he is critical of the many victims in the civil war (Latinus' speech about the many victims in the war with Aeneas). Contrary to many scholars, I conclude that Vergil held Cleopatra in high regard.

5 Vergil's Political Views. Was He His Master's Voice?

Since the 1930s much has been written about Vergil's and other Augustan authors' political views and how these come across in their poetry. The focus of many critics has long been on the *personae* featured in the poetry and their individual experiences. However, in more recent criticism the significance of these experiences for the wider social and political system has also received attention. I examine Vergil's poetry from this latter, socio-political perspective. I do not examine these issues within the standard frameworks, approaching questions such as whether Vergil was pro- or anti-Augustan or in the middle, or whether the *Aeneid* should be considered an epic or a tragedy or both. Instead, I concentrate on questions such as: what do the experiences of the shepherds in the *Eclogues* tell us about the social and political state of affairs in Italia's countryside, or what does the poet's portrayal of Cleopatra and Dido mean for the role of women in Roman society? In short, I will look for themes in Vergil's poetry. I will argue the hypothesis that Vergil was very much an independent political poet, who was both supportive and critical of Octavian/Augustus and the ruling elite, and who stuck to his opinions during most of his writing career. Finally, I will explore briefly whether Vergil was Augustus' mouthpiece writing propaganda. My conclusion is that he was not: he gave his comments on contemporary issues freely and independently.

The chapter is divided accordingly. In section 5.1 I will explore Vergil's political views. In this section I will also identify whether a poem is critical of Augustus. Section 5.2 will be about the question whether Vergil wrote propaganda for Augustus.

5.1 Vergil's Political Views

In this section Vergil's political views will be evaluated from the evidence in the *Eclogues*, the *Georgics* and the *Aeneid*. I refer to the short summaries at the end of section 3.1 (*Eclogues*), at the end of section 3.2 (*Georgics*), and that at the end of chapter 4 (*Aeneid*).

I am very sympathetic to Dominik's (2009, 111) conclusion that "Vergil is indeed a political poet: so persistent is the intrusion of political issues and themes at every level of discourse in the *Eclogues*, *Georgics* and *Aeneid* that it can be said that the poems constitute a political and ideological statement." I identify five major political themes. Three of these are explored at numerous places in the older and recent secondary literature. Vergil's views on the violation of the countryside, on his hope that peace and stability could return under Augustus, and on the horrors of the civil war and his rejection of violence have already been examined by many scholars. In the case of the fourth major theme, the kingship of Augustus, I will extend the arguments which were put forward particularly by Cairns (1989, 1-84) in his study of kingship in the *Aeneid*.

I will argue that Vergil also expressed views on this subject in *Ecl.*4 and in the *Georgics*. The fifth major theme concerns Vergil's views on the position and role of women. It is only relatively recently that scholars interested in gender have put this subject on the scholarly agenda[166]. Against the widespread opinion that Vergil presents a very negative view of Cleopatra, I will contend that Vergil's Cleopatra needs redeeming, and that his ideas about the role of women were more "liberal" than has been yet recognised.

Although *Ecl.*1 is probably not Vergil's first, he most likely wrote the poem early in his career (41 or 40 B.C.). In this early work he is already concerned with the violation of the countryside and its effects. The theme emerges for the last time in *A.*12.766-771 (the cutting of the sacred olive tree), written at the end of his life some twenty years later. Although I may have overlooked some, I have identified in the whole of Vergil's oeuvre a total of twenty-two poems or passages with this theme, of which the majority occurs in the *Eclogues* (see Index: Vergil, political views).

In the *Eclogues*, Vergil addresses political themes with the emphasis on the civil war, particularly the land expropriations and the destruction of the traditional life of the indigenous population. Behind this lies his deep love of the countryside and rural life. Vergil had seen the horrendous death toll of the power struggles in the last days of the Republic and the devastation of the countryside in his own native region of Mantua, in particular by the dispossessions and the might of arms. It is known that in his younger days his sympathies lay with Iulius Caesar, who had improved the situation of the population of his native area and conferred Roman citizenship to the towns of the *Transpadana* region in 49 B.C.. However, no sooner had this come about than it was wrecked again in the last days of the Republic and during the instability after Caesar's death in 44 B.C.: Philippi in 42 B.C., the Perusine war in 41-40 B.C., the defeat of Sextus Pompeius in 35 B.C.. The *Eclogues*, written between 42 and 35 B.C., echo these troubled times. *Eclogues* 1, 6, 9 and 10 refer directly to the expropriations and the expulsions in the Mantua region. In *Eclogues* 2, 3, 5, 6, 7, 8 and 9 Vergil writes about the effects of the changes. Four poems (5, 7, 8 and 9) contain a description of the indifference of and exploitation by the new owners. The threat to pastoral life (*Ecl.*2, 3 and 9), the destruction of rural communities (*Ecl.*6, 8 and 9), and the disappearance of essential values (*Ecl.*3 and 8) are also described. In half of the poems Vergil is openly critical of Octavian (1, 6, 7, 8 and 9) and he makes an urgent appeal to him to bring about change. The theme of the violation of rural life is also found in the *Georgics* and the *Aeneid*, although not as much as in the *Eclogues*. The poet addresses the desolate state of farming and the pitiful life of the farmers in the proem to book 1, and at the end of books 2 and 4 of

---

[166] In chronological order: Pomeroy, 1975; Pomeroy, 1984; Wyke, 2004 (first publ. 1992); Oliensis, 2000; Kleiner, 2005b; Oliensis, 2007.

the *Georgics*. A nice detail is that the book of *Georgics* ends with virtually the same line as that which opens the book of *Eclogues*, thus symbolizing the continuity of his concern about the state of the countryside. Although Vergil refers scarcely to the subject of the violation of the countryside in the *Aeneid*, he does so at a significant point (*A*.12.766-771), virtually at the close of the epic. At that point in time Aeneas' (Augustus') victory is within reach, an end to war and destruction might be expected and order will be established.

In three *Eclogues*, Vergil expresses not so much hope that an end to the destruction of the countryside and to the civil war might one day be achieved, but rather despair that such a day may never come. In *Ecl*.4 he places his trust in a baby still to be born, who turned out to be a daughter of Antony. *Ecl*.5 also refers to a distant future, and in one of his earliest poems, *Ecl*.9, his words are a prayer for peace and stability while the war was still raging. In the *Georgics* however, he introduces a change of emphasis with his hope, later even his expectation, that Octavian/Augustus might improve the farmers' situation by restoring peace and order. The poet testifies of this in *G*.1.40-41, the proem of *G*.3, and the epilogue of *G*.4. After this, in the *Aeneid* – in *A*.6.792-794 and *A*.8.626-731, and especially in *A*.8.714-728 – Vergil's hope of Augustan peace is clearly transformed into high expectations for Augustus' reign.

I suggested above that Vergil had strong sentiments about the evictions of the farmers and the social disruption at the end of the civil war, which he aired frequently in the *Eclogues*. It seems that in particular the effects of war disturbed him, rather than waging war itself. This can be deduced for instance from the emphasis in the *Aeneid* on Aeneas having to fulfil his duty of founding a new *imperium* in spite of all the concomitant war and violence. However, in the very last scene of the *Aeneid* Vergil shows the other side of this picture. Was the violence of the killing of Turnus justified? I argue that Vergil's view was that such a brutal killing went too far and that through this he implicitly criticizes Augustus for the violence of the war. Vergil suggests that the moral justification of the killing was tainted by the brutality of it. This corresponds with the poet's view that war is a messy business, in which men – Augustus and Aeneas alike when involved in war – show their weakness, which always goes paired with cruelty and violence. Augustus had been accused of cruelty in the civil war, for instance in the case of the farmers' evictions of their land, which had caused many casualties, and in the case of the slaughter at the surrender of Perusia. There are also other indications of Vergil rejecting violence, both in the *Georgics* and in the *Aeneid*. In *G*.1.489-497, he gives a harrowing condemnation of the slaughter at Philippi, which reminds one of the fields of Flanders. *G*.4.554-558 expresses the cost with which Octavian attained his final victory when he won control over the Roman state, and shows Vergil's concern regarding the way the Principate has been established and the havoc it has created. He also condemns the violence in the civil war in *A*.11.100-105, *A*.11.372-373, and *A*.12.35-36. In *A*.6.847-853, he suggests that the price for imperial success was often too high. These passages are all critical of the manner in which Augustus operated in the years he established the new political situation, although Vergil does not suggest that there was a better candidate than Augustus or that someone else would have acted differently.

Vergil has written not only about kingship as such, but in particular also about hereditary kingship. Cairns (1989, 1-84) examines kingship in the *Aeneid* in great detail and gives extensive references to secondary literature. Consequently, I will present only limited evidence from the *Aeneid*, and I refer for further reading to his book[167]. In the opening pages of his book Cairns (1989, 1), states the following: "A striking and *neglected* feature of the *Aeneid*, and of its first book in particular, is the frequency with which references to kingship appear," and in (1989, 8): "It is the ease with which *Virgil takes for granted a positive view of kingship*, and indeed a positive reaction to it from his audience, which argues loudest for the thesis offered here about the exploitation of ancient kingship theory." It is not only the feature of kingship as described in the *Aeneid* that has been neglected, but also that in the *Eclogues* and *Georgics*. *Ecl.*4, a poem that has a special place in the book of *Eclogues*, is probably the first place where Vergil referred to a hereditary form. It was written between 40 and 35 B.C., at a time when Mark Antony was still the leading contender for power in Rome. In this poem Vergil expresses his hopes that Antony, and later his son, will establish and maintain peace and stability. When Vergil combines the father and the son he may have been thinking in terms of a dynasty of a single ruler with regal powers. Thus around 40 B.C. he already expressed his leanings towards this form of kingship, to which he returned in his later poetry.

It is plausible that Vergil welcomed the change from the Republic to the emerging Principate of Octavian. This can be read in the *Georgics* written between 35 and 29 B.C., when Vergil had probably come to realise that a stable and strong form of government was needed, and that the time was ripe for a strong leader, perhaps even for a monarch. In the words of Woodman and West (1974, 131): "The importance of contemporary history is most conspicuous in the political poems, the *Eclogue* and *Georgic*. Williams and Lyne [both in Woodman & West, 1974] show again and again how the details of these poems and their emotional tone are to be connected with the emergence of Octavian." Vergil concluded that the traditional Roman state had come to an end and suggested that it was necessary to fundamentally change the order into a kingdom such as the bees enjoyed (*G*.4.1-227). At the time of writing the *Georgics*, Vergil considered Octavian a good candidate, although he did not yet advocate openly that the latter should be the first of a dynasty. It is reasonable to assume that through his education and through his affiliation to the Neoterics he was not only well versed in Hellenistic poetry but was also knowledgeable about the political situation in Asia and Egypt. He knew that these peoples had dynastic monarchies, as can be inferred from *G*.4.210-211. It is generally assumed that he wrote the fourth book in 30 or 29.. In that year Octavian had turned matters to his advantage and Vergil, who was forty-one

---

167 The emphasis in the quotations of Cairns are mine.

years of age, had seen more than twenty years of civil war and destruction. It is likely that Octavian's victory at Actium – at the time when Vergil was finishing the *Georgics* – confirmed Vergil's opinion that it was only Octavian who could bring stability as a monarch.

The idea of kingship is maintained in the *Aeneid*. The end of the relationship between Aeneas and Dido had a powerful meaning for Vergil's own time. Augustus was the Aeneas who did not stay with his love but stayed true to his calling. It indicated that Augustus and not Antony was the right choice. The gods had supported the right man at Actium. This man could bring peace and order, as Vergil suggets in different occasions, such as Iuppiter's promise to Venus in *A.*1.286-296 and, in particular, Anchises' prophecy in *A.*6.788-800. In these lines Vergil expresses not only his hope of Augustus' leadership in Italia, of a new Golden Age and of the restoration of the land, but also of his exploits abroad as for example in *A.*1.286-287 and in *A.*6.794-795. This required a strong leader and by the use of such words as *rex Aeneas*, which can be interpreted as referring to Augustus, Vergil returned to the old theme of kingship, which he had expounded in his previous poems, fifteen or more years earlier: in *Ecl.*4 in 40 B.C and in book 4 of the *Georgics* in 30 B.C.. In the *Aeneid* however, Vergil writes more often about his preference for the hereditary form of kingship. The latter theme is very prominent in *A.*6.860-886, which concerns the death of Marcellus, and, as I argued above, the marriage of Aeneas and Lavinia (*A.*7.96-106) also shows Vergil advocating a form of hereditary kingship. When he referred to the idea of a king as future ruler in the *Aeneid*, this was not a new conviction. It is likely that he remained as convinced as he was before of the need to restore the land and to bring order and stability, and that he saw that the changing world required a more efficient authority, which the Republic could no longer provide. When Alexandria fell in 30 B.C. and Octavian was made *princeps* in 27 B.C., there was not just one major change in the Mediterranean, but two. The end of the Republic coincided with the fall of the last Hellenistic kingdom. The Republic had to be replaced with a new structure and it is possible that the emerging leader looked at how power was organised in the East. As Vergil believed that the restoration of Italia would only be possible in a well-ordered society, he testified in the *Aeneid* to his belief that the new leader should receive wide authority. Vergil did not present this view on the organisation of the state by order of the new regime. Just as in 30 or 29 B.C., the late twenties B.C. were not the right time for Augustus to start a lobby and a propaganda campaign for his elevation. Furthermore, there was no need to press Vergil, as he had already written down his views on the blessings of a monarchy on his own initiative. He was prepared to live under a king, but he expected the king to be *pius* and *iustus*: the *rex* should show his responsibility towards society at large and should be just. Aeneas should be his true example and only by ruling in accordance with the standards which Aeneas had set, could the king succeed.

In chapter 4 I touched briefly on the fifth socio-political theme emerging in Vergil's poetry, that of his attitude towards Cleopatra and women in general. I concluded that

Vergil held Cleopatra in high regard, and held a much more "liberal" view on the role of women in society than the majority of his contemporaries.

Although Vergil did also express a critical view of Cleopatra, I have argued that on balance his opinion of her was positive, and that his esteem for the queen is manifest in his poetry in two complementary ways. Firstly, by many of the direct and indirect references to Cleopatra: direct references in particular can be found in the passage about Aeneas' shield in book 8 of the *Aeneid*. I discussed (section 4.1.2) *A*.8.696-700 in some detail suggesting a new interpretation of this passage. The poet shows kindness and compassion when he portrays the shadow of death hanging over the queen. Indirect references can be found, for example, in *G*.3.26-29 and in *A*.10.495-498. These references have been considered in the appropriate sections. Secondly, I argued that Vergil's high regard for the Egyptian queen is evident by his modelling of Dido on Cleopatra and that the manner in which he portrayed Dido as queen is testament of his appreciation of Cleopatra's qualities. Why should Vergil have chosen Cleopatra as the functional model for Dido's character? The *Aeneid* operates simultaneously on different levels, and one of these levels is the result of the poet's wish to give his view on major contemporary issues. By choosing a contemporary person as model for one of his heroes in the epic, he referred back to Cleopatra through the *persona* of Dido. Thus, the reader associated Dido's story with the events of Vergil's own day, and implicitly the poet gave his views on these events. By considering Vergil's portrayal of both Dido and Cleopatra – the latter by direct and indirect references – it is possible to deduce several of the poet's political views. He gave his Dido unique features which he must have recognized in the Egyptian queen, such as not only her queenship, but also her independence, military and political leadership and intelligence. This suggests that Vergil did not consider Cleopatra an evil woman, but that he approved of and admired her qualities. All this may have inspired him to conclude that these attributes were also the right ones for the *princeps* of the Roman state and that the continuity of the dynastic model would be advantageous for Rome.

There are indications that Vergil was not the only one who had a high regard for Cleopatra, but that Octavian shared these feelings. After her death in 30 B.C. Octavian treated the queen's memory with respect. For instance, he did not remove her gilded statue from the temple of Venus Genetrix, where Iulius Caesar had placed it. Kleiner (2005b, 274), quoting *A*.8.709-713, recognizes this, but she interprets the *princeps'* action as clever propaganda: "The [Augustan] poets who gave literary life to Augustus' regime were perfectly amenable to using their lyrics to give rise to Cleopatra's legend. The famous shield scene in Virgil's *Aeneid* highlights Actium, Cleopatra's presence there, and her inevitable flight in the face of Octavian's omnipotence: [...]. The shift of Cleopatra post mortem *from harlot to noble queen*" (emphasis is mine). Although Octavian may have had political motives for his action, such as demonstrating his position as the new ruler of Egypt in the Ptolemaic line of succession, his action made clear that he saw Cleopatra as a queen in her own right, whose memory could not just simply be blotted out.

Modern scholars argue that Vergil – like other Augustan poets – presents a hostile view of Cleopatra, which was exemplary of his views of women in general[168]. On this issue Oliensis' (2000, 303) summary may be illustrative: "In certain respects, the articulation of gender in the *Aeneid* proceeds along familiar lines: Virgil associates the feminine with unruly passion, the masculine with reasoned (self-) mastery. In narrative terms, this tends to mean that women make trouble and men restore order." She (2000, 303) also states that in Vergil's portrayal "women are 'primitive' in the *Aeneid* in that they are linked to (maternal, material, narrative) origins." I have argued above that there is ample evidence that Vergil's view on Cleopatra was positive, which is also manifest in his depiction of Dido, about whom he generally writes sympathetically, although not unreserved. This is in keeping with Vergil's positive attitude to women in general. It is evident that Vergil felt more attracted to Dido than to Lavinia, whom he portrayed as the dutiful, demure girl. His rather flat depiction of Lavinia, the paradigm of the dutiful Roman woman is in strong contrast with Dido, who surpassed Lavinia in every aspect of her private and public role. It would not be possible to meet a second woman like Dido in Rome in 25 B.C.: not because Dido was a mythical figure, but because she would have been unique.

There are also several indications of Vergil's positive attitude towards women other than these references in the *Aeneid*. In *Ecl*.1, frugal Amaryllis looks after Tityrus' domestic affairs so well that he can purchase his freedom. In *Ecl*.8, the girl Nysa is not given away in marriage to a shepherd, but to a newcomer who offers her a better future instead. Similarly, in *Ecl*.10, Lycoris, Gallus' love, runs off with a soldier. Vergil does not disapprove of Nysa or Lycoris, who both go their own ways. The woman in Alphesiboeus' song in *Ecl*.8 loses her husband to a girl who does not belong to her world. Vergil portrays the woman with the positive values of pastoral life, such as home, fidelity and genuine love, and gives her her own independent views on the events which have overturned her life in the countryside. See also the relevant discussions in section 3.1.

At the risk of introducing psychological speculation, I offer some suggestions about Vergil's attitude to life. The violation of the countryside – most likely that of his native region – has left a deep and lasting impression upon him. He did not only write many *Eclogues* about the destruction and grief this brought to the original population, but he also referred to these over a period of more than thirteen years. This is very apparent from the closing line of *G*.4 (*Tityre, te patulae cecini sub tegmine fagi*) being nearly identical to the opening line of *Ecl*.1 (*TITYRE, tu patulae recubans sub tegmine fagi*). This could indicate that the great social change in the countryside upset him not only because he was personally involved, but also because he was a sensitive man, "a man of sorrows, and acquainted with grief." His rejection of the violence in war also points that way. It seems that Vergil abhorred the political power struggle and

---

[168] See section 4.1.2, and note 136.

the resulting slaughter and devastation so much, that he was prepared to accept the social and political disadvantages of a new form of leadership: hereditary kingship. Re-establishing peace and stability in Italia, which would make it possible for the farmers to return to work, had in his opinion a higher priority than the dangers of the concentration of power, which was in the hands of a small circle of men anyway. Vergil's attitude towards women and Cleopatra indicates that he had an independent mind and was not averse to a radical change of long established *mores*.

5.2 Vergil: His Master's Voice?

Vergil's – and Horace's, Propertius' and Ovid's – putative participation in a supposed Augustan propaganda programme is much discussed. It is still a topical question considering the number of papers and books addressing the subject in general as well as specific terms, for instance the case of the propaganda against Cleopatra[169]. In section 2.4 I argued that poetry was most likely a very unsuitable medium for propaganda, as the poet's view on political matters was for their elite audiences one of many, and perhaps not even the most authoritative one. As Vergil's political engagement is visible through the number of poems about political or social issues, his texts should also be examined with respect to the likelihood of his participating in an Augustan propagandistic programme, if one existed.

Looking closer at Vergil's five political themes, it appears that he was consistent in his opinions during long periods. He wrote about the violation of the countryside from the beginning of his poetic career – as far as transmitted to us – in the first *Eclogue* until the last book of the *Aeneid*. The theme of his hope of a better future for the people in the countryside is found already in *Ecl.5*, and was turned into a specific suggestion to Octavian to work towards improving the fate of the farming population in the proem to the first book of the *Georgics*. At the end of the *Georgics*, Vergil's hope and prayer for Octavian's strong leadership became an expectation that Augustus would deliver; the latter view is obviously one of the leading themes in the *Aeneid*. Vergil referred to the third theme of the horrors of the civil war and the violence in war in general only implicitly when he described the dispossessions of the small farmers and the destruction of the countryside in many of the *Eclogues*. Violence in war appears with great literary impact in the first book of the *Georgics*, when Vergil

---

[169] A selection of titles on propaganda in the Augustan age in general which have been published or reprinted since 2000 includes (in chronological order): Powell (Ed.), (2004, 141-174); Brown (2007, 13-14); Adler, 2003; White (2005, 321-339); Davis (2006, 9-14, 16-18); Dominik, Garthwaite & Roche (Eds.), 2009; Davis, G. (Ed.) (2010, 34-90); Le Doze, 2014. On propaganda against Cleopatra by Augustus and the poets, see: Pomeroy (1975, 185, 229); Pomeroy (1984, 24-28); Wyke (2004, 98-140); Kleiner (2005b, 136-137, 274); Schäfer (2006, 181-196); Oliensis (2007, 226).

describes the ravages after the battle of Philippi and, significantly, connects the portrayal of the remains of the slaughter with the work of the farmer. And violence is prominent at the close of the *Aeneid*, when Aeneas kills Turnus. Vergil's positive view on kingship is visible for the first time in *Ecl*.4, is maintained in the *Georgics*, and is very much apparent in the *Aeneid*. Finally, Vergil's positive opinion of women is already indicated by his portrayal of frugal Amaryllis in *Ecl*.1, and later resurfaces in the *Aeneid* in, for instance, the difference between his positive depiction of his heroine Dido and the flat image of obedient Lavinia. His appreciation of Cleopatra's qualities comes obviously only to light in the *Aeneid*; using her as a functional model for Dido reflects also his view on the potential of women at the top of society.

My point is that Vergil's political views were not fancy or fashionable ideas, but were well considered and maintained throughout his writing. He addressed major issues, which stood at the centre of the contemporary political scene. A good example of this is Vergil's view on hereditary kingship, the most far-reaching of his five political themes. It is very likely that Vergil expressed his private opinion on his own initiative. An important argument lies in the fact that he already recommended a monarchy in *Ecl*.4, probably written in 40 B.C., but no later than 37 B.C., when he saw Antony as the right candidate. Later he did the same in *G*.4, written around 30 B.C.. It is very improbable that he wrote on Octavian's orders about a kingship of Octavian in 30 B.C., because the timing would be wrong. The First Settlement is of January 27 B.C. when Octavian accepted only a restricted position of power for a limited period. It is likely that Octavian had set his mind on absolute power in the future, but not at that juncture. He had to manoeuvre between achieving his long-term goal and keeping the loyalty of the Senate and the leading elite in general. The next and much more meaningful step on the way to absolute rule came in 23 B.C.. The book of *Georgics* was released three years before the First Settlement. Is it really plausible, that Octavian, at the time when he was in the middle of his struggle with Antony and Cleopatra and needed all the support of the Roman political and social elite he could get, should start a propaganda campaign for his elevation to kingship in the late 30s? Vergil indeed wrote poetry which was supportive of Augustus, the high point being the *Aeneid*. In his supportive poetry he voiced political ideas which he held consistently during the whole course of his authorship, from a point in time well before Octavian was in control. It is feasible that Vergil expressed these views in his supportive poetry irrespective of any outside propagandistic pressure, if it was applied at all.

Vergil, on the one hand, wrote poetry supportive of Augustus, but, on the other, he dared also to be critical of him and his policies. I have identified many critical poems and passages which also span the whole of his career. Five out of ten *Eclogues*, parts of books 1, 2 and 4 of the *Georgics*, and several passages of the *Aeneid* are critical of Octavian and later Augustus. Vergil believed that after the demise of the Republic strong leadership was required and, although he had come to the conclusion that Octavian was the most suitable candidate, he was also consistent in his criticism of him. This criticism was often directed at Octavian personally, as for instance with regard to his involvement in the violation of the countryside, his conduct in war, or his violence. It is unlikely that Vergil's criticism of some of Augustus' essential policies or actions was a result of a request or pressure to write propaganda. I suggest that Vergil's political views as they emerge in his poetry should be explained as independent commentary by an intelligent, well-educated man who was informed of what was going on. Vergil was a commentator and not a member of Augustus' putative propaganda machine[170]. It was his position in Augustan society which gave Vergil his overall view. Combined with his desire to maintain his personal freedom and independence of mind, he positioned himself as a commentator holding well-informed views on many aspects of life, and with the best information at his disposal thanks to his connections.

---

170 Cf. Putnam (1995, 14), who states: "In partially rejecting the nineteenth-century attitude about the *Aeneid* as the glorification of Augustan Rome, with Virgil merely pulling the strings at the emperor's puppet show," and "The poet, on the other hand, comments, teaches, argues from an intellectual and emotional distance which prods society by applying the goad of quality." See also Yavetz (1993, 40) who makes a similar point about Horace.

Bibliography

Adler, E. (2003). Vergil's Empire, Political Thought in the Aeneid. Oxford: Rowman & Littlefield.
Anderson, R.D., Parsons, P.J. & Nisbet, R.G.M. (1979). Elegiacs by Gallus from Qaşr Ibrîm. The Journal of Roman Studies, 69, 125-155. Reprinted in S.J. Harrison (Ed.). (1995). R.G.M. Nisbet. Collected Papers on Latin Literature (pp. 101-131). Oxford: Clarendon Press.
Anderson, W. (2010). Horace's Friendship: Adaptation of a Circular Argument. In G. Davis (Ed.), A Companion to Horace (pp. 34-52). Chichester, U.K. & Malden MA: Blackwell.
Armstrong, D. (2010). The Biographical and Social Foundations of Horace's Poetic Voice. In G. Davis (Ed.). A Companion to Horace (pp. 7-33). Chichester, U.K. & Malden MA: Blackwell.
Barchiesi, A. (2005). Learned Eyes: Poets, Viewers, Image Makers. In K. Galinsky (Ed.). The Cambridge Companion to the Age of Augustus (pp. 281-305). Cambridge: Cambridge University Press.
Basson, A.F. & Dominik, W.J. (Eds.) (2003). Literature, Art, History: Studies on Classical Antiquity and Tradition (in honour of W.J. Henderson). Frankfurt am Main: Peter Lang
Bauer, L. (Ed.) (1890). Sili Italici: Punica, Vol. 1, Books I-X. Leipzig:Teubner.
Bessone, F. 2013. Latin precursors, in T.S. Thorsen (Ed.).The Cambridge Companion to Latin Love Elegy (pp. 39-56). Cambridge: Cambridge University Press.
Binder, G. (1971). Aeneas und Augustus: Interpretationen zum 8. Buch der Aeneis. Meisenheim am Glan: Verlag Anton Hain.
Bivar, A.D.H. (1983). The political History of Iran under the Arsacids. In E. Yarshater (Ed.) The Cambridge History of Iran, vol. 3.1;The Seleucid, Parthian and Sasanian Periods (pp. 21-99). Cambridge: Cambridge University Press.
Blänsdorf, J. (1995). Fragmenta Poetarum Latinorum Epicorum et Lyricorum praeter Ennium et Lucilium, post W.Morel nouis curis adhibitis edidit Carolus Buechner, editionem tertiam auctam curauit. Stuttgart/Leipzig: Jürgen Blänsdorf, Teubner.
Blundell, S. (1995). Women in Ancient Greece. London: British Museum Press.
Boatwright, M.T., Gargola, D.J. & Talbert, R.J.A. (2004). The Romans: from Village to Empire. A History of Ancient Rome from Earliest Times to Constantine. Oxford: Oxford University Press.
Bond, R. (2009). Horace's Political Journey. In W.J. Dominik, J. Garthwaite & P.A. Roche (Eds.), Writing Politics in Imperial Rome (pp.133-152). Leiden: Brill.
Boucher, J.P. (1966). Caius Cornelius Gallus. Paris: Société d'Édition "Les Belles Lettres."
Bourdieu, P. F. (1977). Outline of a Theory of Practice. (original title Esquisse d'une théorie de la practique, précédé de trois études d'ethnologie kabyle (1972). Geneva: Librairie Droz. translated by R. Nice). Cambridge: Cambridge University Press.
Bowditch, P. Lowell (2001). Horace and the Gift Economy of Patronage. Berkeley, CA: University of California Press.
Bowditch, P. Lowell (2010). Horace and Imperial Patronage. In G. Davis (Ed.), A Companion to Horace (pp. 53-74). Chichester, U.K., & Malden MA: Blackwell.
Bowersock, G.W. (1971). A Date in the Eighth Eclogue. Harvard studies in classical philology, 75, 73-80.
Bowersock, G.W. (1993). The Pontificate of Augustus. In K.A. Raaflaub & M. Toher (Eds.). Between Republic and Empire. Interpretations of Augustus and his Principate (pp. 380-394). Berkeley, CA: University of California Press.
Bowman, A.K., Champlin, E. & Lintott, A. (1996). The Cambridge Ancient History. Vol. 10: The Augustan Empire, 43 B.C. – A.D. 69. Cambridge: Cambridge University Press.
Bowra, C.M.(1945). From Virgil to Milton. London: MacMillan.
Boyle, A.J. (1986). The Chaonian Dove: Studies in the Eclogues, Georgics, and Aeneid of Virgil. Leiden: Brill.

Bradshaw, A. (1989). Horace in Sabinis. In C. Deroux (Ed.). Studies in Latin Literature and Roman History V (pp. 160-186). Brussels: Latomus.
Brink, C.O. (1982). Horace on Poetry; Epistles book II, The Letters to Augustus and Florus. Cambridge: Cambridge University Press.
Brink, C.O. (1982). Horace's Literary Epistles and their chronology: Augustanism in the Augustan Poets. In C.O. Brink (Ed.), Horace on Poetry; Epistles book II, The Letters to Augustus and Florus (pp. 523-577). Cambridge: Cambridge University Press.
Brown, P.M. (2007). Horace, Satires I. Warminster: Aris and Phillips; first edition 1993.
Brunt, P.A. (1988). The Fall of the Roman Republic and Related Essays. Oxford: Oxford University Press.
Brunt, P.A. (1988b). Amicitia in the Roman Republic. In P.A. Brunt. The Fall of the Roman Republic and Related Essays (pp. 351-381). Oxford: Oxford University Press.
Brunt, P.A. (1988c) Clientela. In P.A. Brunt. The Fall of the Roman Republic and Related Essays (pp. 382-442). Oxford: Oxford University Press.
Burnett, A., Amandry, M., Ripollès, P. & Crawford, M. (1994). Roman Provincial Coinage. Athenaeum, 82.2, 593-594.
Cairns, F. (1989). Virgil's Augustan Epic. Cambridge: Cambridge University Press.
Cairns, F. (1992). The power of implication: Horace's invitation to Maecenas (Odes 1.20). In A.J. Woodman & J.C.F. Powell (Eds.). Author and Audience in Latin Literature (pp. 94-109). Cambridge: Cambridge University Press.
Campbell, A.Y. (1970). Horace: a new interpretation. (first ed. 1924). Westport, CT: Greenwood Press.
Casson, L. (2001). Libraries in the Ancient World. New Haven, CT: Yale University Press.
Champion, C.B. (Ed.) (2004). Roman Imperialism: Readings and Sources. Oxford: Blackwell Publishing.
Chaudhuri, P. (2012). Naming nefas: Cleopatra on the shield of Aeneas. Classical Quarterly 62.223-226.
Claes, P. (1988). Echo's echo's: de kunst van de allusie. Amsterdam: De Bezige Bij.
Clausen, W. (2003). A Commentary on Virgil Eclogues. Oxford: Clarendon Press.
Coleiro, E. (1979). An Introduction to Vergil's Bucolics with a critical Edition of the Text. Amsterdam: Grüner.
Coleman, R. (1966). Tityrus and Meliboeus. Greece and Rome, Second Series, Vol. 13, No. 1, 79-97.
Coleman, R. (1981). Vergil: Eclogues. Cambridge: Cambridge University Press.
Conington, J. & Nettleship, H. (Eds.) (1963). The works of Virgil III: The last six books of the Aeneid, (reprint of ed. 1858-1862). Hildesheim: Olms.
Conte, G.B. (1974). Memoria dei poeti e sistema letterario: Catullo, Virgilio, Ovidio, Lucano. Turin: Giulio Einaudi Editore.
Conte, G.B. (1980/1984). Il genere e i suoi confini: Cinque studi sulla poesia di Virgilio. Turin: Editrice Stampatori, enlarged ed.: Garzanti Editore.
Conte, G.B. (1986). The Rhetoric of Imitation, Genre and Poetic Memory in Virgil and other Latin Poets. Translated by C. Segal. Ithaca, NY: Cornell University Press.
Conte, G.B. (2008). An Interpretation of the Tenth Eclogue. In K.Volk (Ed.). Oxford Readings in Classical Studies: Vergil's Eclogues (pp. 216-244). Oxford: Oxford University Press.
Courtney, E. (1993). The Fragmentary Latin Poets. Oxford: Clarendon Press.
Crees, J.H.E. & Wordsworth, J.C. (1927). Apollonius Rhodius; The Story of Medea. Cambridge: Cambridge University Press.
Crook, J.A., Lintot A. & Rawson, E. (1994). The Cambridge Ancient History. Vol. 9: The last Age of the Roman Republic, 146-43 B.C. Cambridge: Cambridge University Press.
Crook, J.A. (1997). review of Galinsky, K. (1996). Augustan Culture; an interpretive introduction. Princeton, NJ: Princeton University Press. The Journal of Roman Studies, 87, 287-288.
Davies, P.V. (Ed.) (1969). Macrobius, The Saturnalia. New York, NY: Columbia University Press.

Davis, G. (1991). Polyhymnia: the rhetoric of Horatian lyric discourse. Berkeley, CA: University of California Press.
Davis, G. (Ed.) (2010). A Companion to Horace. Chichester, U.K. & Malden MA: Blackwell.
Davis, G. (2010). Defining a lyric Ethos: Archilochus lyricus and Horatian melos. In G. Davis (Ed.), A Companion to Horace (pp. 105-127). Chichester, U.K., & Malden MA: Blackwell.
Davis, P.J. (2006). Ovid & Augustus: A political reading of Ovid's erotic poems. London: Duckworth.
Deroux, C. (Ed.) (1989). Studies in Latin Literature and Roman History V. Brussels: Latomus.
Deroux, C. (Ed.) (2010). Studies in Latin Literature and Roman History XV. Brussels: Latomus.
Desmond, M. (1994). Reading Dido; Gender, Textuality and the Medieval Aeneid. Minneapolis, MN: University of Minnesota Press.
Dixon, S. (1993). The Meaning of Gift and Debt in the Roman Elite. Échos du monde classique 37.451-464.
Dominik, W.J., Garthwaite, J. & Roche, P.A. (Eds.) (2009). Writing Politics in Imperial Rome. Leiden: Brill.
Dominik, W.J. (2009). Vergil's Geopolitics. In W.J. Dominik, J. Garthwaite & P.A. Roche (Eds.). Writing Politics in Imperial Rome (pp. 111-132). Leiden: Brill.
Donatus. Commentarii Vergiliani. at: (http://www.intratext.com/IXT/LAT0367/_P3.HTM).
Le Doze, P. (2014). Le Parnasse face à l'Olympe: poésie et culture politique à l'époque d 'Octavien/ Auguste. Collection de l'École française de Rome. Rome: École française de Rome.
DuQuesnay, I.M. Le M. (1984). Horace and Maecenas; The propaganda value of Sermones I. In A.J. Woodman & D.A. West (Eds.). Poetry and Politics in the Age of Augustus (pp. 19-58). Cambridge: Cambridge University Press.
Earl, D. (1968). The Age of Augustus. London: Elek.
Easterling, P.A., & Knox, B.M.W. (1993). The Cambridge History of Classical Literature, Volume 1, part 1-4. Cambridge: Cambridge University Press.
Eden, P.T. (1975). A Commentary on Virgil: Aeneid VIII. Leiden: Brill.
Ellul, J. (1965). Propaganda: the Formation of Men's Attitudes. New York, NY: Vintage Books.
Evans, J.D. (1992). The Art of Persuasion. Political Propaganda from Aeneas to Brutus. Ann Arbor, MI: University of Michigan Press.
Fantham, E., Foley, H.P., & Kampen, N.B., et al. (1994). Women in the Classical World: Image and Text. Oxford: Oxford University Press.
Fantuzzi, M., & Papanghelis, T. (Eds.) (2006). Brill's Companion to Greek and Latin Pastoral. Leiden: Brill.
Farrell, J., & Putnam, M.C.J. (Eds.) (2010). A Companion to Vergil's Aeneid and its Tradition. Chichester: Wiley-Blackwell.
Farron, S. (1993). Vergil's Aeneid: a Poem of Grief and Love. Leiden: Brill.
Fordyce, C.J., & Christie, J.D. (Eds.) (1977). P. Vergili Maronis, Aeneidos libri VII-VIII. Oxford: Oxford University Press.
Fowler, D. (2000). Roman constructions: readings in postmodern Latin. Oxford: Oxford University Press.
Frischer, B., Crawford, J., & De Simone, M. (Eds.) (2006). The Horace's Villa Project, 1997-2003, Vol. 1; report on new fieldwork and research. Oxford: Archaeopress.
Frischer, B. (2010). The Roman Site Identified as Horace's Villa at Licenza, Italy. In G. Davis (Ed.), A Companion to Horace (pp. 75-90). Chichester, U.K., & Malden MA: Blackwell.
Galinsky, K. (1988). The Anger of Aeneas. The American Journal of Philology, 109.3, 321-348.
Galinsky, K. (1996). Augustan Culture; an interpretive introduction. Princeton, NJ: Princeton University Press.
Galinsky, K. (2003). Horace's Cleopatra and Virgil's Dido. In A.F. Basson & W.J. Dominik (Eds.), Literature, Art, History: Studies on Classical Antiquity and Tradition (in honour of W.J. Henderson) (pp. 17-23). Frankfurt am Main: Peter Lang

Galinsky, K. (Ed.) (2005). The Cambridge Companion to the Age of Augustus. Cambridge: Cambridge University Press.
Galsterer, H. (1993). A Man, a Book, and a Method: Sir Ronald Syme's Roman Revolution after Fifty Years. In K.A. Raaflaub & M. Toher (Eds.), Between Republic and Empire. Interpretations of Augustus and his Principate (pp. 1-20). Berkeley, CA: University of California Press.
Gibson, R.K. (2012). Gallus: The First Roman Love Elegist. In B.K. Gold (Ed.), A Companion to Roman Love Elegy (pp. 172-186). Malden, MA: Wiley-Blackwell.
Gold, B.K. (Ed.) (1982). Literary and Artistic Patronage in Ancient Rome. Austin, TX: University of Texas Press.
Gold, B.K. (1987). Literary Patronage in Greece and Rome. Chapel Hill, NC: University of North Carolina Press.
Gold, B.K. (Ed.) (2012). A Companion to Roman Love Elegy. Malden, MA: Wiley-Blackwell.
Gold, B.K. (2012a). Patronage and the Elegists: Social Reality or Literary Construction? In B.K. Gold (Ed.), A Companion to Roman Love Elegy (pp. 303-317). Malden, MA: Wiley-Blackwell.
Goold, G.P. (1992). The Voice of Virgil: The Pageant of Rome in Aeneid 6. In A.J. Woodman & J.G.F. Powell (Eds.), Author and Audience in Latin Literature (pp. 110-123). Cambridge: Cambridge University Press.
Goold, G.P. (Ed.) (2002). Virgil, Aeneid 7-12, Appendix Vergiliana. Cambridge, MA: Loeb, Harvard University Press.
Goold, G.P. (Ed.) (2006). Virgil, Eclogues, Georgics, Aeneid 1-6. Cambridge, MA: Loeb, Harvard University Press.
Gow, A.S.F. (1986).Theocritus; edited with a translation and commentary, vol. I. Text, vol. II. Commentary. Cambridge: Cambridge University Press.
Gransden, K.W. (Ed.) (1976). Virgil Aeneid Book VIII. Cambridge: Cambridge University Press.
Griffin, J. (1979). The Fourth Georgic, Virgil and Rome. Greece and Rome, Second Series, 26.1, 61-80.
Griffin, J. (2004). Latin Poets and Roman Life. London: Duckworth.
Griffin, J. (2005). Augustan Poetry and Augustanism. In K. Galinsky (Ed.), The Cambridge Companion to the Age of Augustus (pp. 306-320). Cambridge: Cambridge University Press.
Guillemin, A-M. (1937). Le public et la vie littéraire à Rome. Paris: Les Belles Lettres.
Gurval, R. A. (1998). Actium and Augustus: The Politics and Emotions of Civil War. Ann Arbor, MI: The University of Michigan Press.
Hardie, C. (Ed.) (1966).Vitae Vergilianae antiquae; Vita Donati; etc. (OCT). Oxford: Clarendon Press.
Hardie, P.R. (1989). Virgil's Aeneid: Cosmos and Imperium. Oxford: Clarendon Press.
Hardie, P.R. (2000). Virgil and tragedy. In C. A. Martindale (Ed.), The Cambridge Companion to Virgil (pp.312-326). Cambridge: Cambridge University Press.
Hardie, P.R. (2006). Virgil's Ptolemaic Relations. The Journal of Roman Studies, 96, 25-41.
Harris, W.V. (1991). Ancient Literacy. Cambridge, MA: Harvard University Press.
Harrison, S.J. (Ed.) (1995a). Homage to Horace: A Bimillenary Celebration. Oxford: Clarendon Press.
Harrison, S.J. (1998). The Sword-belt of Pallas: Moral Symbolism and Political Ideology (Aen.10.495-505). In H.P.Stahl (Ed.), Vergil's Aeneid: Augustan Epic and Political Context (pp. 223-242). London: Duckworth.
Harrison, S.J. (Ed.) (2007a). Oxford readings in Vergil's Aeneid, collection of papers and essays from 1933-1987. Oxford: Oxford University Press.
Harrison, S.J. (Ed.) (2007b). The Cambridge Companion to Horace. Cambridge: Cambridge University Press.
Harrison, S.J. (2007c). Generic Enrichment in Vergil and Horace. Oxford: Oxford University Press.
Hekster, O. (2004). Hercules, Omphale, and Octavian's 'Counter-Propaganda'. BABESCH, Bulletin Antieke Beschaving, 79, 159-166.
Hekster, O. (2009). Romeinse Keizers: de Macht van het Imago. Amsterdam: Bert Bakker.

Hermes, J. (1980). C. Cornelius Gallus und Vergil. Das Problem der Umarbeitung des vierten Georgica-Buches. Dissertation at Westfälischen Wilhelm-Universität zu Münster.

Heyworth, S.J. (2007a). Cynthia: a Companion to the Text of Propertius. Oxford: Oxford University Press.

Heyworth, S.J. (2007b). Propertius, patronage and politics. Bulletin of the Institute of Classical Studies of the University of London, 50, 93-128.

Hinds, S. (1998). Allusion and intertext: Dynamics of appropriation in Roman poetry. Cambridge: Cambridge University Press.

Horsfall, N.M. (1995). Virgil: his life and times. In N.M. Horsfall (Ed.), A Companion to the Study of Virgil (pp.1-25). Leiden: Brill.

Horsfall, N.M. (1995). Aeneid. In N.M. Horsfall (Ed.), A Companion to the Study of Virgil (pp.101-216). Leiden: Brill.

Horsfall, N.M. (Ed.) (1995). A Companion to the Study of Virgil. Leiden: Brill.

Horsfall, N.M. (2003). The Culture of the Roman Plebs. London: Duckworth.

Horsfall, N.M. (2007). Dido in the Light of History. In S.J. Harrison (Ed.), Oxford readings in Vergil's Aeneid, collection of papers and essays from 1933-1987 (pp. 127-144). Oxford: Oxford University Press.

Hunink, V. (2006a). *Quintus Ennius*; Annalen. 's-Hertogenbosch: Voltaire.

Hunink, V. (2006b). Muzen, bezing mij...: Rome's oudste heldendichten, Livius Andronicus 'Odyssee', Gnaeus Naevius 'de Punische Oorlog'. 's-Hertogenbosch: Voltaire.

Hunter, R.L. (1999). Theocritus: A Selection. Idylls 1, 3, 4, 6, 7, 10, 11 and 13. Cambridge: Cambridge University Press.

Isaac, B.H. (2004). The Invention of Racism in Classical Antiquity. Princeton, NJ: Princeton University Press.

Jacoby, F. (Ed.) (1950). Timaios von Tauromenion in Die Fragmente der griechischen Historiker: Geschichte von Städten und Völkern, iiib, 566F82. (also available on BrillOnLine Reference Works). Leiden: Brill.

Janan, M. (2001). The Politics of Desire: Propertius IV. Berkeley, CA: University of California Press.

Jenkyns, R. (1989). Virgil and Arcadia. The Journal of Roman Studies, 79, 26-39.

Jenkyns, R. (1998). Virgil's Experience: Nature and History; Times, Names, and Places. Oxford: Oxford University Press.

Johnson, W.R. (1976). Darkness visible: a study of Vergil's 'Aeneid'. Berkeley, CA: University of California Press.

Jones, P.J. (1971). Cleopatra; a Sourcebook. Norman, OK: University of Oklahoma Press.

Jong de, J.F., & Sullivan, J.P. (1994). Modern critical theory and classical literature. Leiden: Brill.

Kellum, B. (1985). Sculptural programs and propaganda in Augustan Rome: the temple of Apollo on the Palatine. In R. Winkes (Ed.), The Age of Augustus: interdisciplinary conference held at Brown University, april 30-May 2, 1982 (pp. 169-176). Louvain, Collège Érasme: Institut Supérieur d'Archéologie et d'Histoire de l'Art.

Kennedy, D.F. (2004). 'Augustan' and 'Anti-Augustan': Reflections on Terms of Reference. In A. Powell (Ed.), Roman Poetry and Propaganda in the Age of Augustus (pp. 26-58). (first published 1992). London: Duckworth.

Keppie, L. (1981). Vergil, the Confiscations, and Caesar's Tenth Legion. Classical Quarterly, NS 31.2, 367-370.

Kleiner, D.E.E. (1992). Roman Sculpture. New Haven, CT: Yale University Press.

Kleiner, D.E.E. (2005a). Semblance and Storytelling in Augustan Rome. In K. Galinsky (Ed.), The Cambridge Companion to the Age of Augustus (pp.197-233). Cambridge: Cambridge University Press.

Kleiner, D.E.E. (2005b). Cleopatra and Rome. Cambridge, MA: Harvard University Press.

Knauer, G.N. (1979). Die Aeneis und Homer: Studien zur poetischen Technik Vergils. Göttingen: Vandenhoeck und Ruprecht.
Leo, F. (1903). Vergils erste und neunte Ecloge. Hermes, 38, 1-18.
Lefkowitz, M.R., & Fant, M.B. (1982). Women's Life in Greece and Rome: a Source Book etc. London: Duckworth.
Levick, B. (1982). Propaganda and Imperial Coinage. Antichthon, 16, 104-116.
Linderski, J. (1993). Mommsen and Syme: Law and Power in the Principate of Augustus. In K.A. Raaflaub & M. Toher (Eds.), Between Republic and Empire. Interpretations of Augustus and his Principate (pp. 42-53). Berkeley, CA: University of California Press.
Loraux, N. (1981). Les enfants d'Athéna: idées athéniennes sur la citoyenneté et la division des sexes. Paris: Maspero.
Lowrie, M. (2007). Orientations: Horace and Augustus. In S.J. Harrison (Ed.), The Cambridge Companion to Horace (pp. 77-89). Cambridge: Cambridge University Press.
Lowrie, M. (2009). Writing, Performance, and Authority in Augustan Rome. Oxford: Oxford University Press.
Lyne, R.O.A.M. (1974). SCILICET ET TEMPVS VENIET….: Virgil, Georgics 1.463-514. In A.J. Woodman & D.A. West (Eds.), Quality and Pleasure in Latin Poetry (pp. 47-66). Cambridge: Cambridge University Press.
Lyne, R.O.A.M. (1980). The Latin love Poets: from Catullus to Horace. Oxford: Clarendon Press.
MacDonough, Chr.M., Prior, R.E., & Stansbury, M. (Eds.) (2004). Servius' Commentary on Book Four of Virgil's Aeneid: an annotated translation. Mundelein, IL: Bolchazy-Carducci Publishers, Inc.
MacMullen, R. (2004). Romanization in the Time of Augustus. In C.B. Champion (Ed.), Roman Imperialism: Readings and Sources (pp. 215-231). Oxford: Blackwell Publishing.
Manders, E.E.J. (2008). Coining Images of Power: Patterns in the Representation of Roman Emperors on Imperial Coinage, A.D. 193-284. Dissertation Radboud Universiteit Nijmegen.
Manuwald, G. (2007). Cicero, Philippics 3-9. Vol.2: Commentary. Berlin: W. de Gruyter.
Manzoni, G.E. (1995). Foroiuliensis poeta. Vita e poesia di Cornelio Gallo. Milan: Pubblicazioni dell'Università Cattolica.
Marichal, R. (1963). L'écriture latine et la civilisation du Ier au XVIe siècle. In M.S.R. Cohen (Ed.), L'écriture et la psychologie des peoples (XXIIe semaine de Synthèse) (pp. 199-247). Paris: Colin.
Martindale, C. A. (1993). Redeeming the Text: Latin Poetry and the Hermeneutics of Reception. Cambridge: Cambridge University Press.
Martindale, C. A. (Ed.) (2000). The Cambridge Companion to Virgil. Cambridge: Cambridge University Press.
Martindale, C. A. (2000). Introduction: 'The classic of all Europe.' In C. A. Martindale (Ed.), The Cambridge Companion to Virgil (pp.1-18). Cambridge: Cambridge University Press.
Martindale, C. A. (2000). Green politics: the Eclogues. In C.A. Martindale (Ed.), The Cambridge Companion to Virgil (pp.107-124). Cambridge: Cambridge University Press.
Martindale, C.A. (2013). Reception – a new humanism? Receptivity, pedagogy, the trans-historical. Classical Receptions Journal, 5.2, 169-183.
Mauss, M. (1954). The Gift: Forms and Functions of Exchange in Archaic Societies. (original title Essay sur le don: forme archaïque de l'échange (1925). translated by E. Cunnison). London: Cohen and West.
Mayhoff, C. (Ed.) (1967). C. Plini Secvndi Natvralis Historiae, Vol. 3, Books XVI-XXII. Stuttgart: Teubner.
McKay, A.G. (1998). Non enarrabile textum? The Shield of Aeneas and the Triple Triumph in 29 BC (Aen.8.630-728). In H.P.Stahl (Ed.), Vergil's Aeneid: Augustan Epic and Political Context (pp.199-222). London: Duckworth.
Millar, F. (1981). Style Abides; (review of Roman Papers I-II). The Journal of Roman Studies, 71, 144-152.

Miller, J.F. (2009). Apollo, Augustus, and the Poets. Cambridge: Cambridge University Press.
Mols, S.T.A.M. (2006). Fragments of Wall Painting from 'Horace's Villa'. In B. Frischer, J. Crawford & M. De Simone (Eds.), The Horace's Villa Project, 1997-2003, Vol. 1; report on new fieldwork and research (pp. 267-272). Oxford: Archaeopress.
Monti, R.C. (1981). The Dido Episode and the Aeneid; Roman Social and Political Values in the Epic. Leiden: Brill.
Morel, W. (later Büchner, K. & Blänsdorf, J.) (Eds.) (1995). Fragmenta poetarum latinorum epicorum et lyricorum praeter Ennium et Lucilium. Stuttgart: Teubner.
Morwood, J. (1998). Virgil's Pious Man and Menenius Agrippa: A Note on 'Aeneid' 1.148-53. Greece and Rome, Second Series, Vol. 45.2.195-198.
Moscati, S. (1968). transl. by A. Hamilton. The World of the Phoenicians. London: Phoenix.
Moscati, S. (1984). Die Karthager. Stuttgart: Belser Verlag.
Mountford, J.F., & Schultz, J.T. (1962). Index Rerum et Nominum in Scholiis Servii et Aelii Donati Tractatorum. Hildesheim: Georg Olms Verlagsbuchhandlung.
Muecke, F. (1983). Foreshadowing and Dramatic Irony in the Story of Dido. The American Journal of Philology, 104. no. 2, 134-155.
Muecke, F. (2007). Poetic Genres: The Satires. In S.J. Harrison (Ed.), The Cambridge Companion to Horace (pp. 105-120). Cambridge: Cambridge University Press.
Murray, O. (1990). Introduction. In P. Veyne, Bread and Circuses: Historical Sociology and Political Pluralism (pp. vii-xxii). London: Allen Lane The Penguin Press.
Mynors, R.A.B. (Ed.) (1969). P. Vergili Maronis: Opera. (OCT) Oxford: Oxford University Press.
Mynors, R.A.B. (Ed.) (2003). Virgil, Georgics. Oxford: Clarendon Press.
Nadeau, Y. (1984). The Lover and the Statesman; a study in apiculture (Virgil, Georgics 4.281-558). In A.J. Woodman & D.A. West (Eds.), Poetry and Politics in the Age of Augustus (pp. 59-82). Cambridge: Cambridge University Press.
Nadeau, Y. (2004). Safe and subsidized. Vergil and Horace sing Augustus. Brussels: Éditions Latomus.
Nadeau, Y. (2007). Vergil's Sextus Pompeius Celaeno (and his defeat by Agrippa). Latomus, 66.94-98.
Nadeau, Y. (2008). Erotica for Caesar Augustus – A study of the love-poetry of Horace, Carmina, Books I to III. Brussels: Éditions Latomus.
Nadeau, Y. (2009). Sextus Pompeius Celaeno, Vergil, Lucan, Hell, and Marcus Antonius Salmoneus. Latomus, 68.35-42.
Nadeau, Y. (2010a). Naulochus and Actium, the Fleets of Paris and Aeneas, and the Tree-felling of C. Iulius Caesar Erysichton. In C. Deroux (Ed.), Studies in Latin Literature and Roman History XV (pp. 219-239). Brussels: Latomus.
Nauta, R.R. (2006). Panegyric in Virgil's Bucolics. In M. Fantuzzi & T. Papanghelis (Eds.), Brill's Companion to Greek and Latin Pastoral (pp. 301-332). Leiden: Brill.
Nelis, D.P. (2001). Vergil's Aeneid and the Argonautica of Apollonius Rhodius. Leeds: Francis Cairns.
Nelis, D.P. (2010). Vergil's Library. In J. Farrell & M.C.J. Putnam (Eds.), A Companion to Vergil's Aeneid and its Tradition (pp. 13-25). Chichester: Wiley-Blackwell.
Nicastri, L. (2002). Cornelio Gallo e l'elegia ellenistico-romana. Studio dei nuovi frammenti. Naples: D'Aria.
Nisbet, R.G.M. & Hubbard, M. (2001). A Commentary on Horace Odes, Book I. Oxford: Clarendon Press.
Nisbet, R.G.M. & Hubbard, M. (2004). A Commentary on Horace Odes, book II. Oxford: Clarendon Press.
Nisbet, R.G.M. (1978). Virgil's Fourth Eclogue: Easterners and Westerners. Bulletin of the Institute of Classical Studies, 1978, 25, 59-78. Reprinted in S.J. Harrison (Ed.). (1995). R.G.M. Nisbet. Collected Papers on Latin Literature (pp. 47-75). Oxford: Clarendon Press. Reprinted in K.Volk (Ed.). (2008). Oxford Readings in Classical Studies: Vergil's Eclogues (pp. 155-188). Oxford: Oxford University Press.

Oliensis, E. S. (1998). Horace and the Rhetoric of Authority. Cambridge: Cambridge University Press.
Oliensis, E.S. (2000). Sons and Lovers: sexuality and gender in Virgil's poetry. In C.A. Martindale (Ed.), The Cambridge Companion to Virgil (pp. 294-311). Cambridge: Cambridge University Press.
Oliensis, E.S. (2007). Poetic Themes: Erotics and Gender. In S.J. Harrison (Ed.), The Cambridge Companion to Horace (pp. 221-234). Cambridge: Cambridge University Press.
Otis, B. (1966). Virgil: a study in civilized poetry. Oxford: Oxford University Press.
Pagán, V. (2004). Speaking Before Superiors: Orpheus in Vergil and Ovid. In I. Sluiter & R.M. Rosen (Eds.), Free Speech in Classical Antiquity (pp. 369-390). Leiden: Brill.
Page, T.E. (1960). P. Vergili Maronis: Bucolica et Georgica. (first ed. 1898). London: MacMillan.
Page, T.E. (1962a). The Aeneid of Virgil, books I-VI, vol 1. (first ed. 1894). London: MacMillan.
Page, T.E, (1962b). The Aeneid of Virgil, books VII-XII, vol.2. (first ed. 1900). London: MacMillan.
Pasquali, G. (1951). Stravaganze quarte e supreme. Venice: Neri Pozza.
Pasquali, G. (1964). Orazio lirico. Florence: Le Monnier.
Paton, W.R. (Ed.) (1960). Epigrams of the Planudean Anthology, not in the Palatine Manuscript, part 4. In The Greek Anthology, volume V. Cambridge, MA: Loeb, Harvard University Press.
Patterson, A.M. (1987). Pastoral and ideology: Virgil to Valéry. Berkeley, CA: University of California Press.
Pease, A.S. (1967). Publii Vergili Maronis Aeneidos liber quartus. (reprint of 1935 ed.). Darmstadt: Wissenschaftliche Buchgesellschaft.
La Penna, A. (1985). Didone. In Enciclopedia Virgiliana 2. Rome: Inst. della enciclopedia italiana.
Perutelli, A. (1995). Bucolics. In N.M. Horsfall (Ed.), A Companion to the Study of Virgil (pp. 27-62). Leiden: Brill.
Pomeroy, S.B. (1975). Goddesses, Whores, Wives, and Slaves: Women in Classical Antiquity. New York, NY: Schocken Books.
Pomeroy, S.B. (1984) Women in Hellenistic Egypt: from Alexander to Cleopatra. New York, NY: Schocken Books.
Powell, A. (Ed.) (2004). Roman Poetry and Propaganda in the Age of Augustus. London: Duckworth
Powell, A. (2004). The Aeneid and the Embarrassments of Augustus. In A. Powell (Ed.), Roman Poetry and Propaganda in the Age of Augustus (pp. 141-174). (first ed. 1992). London: Duckworth.
Powell, C. A. & Welch, K. (Eds.) (2002). Sextus Pompeius. London: Duckworth.
Powell, C. A. (2002). An island amid the flame; the strategy and imagery of Sextus Pompeius, 43-36 B.C. In C. A. Powell & K. Welch (Eds.), Sextus Pompeius (pp. 103-133). London: Duckworth.
Putnam, M.C.J. (1970). Virgil's Pastoral Art: Studies in the Eclogues. Princeton, NJ: Princeton University Press.
Putnam, M.C.J. (1995). Virgil's Aeneid: Interpretation and Influence. Chapel Hill, NC: University of North Carolina Press.
Putnam, M.C.J. (2011). The Humanness of Heroes. Studies in the Conclusion of Virgil's Aeneid. Amsterdam: Amsterdam University Press.
Quinn, K.P. (Ed.) (1963). Latin Explorations: critical studies in Roman Literature. London: Routledge and Kegan Paul.
Quinn, K.P. (1963a). Virgil's Tragic Queen. In K.P. Quinn (Ed.), Latin Explorations: critical studies in Roman Literature (pp. 29-58). London: Routledge and Kegan Paul.
Quinn, K.P. (1963b). The tempo of Virgilian Epic: Allusion. In K.P. Quinn (Ed.), Latin Explorations: critical studies in Roman Literature (pp. 216-220). London: Routledge and Kegan Paul.
Quinn, K.P. (1968). Virgil's Aeneid. A Critical Description. London: Routledge & Kegan Paul.
Quinn, K.P. (1979). Texts and contexts: The Roman Writers and their Audience. London: Routledge & Kegan Paul.
Quinn, K.P. (1982). The Poet and his Audience in the Augustan Age. In H. Temporini & W. Haase (Eds.), Aufstieg und Niedergang der römischen Welt (pp.II.30.1, 75-180). Berlin: Walter de Gruyter.

Quint, D. (1993). Epic and Empire: Politics and Generic Form from Virgil to Milton. Princeton, NJ: Princeton University Press.

Raaflaub, K.A. & Toher, M. (Eds.) (1993). Between Republic and Empire. Interpretations of Augustus and his Principate. Berkeley, CA: University of California Press.

Raaflaub, K.A. & Samons II, L.J. (1993). Opposition to Augustus. In K.A. Raaflaub & M. Toher (Eds.), Between Republic and Empire. Interpretations of Augustus and his Principate (pp.417-454). Berkeley, CA: University of California Press.

Raaflaub, K.A. (2004). Aristocracy and Freedom of Speech in the Greco-Roman World. In I. Sluiter & R.M. Rosen (Eds.), Free Speech in Classical Antiquity (pp. 41-62). Leiden: Brill.

Raymond, E. (2013). Caius Cornelius Gallus: 'the inventor of Latin love elegy.' In T.S. Thorsen (Ed.), The Cambridge Companion to Latin Love Elegy (pp. 59-67). Cambridge: Cambridge University Press.

Reinhold, M. (1981/1982). The Declaration of War against Cleopatra. The Classical Journal 77.2. 97-103.

Richardson, J. (2008). The Language of Empire: Rome and the Idea of Empire from the Third Century BC to the Second Century AD. Cambridge: Cambridge University Press.

Rijser, D. (2011). Afterword. In M.C.J. Putnam, The Humanness of Heroes. Studies in the Conclusion of Virgil's Aeneid (pp. 135-150). Amsterdam: Amsterdam University Press.

Ross, Jr., D.O. (1975). Backgrounds to Augustan Poetry: Gallus, elegy and Rome. Cambridge: Cambridge University Press.

Ross, Jr., D.O. (2008). The Sixth Eclogue: Virgil's Poetic Genealogy. In K.Volk (Ed.), Oxford Readings in Classical Studies: Vergil's Eclogues (pp. 189-215). Oxford: Oxford University Press = Ross 1975, 18-38.

Ross Taylor, L. (1925). Horace's Equestrian Career. The American Journal of Philology, 46. no.2, 161-170.

Rostagni, A. (Ed.) (1944). Svetonio de Poetis e biografi minori. Turin: Chiantore.

Rudd, N. (Ed.) (1976). Lines of Enquiry: studies in Latin Poetry. Cambridge: Cambridge University Press.

Rudd, N. (1976). IDEA: Dido's culpa. In N. Rudd (Ed.), Lines of Enquiry: studies in Latin Poetry (pp. 32-53). Cambridge: Cambridge University Press.

Rudd, N. (1976). ARCHITECTURE: theories about Virgil's Eclogues. In N. Rudd (Ed.), Lines of Enquiry: studies in Latin Poetry (pp. 119-144). Cambridge: Cambridge University Press.

Ruikes sma, P.W. (1966). Samenzweringen en intriges tegen Octavianus Augustus Princeps. Dissertation Radboud Universiteit Nijmegen. Maastricht: 'Ernest van Aelst'.

Russell, D.A.F.M. (1979). De Imitatione. In D. West & T. Woodman, Creative Imitation and Latin Literature (pp. 1-16). Cambridge: Cambridge University Press.

Rutledge, S.H. (2009). Writing Imperial Politics: The Context. In W.J. Dominik, J. Garthwaite & P.A. Roche (Eds.), Writing Politics in Imperial Rome (pp. 23-62). Leiden: Brill.

Schäfer, C. (2006). Kleopatra: Gestalten der Antike. Darmstadt: Wissenschaftliche Buchgesellschaft.

Schanz von, M., & Hosius, C. (1914-1935). Geschichte der römischen Literatur bis zum Gesetzgebungswerk des Kaisers Justinian. Tl. I-IV. München: Beck.

Schrijvers, P. H. (2004). Vergilius, Georgica: Landleven. Groningen: Historische Uitgeverij.

Segal, C. (1986). Foreword. In G.B. Conte, The Rhetoric of Imitation, Genre and Poetic Memory in Virgil and other Latin Poets. Ithaca, NY: Cornell University Press.

Shackleton Bailey, D.R. (1986). Tu Marcellus eris. Harvard Studies in Classical Philology, 90, 199-205.

Schmidt, E.A. (2008). Arcadia: Modern Occident and Classical Antiquity. In K.Volk (Ed.), Oxford Readings in Classical Studies: Vergil's Eclogues (pp. 16-47). Oxford: Oxford University Press.

Skutsch, O. (1985). The Annals of Quintus Ennius. Oxford: Clarendon Press.

Sluiter, I., & Rosen R.M. (Eds.) (2004). Free Speech in Classical Antiquity. Leiden: Brill.

Spaltenstein, F. (1986). Commentaire des Punica de Silius Italicus (livres 1 à 8). Genève: Droz.

Stahl, H.P. (1993). The Death of Turnus: Augustan Vergil and the Political Rival. In K.A. Raaflaub & M. Toher (Eds.), Between Republic and Empire. Interpretations of Augustus and his Principate (pp. 174-211). Berkeley, CA: University of California Press.

Stahl, H.P. (Ed.) (1998). Vergil's Aeneid: Augustan Epic and Political Context. London: Duckworth.

Stahl, H.P. (1998). Editors Introduction: Changing Views of the Political Aeneid. In H.P.Stahl (Ed.), Vergil's Aeneid: Augustan Epic and Political Context (pp. xv-xxxiii). London: Duckworth.

Starr, R.J. (1987). The Circulation of Literary Texts in the Roman World. The Classical Quarterly, 37.1, 213-223.

Strzelecki, W. (Ed.) (1964). Cn. Naevii, Belli Punici Carmen. Leipzig: Teubner.

Syed, Y. (2005). Vergil's Aeneid and the Roman Self: Subject and Nation in Literary Discourse. Ann Arbor, MI: The University of Michigan Press.

Syme, R. (1978). History in Ovid. Oxford: Clarendon Press.

Syme, R. (Ed. by E. Badian) (1979). Roman Papers. Oxford: Clarendon Press.

Syme, R (2002). The Roman Revolution. (first ed.1939). Oxford: Oxford University Press.

Tarrant, R.J. (2000). Poetry and power: Virgil's poetry in contemporary context. In C.A. Martindale (Ed.), The Cambridge Companion to Virgil (pp.169-187). Cambridge: Cambridge University Press.

Tarrant, R.J. (2012). Virgil: Aeneid book XII. Cambridge: Cambridge University Press.

Temporini, H., & Haase, W. (Eds.) (1972 -). Aufstieg und Niedergang der römischen Welt. Berlin: De Gruyter.

Theodorakopoulos, E. M. (2000). Closure: the Book of Virgil. In C.A. Martindale (Ed.), The Cambridge Companion to Virgil (pp.155-165). Cambridge: Cambridge University Press.

Thilo, G. (Ed.) (1887). Servii Grammatici qui fervntvr in Vergilii Bvcolica et Georgica Commentarii. Leipzig: Teubner.

Thilo, G. & Hagen, H. (Eds.) (1923). Servii Grammatici qui fervntvr Vergilii Carmina Commentarii, Vol. I. and Vol. II, Aeneidos Librorum. Leipzig: Teubner.

Thomas, R.F. (1982). Catullus and the Polemics of Poetic Reference (Poem 64.1-18). The American Journal of Philology, 103.2, 144-164.

Thomas, R.F. (1986). Virgil's Georgics and the Art of Reference. Harvard Studies in Classical Philology, 90, 171-198.

Thomas, R.F. (Ed.) (1988a). Virgil: Georgics, books I-II, Vol. I; books III-IV, Vol.II. Cambridge: Cambridge University Press.

Thomas, R.F. (1988b). Tree violation and ambivalence in Virgil. Transactions of the American Philological Association, 118, 261-273.

Thorsen, T.S. (Ed.). (2013). The Cambridge Companion to Latin Love Elegy. Cambridge: Cambridge University Press.

Treggiari, S. (2005). Women in the time of Augustus. In K. Galinsky (Ed.), The Cambridge Companion to the Age of Augustus (pp. 130-147). Cambridge: Cambridge University Press.

Veyne, P. (1990). Bread and Circuses: Historical Sociology and Political Pluralism. (original title Le Pain et le cirque. (1976). Paris: Éditions du Seuil. translated by B. Pearce). London: Allen Lane The Penguin Press.

Veyne, P. (1997). Roman Erotic Elegy: Love, Poetry and the West. (original title L'élégie érotique romaine: L'amour, la poésie et L'Occident. (1983). Paris: Éditions du Seuil. translated by D. Pellauer). Chicago: University of Chicago Press.

Volk, K. (2008). Oxford Readings in Classical Studies: Vergil's Eclogues. Oxford: Oxford University Press.

Volkmann, H. (1958). Cleopatra: A Study in Politics and Propaganda. London: Elek.

Wagenvoort, H. (1930). De Vergilii Ecloga prima. Mnemosyne, New Series, Vol. 58, Pars 1/2. Leiden: Brill, 137-159.

Wallace-Hadrill, A. (2005). Augustan Rome. London: Bristol Classical Press, Duckworth.

Warminton, E.H. (1988). Q. Ennius, Annales. In E.H. Warmington. Remains of Old Latin I. Cambridge, MA: Loeb, Harvard University Press.

Warmington, E.H. (2001). Cn. Naevius, Bellum Poenicum, liber I. In E.H. Warmington (Ed.), Remains of Old Latin II. Cambridge, MA: Loeb, Harvard University Press.

Watson, L.C. (2003). A Commentary on Horace's Epodes. Oxford: Oxford University Press.

Watson, L.C. (2007). Poetic Genres: The Epodes: Horace's Archilochus? In S.J. Harrison (Ed.), The Cambridge Companion to Horace (pp. 93-104). Cambridge: Cambridge University Press.

Weeda, L. (2010). The Augustan Poets: Their Master's Voices? A study of the political views of Vergilius, Horatius and Propertius. Dissertation at Radboud Universiteit Nijmegen. The dissertation is available as digital edition at: (http://repository.ubn.ru.nl/handle/2066/85997)

Weeda, L., & van der Poel, M.G.M. (2014). Vergil and the Batavians (Aeneid 8.727). Mnemosyne, 67.4 588-612.

Weeda, L., & van der Poel, M.G.M. (2014/2015). Which River did Lycoris see in Vergil's tenth Eclogue? In progress.

West, D. A., & Woodman A.J. (Eds.) (1979). Creative Imitation and Latin Literature. Cambridge: Cambridge University Press.

West, D.A. (2007). Cernere erat: The Shield of Aeneas. In S.J. Harrison (Ed.), Oxford readings in Vergil's Aeneid, collection of papers and essays from 1933-1987 (pp. 295-304). Oxford: Oxford University Press.

Whitaker, R. (1988). Did Gallus write 'Pastoral' Elegies?. The Classical Quarterly, New Series, 38.2, 454-458.

White, P. (1978). Amicitia and the Profession of Poetry in Early Imperial Rome. The Journal of Roman Studies, 68, 74-92.

White, P. (1982). Positions for Poets in Early Imperial Rome. In B.K. Gold (Ed.), Literary and Artistic Patronage in Ancient Rome (pp. 50-66). Austin, TX: University of Texas Press.

White, P. (1993). Promised Verse. Poets in the Society of Augustan Rome. Cambridge, MA: Harvard University Press.

White, P. (2005). Poets in the New Milieu: Realigning. In K. Galinsky (Ed.), The Cambridge Companion to the Age of Augustus (pp. 321-339). Cambridge: Cambridge University Press.

White, P. (2007). Poetic Themes: Friendship, patronage and Horatian sociopoetics. In S.J. Harrison (Ed.), The Cambridge Companion to Horace (pp. 195-206). Cambridge: Cambridge University Press.

Wilkinson, L.P. (1966). Virgil and the Evictions. Hermes, 94.3, 320-324.

Wilkinson, L.P. (1997). The Georgics of Virgil: a critical survey. (first ed. 1969, Cambridge University Press). Norman, OK: University of Oklahoma Press.

Williams, G. (1962). Poetry in the Moral Climate of Augustan Rome. The Journal of Roman Studies, 52, 28-46.

Williams, G. (1968). Tradition and Originality in Roman Poetry. Oxford: Clarendon Press.

Williams, G. (1974). A Version of Pastoral; Virgil, Eclogue 4. In A.J. Woodman & D.A. West (Eds.), Quality and Pleasure in Latin Poetry (pp. 31-46). Cambridge: Cambridge University Press.

Williams, G. (1982). Phases in political patronage of literature in Rome. In B. K. Gold (Ed.), Literary and Artistic Patronage in Ancient Rome (pp. 3-27). Austin, TX: University of Texas Press.

Williams, G. (1993). Did Maecenas 'Fall from Favor'? Augustan Literary Patronage. In K.A. Raaflaub & M. Toher (Eds.), Between Republic and Empire. Interpretations of Augustus and his Principate (pp. 258-275). Berkeley, CA: University of California Press.

Williams, G. (1995). Libertino Patre Natus: True or False? In S.J. Harrison (Ed.), Homage to Horace: A Bimillenary Celebration (pp. 296-313). Oxford: Clarendon Press.

Williams, R.D. (2006a). Virgil, Aeneid Books I-VI. (first ed.,1972, MacMillan Education). London: Bristol Classical Press, Duckworth.

Williams, R.D. (2006b) Virgil, Aeneid Books VII-XII. (first ed., 1973, Macmillan Education).London: Bristol Classical Press, Duckworth.
Willis, J. A. (Ed.) (1963). Ambrosii Theodosii Macrobii Saturnalia, Vol.I. Leipzig: Teubner.
Wilson, M. (2009). The Politics of Elegy: Propertius and Tibullus. In W.J. Dominik, J. Garthwaite & P.A. Roche (Eds.), Writing Politics in Imperial Rome (pp. 173-202). Leiden: Brill.
Winkes, R. (Ed.) (1985). The Age of Augustus: interdisciplinary conference held at Brown University, april 30-May 2, 1982. Louvain, Collège Érasme: Institut Supérieur d'Archéologie et d'Histoire de l'Art.
Wissowa, G. (1902). Monatliche Geburtstagsfeier. Hermes, 37, 157-159.
Woodman, A.J., & Powell, J.G.F. (Eds.) (1992). Author and Audience in Latin Literature. Cambridge: Cambridge University Press.
Woodman, A.J., & West, D.A. (Eds.) (1974). Quality and Pleasure in Latin Poetry. Cambridge: Cambridge University Press.
Woodman, A.J., & West, D.A. (Eds.) (1984). Poetry and Politics in the Age of Augustus. Cambridge: Cambridge University Press.
Woodworth, D.C. (1930). Lavinia: An Interpretation. Transactions and Proceedings of the American Philological Association, 61, 175-194.
Woolf, G. (2004). Becoming Roman: The Origins of Provincial Civilization in Gaul. In C.B. Champion (Ed.), Roman Imperialism: Readings and Sources (pp. 231-242). Oxford: Blackwell Publishing.
Wyke, M. (2004). Augustan Cleopatras: Female Power and Poetic Authority. In A. Powell (Ed.), Roman Poetry and Propaganda in the Age of Augustus (pp. 98-140). London: Duckworth.
Yavetz, Z. (1993). The Personality of Augustus: Reflections on Syme's Roman Revolution. In K.A. Raaflaub & M. Toher (Eds.), Between Republic and Empire. Interpretations of Augustus and his Principate (pp. 21-41). Berkeley, CA: University of California Press.
Zanker, P. (2010). The Power of Images in the age of Augustus. (original title Augustus und die Macht der Bilder. (1987). München: Beck. translated by A. Shapiro). Ann Arbor, MI: University of Michigan Press.
Zetzel, J.E.G. (1982). The Poetics of Patronage in the Late First Century B.C. In B.K. Gold (Ed.), Literary and Artistic Patronage in Ancient Rome (pp. 87-102). Austin, TX: University of Texas Press.
Zetzel, J.E.G. (2006). Dreaming about Quirinus: Horace's Satires and the development of Augustan poetry. In A.J. Woodman & D.C. Feeney (Eds.), Traditions and contexts in the poetry of Horace (pp. 38-52). Cambridge: Cambridge University Press.
Ziegler, K., & Sontheimer, W. (Eds.) (1969). Der Kleine Pauly, Lexikon der Antike, Vols. I-V. Stuttgart: Alfred Druckenmüller Verlag.

Index

Actium   1, 2, 3, 10, 29, 90, 94
   Vergil reads Georgics to Octavian after Actium   41
Aeneas
   did his duty when he left Dido   132
   difference Dido and Lavinia   132
   uncontrolled anger killing Turnus   111
Amicitia   44, 46
   general
     in HOR.Carm.2.6.24   44
     in HOR.Carm.3.8.13   44
     in HOR.Ep.1.9.5   44
     in HOR.S.1.10.85-87   44
   Horace and Maecenas
     in HOR.Carm.1.1.1-2   47
     in HOR.Carm.1.20.1-5   47
     in HOR.Carm.2.17.3-4   47
     in HOR.Carm.3.16.29-30   47
     in HOR.Carm.3.29.25-26, 32-34   47
     in HOR.Carm.4.11.18-20   48
     in HOR.S.1.5.40-42   48
     in SUET.Vita Horati.2.2   48
   Propertius and Maecenas
     in PROP.2.1 and 3.9   48
   Propertius and Tullus
     in PROP.1.22.2   48
Andromache   133
Antonius, Iullus   2
Antonius, Lucius   2
Anubis,   117
Ara Pacis   104
Aristaeus
   epyllion   95
   bougonia   101
   in G.4.281-558   97
   in G.4.317-332 claim of Octavian to restore order   99
   in G.4.351-356   attacks on heritage of Octavian   99
   in G.4.453-459 Antony and Cleopatra   99
   in G.4.554-558   victory of Octavian over Antony   99
   in G.4 Aristaeus represents two opposite qualities   98
Artemidorus of Tarsus
   Collection of pastoral poetry   55

Audiences of the poet   31, 36, 39
   audience of Georgics   86
   conditions not ideal for propaganda   43
   Latin poetry read outside Rome?   36
     Horace writes about this in Carm.2.20, and in Ep.1.20   36
   performance on stage   40
     Horace dismissive of performance on stage   42
       in HOR.Ars.212-213   42
       in HOR.Ep.1.19.41-44   42
       in HOR.Ep.2.1.156-218   42
       in HOR.S.1.10.39 and 73-74   41
       in SERV.Ecl.6.11   40
       in St. Augustine   40
       in Vita Donati.26   40
     poetry of Vergil and Horace on stage   40
   private reading   23, 41
   public reading   23
   reading in small group   39
     PROP.3.16.29-30   42
     SERV.A.4.323   41
     SERV.A.6.861   41
     Vita Donati.16 and 27   41
   reciting poetry with political content   39
Augustan poetry   23
   involvement in contemporary issues   23
   Neoterici   23
   sources of inspiration
     Hellenistic poetry   23
   use of references   24
Augustus. See also Octavian
   auctoritas   43
   high regard for Cleopatra   147
   opposition to Augustus   1
     in SUET.Aug.14-18   2
     in SUET.Aug.19.1   2
     in TAC.Ann.1.9-1.10   2
   parallels between Lavinia/Aeneas and Livia/Augustus   132, 138
   propaganda
     Augustus and propaganda   149
Batavians   107
Book circulation
   book dealers   38
   Horace on Sosii in HOR.Ep.1.20.1-2 and in

HOR.Ars.344-346   38
poor quality of bookdealers in CIC.Q.fr.3.6.1   38
sale of his book in HOR.Ep.1.20.1-2   38
borrowing books   37
borrowing books in CIC.Att.8.11.7; 8.12.6; 13.31.2; 13.32.2   37
gift copies   37
libraries   37
library at Porticus Octaviae in HOR. Ep.2.1.216-217   37
library of Lucullus in CIC.Fin.3.2.7   37
library of Sulla in CIC.Att.4.10.1   37
library on the Palatine in OV.Tr.3.1.63-64   38
Brundisium
pact of   62
Caepio, Fannius   2, 139
Catilina
in VERG.A.8.668-669   108
Cleopatra
Antony and Cleopatra   101, 132
Cleopatra and Dido compared   135
functional model for Dido   122, 136, 147
in VERG.G.4.453-459   99
Context
conclusions   53
Cytheris. See Gallus
in Ecl.10 Cytheris is Lycoris   77
in Ecl.10 it is unlikely that Cytheris followed Mark Antony to the Rhine   78
Danaids
in VERG.A.10.495-498 myth of Danaids on Pallas' sword-belt   119
Dido
analogy with Cleopatra   136
analogy with Cleopatra in secondary literature   135
Dido and Cleopatra compared   135
in Ennius' Annales   126
in VERG.A.04.300-303, A.04.365-392, A.04.584-629 Dido acts without self-control   129
in VERG.A.04.327-330 frustrated that she will not get a son by Aeneas   129
in VERG.A.04.622-626 Dido's anger also at Aeneas' descendants   130
in VERG Aeneid   127
lack of analogy with Andromache   133

lack of analogy with Medea   134
myths about Dido   124, 133
political status   137
unique features   133
Vergil's portrayal of Dido   130
was Dido a historical woman?   124
Donatus
evidence re. land commission unreliable   56
Elissa of Tyros   124
founder of Carthage   125
Emathia
in VERG.G.1.491 Homeric word for part of Macedonia   88
Ennius
Annales
Dido in Annales   125, 126
Freedom of speech   52
Functional frame   4, 11, 120
definition of functional model   VII, 12
functional model   12
and historic representation   140
Augustus model for Aeneas   109, 132, 140
Cleopatra model for Dido   13, 122, 136, 140, 147
in VERG.A.06.162-174 Aeneas' problems near Sicily indicating Octavian's struggle with Sextus Pompeius   138
in VERG.A.08.626-731 prophecy of Actium/ triple triumph indicating peace under Octavian's leadership   108
in VERG.Aeneid   120
in VERG.Ecl.04.17 indicating Hercules   62
in VERG.Ecl.04.62-63 indicating Hercules   62
in VERG.Ecl.05 name of Mopsus   63
in VERG.Ecl.06 song of Silenus   66
in VERG.Ecl.06 Varus and Gallus indicating political roles in countryside   66
in VERG.Ecl.07 name of Thyrsis   69
in VERG.Ecl.08 Mopsus soldier who received land   71
in VERG.Ecl.09.07-09 indicating that region is not Mantuan   73
in VERG.Ecl.09.58-61 tomb of Bianor   75
in VERG.Ecl.10 Gallus in Arcadia indicating that he does not belong to the pastoral world   81

in VERG.G.2.136-176 reference to Alexander the Great indicating that Augustus will restore greatness of Italia 90
in VERG.G.2.460 tellus indicating traditional view on use of land 91
in VERG.G.2.494 Pan, Silvanus and Nymphs indicating country life 91
in VERG.G.2.532-533 Sabini, Remus and Etruria indicating foundation of Rome 93
in VERG.G.2 Jason ploughing in Colchis indicating peaceful Italia 89
in VERG.G.3.17-18 Pindaric picture 94
in VERG.G.4 allegory for Octavian and Antony 98
in VERG.G.4 bees indicating nation 96
in VERG.G.4 bougonia indicating the resurrection of the nation 101
in VERG.G.4 Octavian-Aristaeus victor indicating Octavian as new leader 101
opening PIND.O.2 for HOR.Carm.1.12 13
functional objective 12
single reference and functional frame 11
Gallus, C. Cornelius 34, 56, 67, 95
  Cytheris 40, 76
  in Ecl.10 Gallus in love with Lycoris/Cytheris who leaves him 76
  fragment 78
    date of writing 41 or 40 B.C 79
    found in 1978 in Egypt 78
    Gallus expressed confidence in Octavian 79
  friend of Vergil 76
  in Ecl.06 Gallus' poetical orientation 67
  in Ecl.06 involved in land expropriations? 65, 67
  in Ecl.06 praise by Vergil 67
  in Ecl.09 involved in attempt to exempt Mantua in expropriations? 74
  in Ecl.09 involved in land expropriations? 65
  in Ecl.09 mediates between Varus and family of Vergil? 73, 81
  in Ecl.10 involved in land expropriations? 65
  in Ecl.10 poet in Arcadia 76
  in Ecl.10 suffering when Lycoris/Cytheris runs off with soldier 77
  in G.4 suicide, damnatio memoriae 95

Lycoris 78
  in Ecl.10 Lycoris mistress of Gallus 78
poetic genre
  in Ecl.06 68
Garamantes 105
Gifts 49
  gift economy as a development of Greek euergetism 50
  Horace
    Sabine estate 50
good king/queen versus bad king/queen
  Aeneas killing Turnus 113
  Dido good queen 128
  Dido's fury at Aeneas' departure 129
Haemon
  in G.1.491 now the Great Balkans in northern Thrace 88
Hermus
  in G.2 river in Lydia 90
Horace 47
  friendship for Maecenas. See Amicitia
  pressure by Maecenas 51
  Sabine estate 50. See Gifts:Horace
  social position 44
  in
    HOR.S.1.6.76-78 44
    HOR.S.2.7.53-54 44
Independence of the poets 44, 50
INDEX LOCORUM
  AELIUS DONATUS
    Life of Vergil
      Vita Donati.16 41
      Vita Donati.26 40
      Vita Donati.27 41
  ARISTOTLE
    Nic.Eth.1149a25-1149b27 111
  AUGUSTUS
    Res Gestae.019.01 15
    Res Gestae.020.01 15
  CICERO
    Att.04.10.01 37
    Att.13.31.02 37
    Att.13.32.02 37
    Fin.03.02.07 37
    Phil.03.13 80
    Q.fr.03.06.01 38
  ENNIUS
    Annales
      book 07.fr.inc.27 126
      book 08.fr.8.24 126

HOMER
  Iliad
    Il.06.407-613   133
    Il.06.484-492   134
HORACE
  Art of Poetry
    Ars.212-213   42
    Ars.344-346   38
  Carmen Saeculare
    Saec.   45
  Epistles
    Ep.01   50
    Ep.01.09.05   44
    Ep.01.19   42
    Ep.01.19.41-44   42
    Ep.01.20.01-02   38
    Ep.01.20.10-13   36
    Ep.01.20.17-18   32
    Ep.01.20.20-23   33
    Ep.02.01   42
    Ep.02.01.156-218   42
    Ep.02.01.214   42
    Ep.02.01.216-217   37
  Odes
    Carm.01.01.01-02   47
    Carm.01.12   13
    Carm.01.20.01-05   47
    Carm.01.37.06-14   115
    Carm.01.37.30-32   135
    Carm.02.06.24   44
    Carm.02.09   49
    Carm.02.12   19
    Carm.02.17.03-04   47
    Carm.02.20   36
    Carm.03.04   19
    Carm.03.08.13   44
    Carm.03.16.29-30   47
    Carm.03.29   92
    Carm.03.29.25-26   47
    Carm.03.29.32-34   47
    Carm.04.11.18-20   48
  Satires
    S.01.05.040-042   48
    S.01.06.076-078   44
    S.01.10.39   42
    S.01.10.73-74   41
    S.01.10.74-76   32
    S.01.10.85-87   44
    S.02.07.053-054   44

MACROBIUS
  Saturnalia
    Sat.05.17.04   123
    Sat.05.17.05-06   126
    Sat.06.02.30-31   125
NAEVIUS
  Bellum Poenicum
    book 01, fr.18   125
    book 01, fr.19   125
    book 01, fr.20   125
OVID
  Amores
    Am.1.15.30   77
  Ars Amatoria
    Ars 3.527   77
  Tristia
    Tr.02.445   77
    Tr.03.01.63-64   38
PINDAR
  Odes
    Ol.02   13
PLINY THE YOUNGER
  Epistles
    Ep.06.21   40
PROPERTIUS
  Elegies
    El.01.22.02   48
    El.02.01   49
    El.03.09   49
    El.03.11.030-058   115
    El.03.16.29-30   42
QUINTILIAN
  The Orator's Education
    Inst.10.1.91-92   70
SENECA MAIOR
  Con.4.2   43
SERVIUS
  Comment. on Vergil Aeneid
    on A.04.09   125
    on A.04.323   41
    on A.04.682   126
    on A.06.861   41
  Comment. on Vergil Eclogues
    on Ecl.06.11   40
    on Ecl.09.7-10   73
SUETONIUS
  Aug.014-018   2
  Aug.019.01   2
  Aug.070-071   15
  Vita Horati   15

Vita Horati.02.02   48
Vita Verg.19   74

TACITUS
  Annals
    Ann.01.09.001-010   2

VERGIL
  Aeneid
    A.01.148-153   138
    A.01.254-296   109
    A.01.267-268   105
    A.01.286-291   105
    A.01.286-296   146
    A.01.294-296   105, 140
    A.01.338-368   127
    A.01.343   124
    A.01.490-504   128
    A.01.496   128
    A.01.496-504   121
    A.01.499   128
    A.01.507   128
    A.01.507-508   128
    A.01.573-574   128
    A.01.748-749   128
    A.03.059   117
    A.03.209-267   138
    A.04.054-173   129
    A.04.066-073   121
    A.04.074-075   128
    A.04.126-127   128
    A.04.129-159   128
    A.04.165-166   128
    A.04.170-171   128
    A.04.189-197   136
    A.04.259-278   136
    A.04.327-330   129
    A.04.328-329   129
    A.04.376   111
    A.04.584-629   119
    A.04.600-603   130
    A.04.622-626   130
    A.04.644   117
    A.06.069-070   108
    A.06.162-174   138
    A.06.763-765   131
    A.06.788-800   146
    A.06.789-795   105, 109
    A.06.792-794   105, 141, 144
    A.06.794-795   146
    A.06.847-853   109, 141, 144
    A.06.851-853   113
    A.06.854-886   139
    A.06.860-886   108, 141, 146
    A.07.021   117
    A.07.052-106   131
    A.07.096-106   146
    A.07.313-322   131
    A.08.319-322   105, 141
    A.08.357   105
    A.08.494   112
    A.08.608-731   115
    A.08.626-731   106, 141, 144
    A.08.635-637   108
    A.08.642-645   108
    A.08.668-669   108
    A.08.671-710   116
    A.08.671-713   106, 118
    A.08.671-728   140
    A.08.675-728   105
    A.08.682-683   106
    A.08.685   118
    A.08.685-688   115
    A.08.688   118
    A.08.696-700   115, 117, 147
    A.08.697   116
    A.08.707-713   118
    A.08.709   117
    A.08.709-713   147
    A.08.714-728   106
    A.08.727   77
    A.10.310-311   110, 141
    A.10.480-505   98
    A.10.495-498   11, 119, 147
    A.10.500   98
    A.11.100-105   110, 141, 144
    A.11.372-373   110, 141, 144
    A.11.479   132
    A.12.035-036   110, 141, 144
    A.12.192-194   132
    A.12.383-429   139
    A.12.680   112
    A.12.681-696   112
    A.12.766-771   110, 141, 143, 144
    A.12.770-771   110
    A.12.933-934   113
    A.12.937   132
    A.12.941-949   98
    A.12.945-952   11, 110, 113, 141, 144
    A.12.946-947   111
    A.12.947-948   98

Eclogues
- Ecl.01   57, 59, 72, 143, 148
- Ecl.01.01   103
- Ecl.01.42   57
- Ecl.01.42-43   59, 84
- Ecl.01.46-47   60
- Ecl.01.67-72   60
- Ecl.02   58, 60, 143
- Ecl.03   58, 61, 143
- Ecl.03.11   61
- Ecl.03.17-18   61
- Ecl.03.88-89   61
- Ecl.03.92-103   61
- Ecl.04   57, 61, 144
- Ecl.04.04-05   61
- Ecl.04.08-10   62
- Ecl.04.15-17   62
- Ecl.04.36   63
- Ecl.04.53-54   63
- Ecl.04.62-63   62
- Ecl.05   57, 63, 143, 144
- Ecl.05.08-09   64
- Ecl.05.20-44   64
- Ecl.05.34-39   64
- Ecl.05.43   64
- Ecl.05.51-52   64
- Ecl.05.56-61   64
- Ecl.05.60-61   65
- Ecl.05.78-80   65
- Ecl.06   8, 66, 72, 143
- Ecl.06.06-08   65
- Ecl.06.06-12   84
- Ecl.06.07   56
- Ecl.06.10   56
- Ecl.06.11-12   65
- Ecl.06.12   56
- Ecl.06.31-42   65
- Ecl.06.43-73   66
- Ecl.06.46-60   66
- Ecl.06.47   67
- Ecl.06.52-60   66
- Ecl.06.64   56, 84
- Ecl.06.64-66   67
- Ecl.06.69-70   66
- Ecl.06.74-81   66
- Ecl.07   69, 72, 143
- Ecl.07.04   68
- Ecl.07.05   68
- Ecl.07.29   68
- Ecl.07.33-34   57, 68
- Ecl.07.46-47   69
- Ecl.08   57, 63, 70, 143, 148
- Ecl.08.006-013   60
- Ecl.08.026   71
- Ecl.08.027-028   71
- Ecl.08.029   71
- Ecl.08.032-033   71
- Ecl.08.059-060   71
- Ecl.08.064-068   71
- Ecl.08.069-070   71
- Ecl.08.108   72
- Ecl.08.109   72
- Ecl.09   58, 72, 143, 144
- Ecl.09.01-06   72
- Ecl.09.07   73
- Ecl.09.07-29   73
- Ecl.09.10   57, 73
- Ecl.09.11-13   73
- Ecl.09.26-27   56
- Ecl.09.26-29   73, 84
- Ecl.09.27-28   56
- Ecl.09.35-36   74
- Ecl.09.46-50   74
- Ecl.09.51   75
- Ecl.09.58-61   75
- Ecl.10   56, 57, 76, 143, 148
- Ecl.10.01-10   84
- Ecl.10.02-03   77
- Ecl.10.14-17   77, 81
- Ecl.10.21-49   77
- Ecl.10.22-23   78, 80, 84
- Ecl.10.46-49   77
- Ecl.10.47   56, 80
- Ecl.10.62-63   76
- Ecl.10.69   81
- Ecl.10.72-73   84
- Ecl.10.73-74   76

Georgics
- G.1   87
- G.1.001-005   86
- G.1.024-028   85, 86
- G.1.040-041   87, 144
- G.1.121-123   87
- G.1.121-146   87
- G.1.147   87
- G.1.461-514   88
- G.1.489-497   88, 144
- G.1.498-514   89
- G.1.506-508   89
- G.2   87

G.2.042 89
G.2.042-044 86
G.2.061-062 89
G.2.136-138 89
G.2.136-170 93
G.2.136-176 90
G.2.140-143 89
G.2.458-460 90
G.2.458-494 90
G.2.458-540 93
G.2.458-542 90
G.2.490-494 91
G.2.495-498 91
G.2.498-503 92
G.2.523-531 92
G.2.532-534 92
G.2.532-542 92
G.2.538-540 92
G.3 87, 93
G.3.001-048 93
G.3.012-016 93
G.3.017-018 93
G.3.026-029 10, 94, 147
G.3.040-048 94
G.3.049 94
G.3.103 94
G.3.157-203 94
G.3.284-294 93
G.3.284-566 94
G.4 87, 95
G.4.001 95
G.4.001-002 96
G.4.001-227 97
G.4.001-280 95
G.4.001-314 103
G.4.003-005 96
G.4.067-068 96
G.4.067-103 96
G.4.089-090 96
G.4.147-148 87
G.4.149-227 96
G.4.210-211 145
G.4.210-218 96
G.4.281-314 95, 97
G.4.281-558 97
G.4.283 97
G.4.287-288 99
G.4.290 99
G.4.301-302 97
G.4.315 99
G.4.315-558, Aristaeus epyllion 95
G.4.317-332 99
G.4.326-328 99
G.4.351-354 100
G.4.351-356 99
G.4.360 99, 100
G.4.448-449 100
G.4.453-459 99, 100
G.4.460-527 101
G.4.554-558 99, 101, 144
G.4.559-562 85
G.4.559-566 101
G.4.566 103
Iulia the Elder (the daughter of Augustus and Scribonia) 2
Iulia the Younger (Augustus' granddaughter) 2
Land expropriations. See Gallus and Varus
  in Ecl.06 dubious if Varus and Gallus were involved 65
  in Ecl.06 Varus and Gallus typify involvement of high-ranking Romans 67
  in Ecl.06 Vergil's farm? 65
  in Ecl.10 involvement of Gallus and Varus in Mantua dubious 81
  in Mantua region 74, 80, 83
Lavinia
  portrayed as dutiful girl 132, 148
  Vergil's portrayal of Lavinia 131
Literacy 31
  communication 34
    letters 34
  definition 31
  education 32
    grammaticus 32
      Horace on teaching by grammaticus 32
    schoolsystem 32
  literacy rates 33
    in army, administration and trade 33
    latinisation and bilingualism 35
    literacy among different strata of the population 35
    literacy in Rome 33, 35
    literacy in the provinces 35
Literary frame 10, 120
  literary model 10
    Apollonius' Medea literary model for Dido acc. to Nelis 10, 134
    Iliad battles model for martial encounters in Aeneid 10

in VERG
    Aeneid   120
    self-reference in G.4.566 to Ecl.1.1   102
literary objective and literary continuity
    VII, 10
literary predecessors of Georgics   86
Livia Drusilla   132
Lycoris
    girl friend of Gallus who runs off with soldier to the southern Alps crossing the Reno   80
Macrobius
    says that Naevius had great influence on Aeneid   125
Maecenas
    minister of propaganda. See Propaganda
    withdraws from public life   52
Mantua
    in Ecl.09. affected by land expropriations   74
    land expropriations   83
Marcellus   108
    in VERG.A.06.860-886 referred to as Augustus' successor   108, 139
Marcus Lepidus   2
Mark Antony   1, 2
    and Cytheris, See Cytheris   78
    broke with Octavia   61
    in VERG.A.08.675-728   105
    in VERG.A.08.685-688 Antony's position in Alexandria and failure of Eastern campaign ridiculed   118
    in VERG.Ecl.10 governor of Gallia   78
    in VERG.G.4.453-459 Antony and Cleopatra   99
Medea   10, 123, 134, 135
Messalla, M. Corvinus   22, 44, 49
Methodological features   5
    political content   6
        test of dates of writing   7
        test of matters of current interest   6
        test of references   6
    political or private political poems   6
    summary of scheme of analysis   20
Mettus Fuffetius
    in VERG.A.8.642-645   108
Mezentius   112
Mincius, river near Mantua   93
Mopsus. See also Vergil, functional model
    functional model in Ecl.05 and Ecl.08   63

Murena, Licinius Varro   2, 139
Naevius
    Bellum Poenicum
        acc. to Servius in his commentary on VERG.A.04.09 Naevius mentioned Dido   125
        Dido in Bellum Poenicum   125
        Macrobius says that Bellum Poenicum had great influence on Aeneid   125
Octavia
    broke with Mark Antony   61
Octavian. See also Augustus
    dedicatee of Ecl.08   70
    in Aristaeus epyllion   99
    propaganda
        Octavian and propaganda   149
    triple triumph
        in A.08.714-728   106
Panegyric poetry   18
    definition   19
    Horace's panegyrics for Augustus   52
    in Vergil's Eclogues   57, 84
Pasiphaë
    in Ecl.06
        destruction of countryside by human aberrations   66
    in Ecl.06.   66
Patronage or amicitia   43
    gift   49
    independence of the poets   44, 50
    scholarly view that Horace accepted patronage of Maecenas   51
Paullus, L. Aemilius   2, 37
Perusia   2, 59
Pietas   140
Pindar
    in VERG.G.3 proem Pindaric influences   93
Planudes
    Anthology
        Dido in Anthology   126
        translated by Ausonius   125
Poets. See also Propaganda
    and performative medium   24
    and propaganda   17
        pressure by Maecenas and Messalla   22
    as commentators   17, 18, 51, 114, 151
    earning potential   45
        Vergil and Horace relatively rich   45
    personal opinion   25, 50
    social position   44

use of persona 25
Pollio, C. Asinius 34, 40, 44
　birth of child to Mark Antony in Ecl.04 62
　consul in 40 B.C. 62
　friend of Vergil 61, 62
　in Ecl.08 70
Propaganda 3, 13
　ancient authors about propaganda 15
　　in Res Gestae. 19.1, 20.1 15
　　in SUET Divus Augustus.70-71 15
　　in SUET Vita Horati 15
　by coinage. See Visual media
　by Vergil 149
　court poetry 14
　definition 14
　did Maecenas encourage the writing of propaganda? 17, 51
　in 1930's 14
　poetry and propaganda 16, 17
　　poems critical of Augustus 20, 150. See also Vergil, critical poems
　　poems supportive of Augustus 20, 150
　　representation of power 16
　Vergil was independent commentator 151
Quintilian 70
Recusatio 19
　Vergil
　　in Ecl.06 declines to write about Varus 65
References 4, 8. See Augustan poetry
　allusive reference 10
　　definition 11
　　to Augustus' conduct in civil war in VERG.A.12 110
　　to Augustus in VERG.A.12.945-952 11, 113
　　to Cleopatra in VERG.A.10.495-498 11, 119
　　to Octavian/Augustus stealing others' women in VERG.A.07.52-106 132
　Conte's ‚the letter' and ‚the sense' 13
　direct reference
　　to Augustus in VERG.A.01.286-296 105
　　to Augustus in VERG.A.06.789-795 105
　　to Augustus in VERG.A.08.675-728 105
　　to Cleopatra in VERG.A.08.608-731 115
　functional frame 4, 11
　indirect reference 10
　　in Aeneid rex and pius Aeneas refers to Augustus 139

　　to Augustus in VERG.A.06.69-70 and VERG.A.06.860-886 108
　　to Cleopatra in VERG.G.3.26-29 10
　　to future kingship of Augustus in VERG.A.08.319-322 105
　　to land expropriations by Augustus in VERG.A.12.766-771 110
　in the Aeneid to Cleopatra and Augustus 104
　literary frame 4
　single reference. See Functional frame
　Thomas' model of classification 8
Rex. See also Vergil, political views
　word often used in Aeneid 139
Rhenus
　bicornis
　　Rhine near Nijmegen 107
　mentioned only twice by Vergil 77
　river in Northern Italia (Reno) 56
　　in Ecl.10 river crossed by Lycoris 79
Rufus, M. Egnatius. See opposition to Augustus
Rufus, Plautius 3
Servius
　commentary on Aeneid
　　in commentary on VERG.A.04.09 says that Naevius mentioned Dido 125
　　in commentary on VERG.A.04.682 says that Varro wrote that Anna loved Aeneas 126
　evidence re. land commission unreliable 56
Sextus Pompeius 2, 138
Silenus. See also Varus
　in Ecl.06 65
　voice of common farmer 67
Theocritus
　functional model
　　in Ecl.07 Thyrsis 69
　Idylls in collection of Artemidorus 55
　literary model for Vergil's Eclogues 55
　　in Ecl.02 THEOC.Id.11. Corydon modeled on Polyphemus 60
　　in Ecl.03 THEOC.Id.5 61
　　names in Eclogues taken from Idylls 63
Thyrsis. See also Vergil, functional model
　functional model in Ecl.07 69
Timaios, 124
Timavus
　river in Northern Italia 70
Tityrus 59

Tityrus in Ecl.01 does not represent Vergil 59
Turnus. See also Vergil, political views, Aeneid
   death   110
Varus, Alfenus   56
   in Ecl.06 involved in land expropriations?   65, 67
   in Ecl.06 Varus, Gallus and Silenus indicating the ruined countryside   67
   in Ecl.06 Vergil needs his goodwill   65
Vergil
   Aeneid
      Aeneas' shield   106, 108
         expectation of better times   108
         in A.8.635-637 rape of the Sabine women   108
      destruction of manuscript after Vergil's death   114
      literary model
         in A.01.496-504 first meeting of Aeneas and Dido   121
         in A.4.66-73 wounding of Dido   121
         in Aeneid Medea acc. to Nelis literary model for Dido   134
         summary   140
      Vergil's two objectives writing Aeneid   121
   Cleopatra
      regard (high or low) for Cleopatra   115, 147
   commentator on contemporary issues   114, 151
   critical poems   150
      A.06.847-853   109, 141, 144
      A.07.52-106   132
      A.10.310-311   110
      A.11.100-105   110, 141, 144
      A.11.372-373   110, 141, 144
      A.12.35-36   110, 141, 144
      A.12.766-771   110, 141, 143
      A.12.945-952   112, 113, 141
      Ecl.01   60, 84, 143
      Ecl.06   68, 84, 143
      Ecl.07   69, 84, 143
      Ecl.08   72, 84, 143
      Ecl.09   75, 84, 143
      G.1.489-497   88, 144
      G.2.458-540   93
      G.4.554-558   101, 144

Dido
   in A.04 Vergil's portrayal of Dido   130
Eclogues
   Arcadia in Ecl.10   81
   date of writing between 42 and 35 B.C.   60, 70
   date of writing of Ecl.09 ca. 40 B.C.   74
   date of writing of Ecl.10   41 or 40 B.C. 79
   interpretation of Ecl.06 differs much   67
   literary model. See Theocritus
   panegyric versus critical poetry   57
   referring to personal knowledge   56
   summary   83
functional model. See Functional frame
   in A.06.162-174 Aeneas' problems near Sicily indicating Octavian's struggle with Sextus Pompeius   138
   in A.08.626-731 Aeneas' shield indicating Octavian's peaceful leadership   108
   in Aeneid Augustus and Cleopatra functional models for Aeneas and Dido   140
   in Aeneid Cleopatra functional model for Dido   122, 147
   in Aeneid relationship between historic Augustus and Cleopatra and models for Aeneas and Dido   140
   in Ecl.04.17 indicating Hercules   62
   in Ecl.04.62-63 indicating Hercules   62
   in Ecl.05 and Ecl.08 Mopsus indicating newcomer   63
   in Ecl.06 Pasiphaë in Silenus' song indicating destruction of countryside   66
   in Ecl.06 roles of Varus and Gallus   66
   in Ecl.07 contrasting attitudes between farmers and newcomers   69
   in Ecl.07 Thyrsis indicating outsider   69
   in Ecl.08 Mopsus indicating newcomer, soldier   71
   in Ecl.09 indicating region is not Mantuan   73
   in Ecl.09 tomb of Bianor indicating that the farmland is dead   75
   in Ecl.10 Gallus in Arcadia indicating not belonging to pastoral world   81
   in G.2.136-176 reference to Alexander the Great indicating the superiority of Italia   90

in G.2.460 tellus indicating traditional view on use of land 91
in G.2.494 Pan, Silvanus and Nymphs indicating country life 91
in G.2.532-533 Sabini, Remus and Etruria indicating foundation of Rome 93
in G.2 Jason ploughing in Colchis indicating peaceful Italia 89
in G.3.17-18 Pindaric picture indicating link Octavian to rural Italia 94
in G.4 Aristaeus indicating Octavian and Antony 98
in G.4 bees indicating nation 96
in G.4 bougonia indicating the resurrection of the nation 101
in G.4 Octavian-Aristaeus victor indicating Octavian as new leader 101
Georgics 85
  audience of Georgics 86
  date of writing between 35 and 29 B.C. 85
  literary predecessors 86
  not a handbook for farmers 86
  summary 102
Lavinia
  Vergil's portrayal of Lavinia 131
member of circle of Maecenas 85
models for Dido and Aeneas 120
poems critical of Octavian/Augustus 150
poems supportive of Octavian/Augustus 150
political views
  Aeneid
    in A.06.792-794 high expectations of reign of Octavian 105, 144, 146
    in A.06.847-853 high price to be paid for imperial success 109, 144
    in A.06.860-886 Marcellus next in line as successor to Augustus 108, 139, 146
    in A.07.96-106 hope of hereditary kingship of Augustus 138, 146
    in A.08.319-322 emergence of principate 105
    in A.08.626-731 expectation of better times 108
    in A.08.626-731 high expectations of reign of Octavian 108, 144
    in A.08.685-688 Antony's position in Alexandria and failure of Eastern campaign ridiculed 118
    in A.08.696-700 compassion with Cleopatra 117, 147
    in A.10.310-311 concern about expropriations 110
    in A.10.495-498 political murders by Cleopatra and Augustus 119
    in A.11.100-105 and in A.11.372-373 violence in the civil war 110, 144
    in A.12.35-36 the unnecessary violence in civil war 110, 144
    in A.12.766-771 Octavian's violation of the countryside 110, 143, 144
    in A.12.945-952 brutal killing of Turnus 111, 112, 144
    in A.12.945-952 war is a messy business 112
    in Aeneid Augustus' conduct in war 114
    in Aeneid choice of Cleopatra as model for Dido indicates Vergil's approval of extension of women's role 133
    in Aeneid emergence of the Principate 114
    in Aeneid sufferings caused by the civil war 114
    in Aeneid Vergil held Cleopatra in high regard 132, 147
    in Aeneid Vergil's ‚liberal' view on women's role 132
    in Aeneid war with Antony and Cleopatra 114
  Eclogues
    bitter situation after evictions of farmers 72
    concerned about the destruction of rural communities 58
    concerned about the disappearance of farming 57
    deals with substantial problems 57
    in Ecl.01.29-30 positive about role of woman 59
    in Ecl.01 land confiscations after Philippi 59, 143
    in Ecl.02 threat to pastoral life 61, 143
    in Ecl.03 glorifies country life 61
    in Ecl.03 noble values in countryside under threat 61, 143
    in Ecl.03 threat to pastoral life 61, 143
    in Ecl.04 hope for peace 62, 144

in Ecl.04 preference for hereditary, non-elected one-man rule 63
in Ecl.05 arrogance and indifference of newcomers 64, 143
in Ecl.05 hoped-for distant future with peace and stability 65, 144
in Ecl.06 destruction of the traditional society in countryside 68, 143
in Ecl.07 denounces nouveaux riches 69, 143
in Ecl.07 expropriated land is given to outsiders 69
in Ecl.08 destruction of the countryside and the essential values of Italia 72, 143
in Ecl.08 land has been appropriated and given to soldiers (outsiders) 82, 143
in Ecl.08 Octavian should act to stop destruction of life in the countryside 71
in Ecl.09 bitter commentary on social disruption caused by expropriations 75, 143
in Ecl.09 land is appropriated and given to an urban dweller 72, 143
in Ecl.09 Vergil prayed for end of ongoing war and power struggle 75, 144
in Ecl.09 Vergil supporter of party of Iulius Caesar 75
in Ecl.10 Vergil's predicament is the destruction of his familiar environment 83, 143
Vergil uses his personal experience 74
Georgics 85
in G.1.40-41 Octavian to work towards improving fate of farmers 87, 102, 144
in G.1.40-41 poverty of small holders 87, 143
in G.1.489-497 ravages after the battle of Philippi 88, 144
in G.1 destruction of the land 88
in G.1 future of Italia 88
in G.2.136-176 expectation that Augustus will restore Italia's greatness 90
in G.2.458-540 deplores destruction of country life 93, 102
in G.2.458-540 political elite responsible for destruction of country life 93
in G.2.458-542 Vergil gives political statement 93
in G.2.532-542 farmers are the backbone of society 93
in G.2 hope of unified Italia 90
in G.2 laudes Italiae 89
in G.3 proem hope of return to normality for farmers 94, 102, 144
in G.4.1-227 time ripe for strong leader, rex 97, 103, 145
in G.4.554-558 hope of end to war 101, 144
in G.4 Aristaeus epyllion, Octavian as future rex 103
in G.4 epilogue hope that problems of farmers will be resolved 102, 144
in G.4 the word rex used 8 times 96
Vergil praises Octavian in opening of Georgics 86
summary 142
consistency over long period 149
sympathy in his younger days with Iulius Caesar 143
themes
  kingship of Augustus 142, 150
  return of peace under Augustus 142
  role of women 143, 148
  violation of the countryside 142, 143
  violence in war 142
writer of propaganda? 149
  independent commentator 151
Visual media 4, 23, 25
  coinage 26
    coins issued after Naulochus 26
    coins issued by Q. Pomponius Musa 25
    coins with Pax, or Venus or Victoria 27
    Numa coins 27
    propaganda or self-presentation 26
  in private places 29
    Arezzo pottery, Hercules and Omphale 29
    wall paintings in Agrippa's villa in Boscotrecase 30
  in public places 25
    Ara Pacis Augustae 27, 28
    statue of Octavian 26
    temple of Apollo in Circo 28
    temple of Apollo Palatinus 27
  media and Augustan poetry 23